Transforming Viole

This book investigates intractable conflicts and their main verbal manifestation – radical disagreement – and it explores what can be done in the communicative sphere when conflict resolution fails.

Conflict resolution sees radical disagreement as a terminus to dialogue that must be overcome from the outset, not learnt from. The book argues that, on the contrary, radical disagreement – agonistic dialogue – is the key to linguistic intractability. When dialogue for mutual understanding proves premature, it is agonistic dialogue that needs to be acknowledged, explored, understood and managed through a strategic engagement of discourses. This is illustrated through the Israeli-Palestinian conflict. It begins not with exchanges between conflict parties but with inclusive strategic dialogue within them. This approach challenges some of the basic assumptions in the fields of discourse analysis, conflict analysis, and conflict resolution, and opens up new possibilities for discursive engagement. It also has wider implications for cognate disciplines, such as applied ethics, democratic theory, cultural studies, and the philosophy of difference.

This book will be of great interest to students of conflict resolution, peace and conflict studies, ethnic conflict, security studies and international relations, as well as to practitioners and analysts.

Oliver Ramsbotham is Emeritus Professor of Conflict Resolution at the University of Bradford, UK, Chair of the Oxford Research Group, President of the Conflict Research Society, and co-author of *Contemporary Conflict Resolution*.

Routledge Studies in Peace and Conflict Resolution
Series Editors: Tom Woodhouse and Oliver Ramsbotham,
University of Bradford

Transforming Violent Conflict

Radical disagreement, dialogue and survival

Oliver Ramsbotham

Routledge
Taylor & Francis Group

LONDON AND NEW YORK

First published 2010
by Routledge
2 Park Square, Milton Park, Abingdon, Oxon, OX14 4RN

Simultaneously published in the USA and Canada
by Routledge
270 Madison Avenue, New York, NY 10016

Routledge is an imprint of the Taylor & Francis Group, an informa business

Typeset in Times New Roman by Pindar NZ, Auckland, New Zealand
Printed and bound in Great Britain by CPI Antony Rowe, Chippenham,
Wiltshire

British Library Cataloguing in Publication Data
A catalogue record for this book is available from the British Library

Library of Congress Cataloging-in-Publication Data
Ramsbotham, Oliver.
Transforming violent conflict: radical disagreement, dialogue and survival /
Oliver Ramsbotham.
    p. cm.
  1. Sociolinguistics. 2. Social conflict. 3. Violence. 4. Discourse analysis.
  5. Conflict (Psychology) 6. Human behavior. I. Title.
  P40.R36 2010
  306.44—dc22   2009031309

ISBN 10: 0-415-55207-9 (hbk)
ISBN 10: 0-415-55208-7 (pbk)
ISBN 10: 0-203-85967-7 (ebk)

ISBN 13: 978-0-415-55207-3 (hbk)
ISBN 13: 978-0-415-55208-0 (pbk)
ISBN 13: 978-0-203-85967-4 (ebk)

For Meredith, Edward, Ben and Zand

Contents

Figures and boxes

Figures

Boxes

Preface

Human beings do not struggle in silence once conflict parties have formed. In the most serious political conflicts, wars of words play as significant a role as wars of weapons. Wars of words are propaganda battles and contests for media control. But at a deeper level, they are also conflicts of belief. They are clashes of perspective, horizons and visual fields. They are gravitational battles. I call them radical disagreements. The original title of this book was *Radical Disagreement: Managing Agonistic Dialogue When Conflict Resolution Fails.*

Radical disagreement is the chief linguistic manifestation of intense and intractable political conflict. Political conflict is conflict in which conflict parties recommend incompatible outcomes in the one public world – and act accordingly if they have the power to do so. Either a bomb is dropped or it is not dropped. Either a baby is aborted or it is not aborted. Either a sovereign state is created or it is not created. Either a form of government is instituted or it is not instituted. Analysts wedded to deconstructive notions, and practitioners committed to the idea that all conflicts can be transformed, may not like this or want to recognize it. But, crude, brutal and simplistic though it may be, intractable political conflict obstinately persists.

Intense conflict is conflict in which stakeholders mind very much indeed which outcome prevails. And in the war of words, conflict parties cannot 'agree to disagree', when, given the power to do so, they ride roughshod over the other's dearest interests. Intractable conflict is conflict in which attempts at settlement and transformation have so far failed. I say 'so far' because it is always possible that these attempts will succeed in the future, as systemic conflict transformation wants, and as has happened in many other cases. But 'so far' can go on for years, if not decades, during which time unimaginable destruction and damage to human lives and life-hopes is – often unnecessarily – inflicted. This book asks what happens in the communicative sphere during this period, and what, if anything, can be done about it.

The photograph on the front cover of this book shows one result of the physical conflict between Israelis and Palestinians – the Israeli security barrier. What is the equivalent in the war of words? Verbal wars are different to physical wars. They introduce another order of complexity. What is the analogy to combat between armies? What is the equivalent of the territory being fought over? How is victory distinguished from stalemate or defeat? Who decides? One army destroys another army. What is the analogue in the war of words?

Why is it worth trying to find answers to these questions? Because otherwise, there is no prospect of understanding the nature of linguistic intractability. And without an understanding of linguistic intractability, there is no prospect of learning how to manage the communicative aspects of those conflicts that are most resistant to settlement or transformation.

I first became preoccupied with these questions 30 years ago at the time of the Soviet invasion of Afghanistan and the Iranian revolution. Since then, I have written studies of radical disagreement in a number of different arenas:

- public policy, as in the nuclear weapon debate and the humanitarian intervention debate;
- ideological confrontation, as in the religion/secularism debate and the Marxism/Thatcherism debate;
- public issues, as in the abortion debate and the environment debate;
- specific political conflicts, as in the Falklands war or the Israeli-Palestinian conflict.

All of these disagreements are drawn upon in what follows.

The topic of this book – radical disagreement – comes relatively late in the evolution of human conflict. In the long and ferocious history of oppression, exclusion, domination and exploitation, most of the victims – the poor, women, suppressed cultures and peoples, indigenous populations who have been decimated, driven out or enslaved – have suffered in silence over long decades and centuries. These are the inarticulate. And the oppressors want to keep it that way. That is why, although this book begins late when conflict parties have formed and challengers have found a voice, and although as a result this book does not make a contribution before that moment, from then on its topic is not neutral in the ongoing struggle. To take radical disagreement seriously in the first place – to attempt to study, explore, understand and manage it as outlined in Part II – is already to be opposed by internal and external hegemons.

The hegemonic discourse has huge resources for controlling public discursive space. But in radical disagreement –as investigated in this book – the challenger does not vacate public space in response, or try to resist only from the margins, or attempt to transfer the struggle to a new discursive arena supposedly free from domination, or even want to share the public space with the hegemonic discourse. Whatever the power imbalance, right up to the limit where access to public space is denied altogether, the aim of the challenging discourse is to occupy the whole of discursive space in turn. In asymmetric conflict, the promotion of radical disagreement is revolutionary. The fact that one army destroys another army shows the sense in which contending belief systems and discourses do not coexist either. In intractable conflicts, there is no room for this. Such lack of discursive space is at the epicentre of linguistic intractability. A radical disagreement is a singularity in the universe of discourse.

And the same applies to the discourse of peacemaking. As developed from Chapter 6 onwards, in the linguistic struggle to occupy the one discursive space, the discourse of peacemaking is a further discourse struggling to replace the other claimants. The language of discursive 'transformation' may be preferred to the language of discursive elimination, but the preferred direction of transformation is pre-determined or pre-approved by the peacemaker, including the 'elicitive' peacemaker. And the hoped-for change is one in which the transformed discourses are no longer as they were before.

Prologue

Having the first word

Not all conflicts are settled or transformed. The most serious political conflicts are those where settlement and transformation fail – or are yet to succeed. These are the *intractable conflicts*. Intractable conflicts ruin families and engulf whole nations. They drag on for years, destroying lives and persisting in their virulence down the generations. The Israeli-Palestinian conflict, for example, was ignited long before the time of the declaration of the State of Israel in May 1948 and was still raging unquenched when I was writing this early in 2009.

This book is about *radical disagreements*, which are the chief linguistic manifestation of intractable conflicts. They are a key element in that intractability. They cannot be reduced to other determinants. Here is an example of a radical disagreement associated with the Israeli-Palestinian conflict and taken from Palestinian and Israeli school textbooks (Center for Monitoring the Impact of Peace 2000–1: selected and rearranged):

|'Before the partition of Palestine in 1947 the Palestinian population of 1,364,330 made up 69% and the Jewish population of 608,230 made up 31% of the overall population. The Palestinians owned some 95% of the land where they had lived for centuries. Nearly all the Jewish people were recent immigrants – in 1922 there were only 84,000 (census data). Yet UN Resolution 181 called for a division in which Palestinian land would be 42.88% and Jewish land 57.12%. The word 'catastrophe' actually expresses what happened to this nation, which was subjected to massacres about which only a little is known. There are still facts which are so dreadful that pens cannot write them. What happened to the Palestinian people is the assassination of rights, murder of the land and uprooting of human beings. David Ben-Gurion said: "We should destroy Arab pockets in Jewish areas, such as Lod, Ramlah, Beisan and Zir'in, which will constitute a danger when we invade and thus may keep our forces engaged." The destruction of 418 Palestinian villages inside the pre-67 Israeli border, concealing the landmarks of Palestinian life and the massacres against the Palestinian people, are the best evidence for the brutality to which Palestinians were exposed. They were dispersed throughout the world. The Jewish State of Israel was declared in May 1948. By the time of the ceasefire in 1949 Israel held 78% of historic Palestine and the Palestinians were left

with 22%. Nearly 1,400,000 inhabited Palestine in 1948. After the catastrophe about 750,000 Palestinians wandered with nowhere to go. In 1967 Israel occupied the remaining 22% of the land of Palestine – and began building settlements even on that land, encroachments that have expanded to this day.'

'The land of Israel was the birthplace of the Jewish people. Here their spiritual, religious and national identity was formed. Here they achieved independence and created a culture of national and universal significance. Here they wrote and gave the Bible to the world. Exiled from Palestine, the Jewish people remained faithful to it in all the countries of their dispersion, never ceasing to pray and hope for their return and for the restoration of their national freedom. On November 29 1947 the General Assembly of the United Nations adopted a Resolution for the establishment of an independent Jewish State in Palestine. We offered peace and unity to all the neighbouring states and their peoples. But what we were then up against was as clear as daylight for us. Until this very day I can't understand how people don't realize that we faced a continuation of the European Holocaust, that we, the Jews in the land of Israel, were facing extermination. That was the plan and we saw and heard it. There were gangsters and murderers throughout the land – on roads and in settlements – and then came the invasions by seven Arab states. The bitter understanding that if we don't win we will be wiped out was one of the formative experiences of the generation. Thus we fought.'|

I take what appears here – tokens of speech acts indicated by sets of inverted commas – as an *example* of radical disagreement in written notation and mark it out as such between bar lines | |. If the bar lines are empty, there is not enough in common for there to be radical disagreement. This is mutual misunderstanding. If the bar lines disappear, there is too much in common. This is mutual convergence. These are *limits* to radical disagreement. Radical disagreements of this kind are integral to the conflicts with which they are associated and which they do so much to feed – the only parts of the conflict that can be reproduced and transmitted in this way.

In the example given above, we do not yet know who is speaking, from what position, in what context, to what end, or with what result. We do not know whether the speakers are directly responding to each other. Strong emotion is expressed, but we do not see gestures or facial expressions, or hear the intensity of tone or voice. This is a translation from Arabic and Hebrew. We do not know how accurate the translation is, or what connotations and meanings, embedded in different social systems, have been 'lost in translation'.

Nevertheless, despite all this, what is recorded is a putative example of radical disagreement. It already stands in need of exploration on its own terms – what I call the 'phenomenology' of radical disagreement or the study of what conflict parties say. If we want to gain insight into the linguistic intractability that lies at the heart of the Israeli-Palestinian conflict, we do well to take it very seriously indeed. The phenomenology of radical disagreement may seem superficial from the perspective of the sociology, or the psychology, or the political economy, or the cultural history of verbal contestation for reasons noted below. But I argue that it is precisely the phenomenology of radical disagreement – the exploration of agonistic dialogue itself – that gives us our deepest insight into the nature of linguistic intractability – an insight not found elsewhere and not reducible to other determinants.

Here is another example of radical disagreement from the same conflict. I use the Israeli-Palestinian conflict as a running theme throughout the book, both because of its intrinsic significance and because in 2007 and 2008 it was my own main field of empirical enquiry into the nature of radical disagreement through a European Union-funded initiative (see Chapter 7). This example comes from Jay Rothman's work on Israeli-Palestinian dialogue:

> |'For we Israelis our past lingers. We do not forget it. We are ultimately the most alone and historically insecure and persecuted people in this world. But we also have a positive self. Not only are we here because we have been chased and murdered and hated and scapegoated, we are also here, in this our own land, in this our own birthright, to develop ourselves as individuals and as a community and to welcome our brethren who come standing upright or bent over with burdens. Jerusalem is our soul. For thousands of years we have prayed to return to it; we say in our prayers, 'If I forget thee, O Jerusalem, let my right hand forget its cunning'. Without Jerusalem we are as if we were not and thus will not be. Our memory of our past provides us strength now and assurance of the future. Jerusalem is ourselves – past, present, and future.'

> 'For we Palestinians, it is very clear, our dignity has been crushed; our ability to determine the fate of our future, to ensure that our children grow up with a sense of purpose and direction, not reactive and hostile but creative, has been undermined. We need to ensure that our grandchildren – it's too late for us and our sons and daughters – do not grow up chased, beaten, and imprisoned, and that they, who are children of a highly educated people, will grow up with a sense of national honor and communal identity. Jerusalem is the core of our cause, the core of ourselves. We must fulfil ourselves through it and by it. We must rule ourselves here. And from Jerusalem the moral, cultural, and spiritual strength of our nation will grow.'|

> (Rothman 1992: 185–6)

How can this conflict be settled or resolved? Innumerable possible solutions to the problem of Jerusalem have been suggested and promoted, some even getting close to formal agreement at certain moments (for example, the idea that West Jerusalem remains Israeli and Arab East Jerusalem becomes the capital of a new Palestinian state, with mutual guarantees of access to holy places). It is possible that an agreement along these lines may be reached in future. But, while the conflict remains intractable, it is radical disagreement of this kind that stands most in need of exploration within the communicative sphere if both the challenge and the possibilities for transformation are to be understood.

Before developing this theme further, I will introduce two issues that will be preoccupations throughout the book. The first is a reservation about taking radical disagreements at face value given human duplicity. The second is the suspicion that the phenomenon of radical disagreement itself, taken as a whole, is contingent on deeper gender and culture differences.

The question of sincerity

Is it not well known that 'all men are liars'? Are human beings not highly skilled at deceiving both others and themselves (Aughey 2002)? There is deliberate deception, as practiced by political propagandists like Goebbels or Stalin ('a lie always has a stronger effect than the truth: the main thing is to obtain one's objective' – Stalin quoted in Montefiore 2007: 349). But also, do people not tend to believe what they want to believe? And are they not shaped in their beliefs by external and internal conditioning and manipulation? Does this not leave ample textual evidence amenable to analysis and exposure by qualified experts? So is it not naive to take what people say in radical disagreements at face value?

The study of radical disagreement does not take what people say at face value. It *begins* with what people say (the phenomenon, or what appears between bar lines in written notation), but in most radical disagreements with which I am familiar, all the points made above are found to be already at issue. There is, I guess, an initial presumption of sincerity along the lines argued by Bernard Williams in his discussion of the relation between truth and truthfulness (2002: 11) – opposed deliberate lies are not normally called disagreement. But radical disagreements are full of mutual accusations of insincerity. Moreover, a minimal and provisional criterion of sincerity of this kind is quite compatible with unconscious external and internal manipulation – which is usually equally disputed. As often as not, even the deliberate lies of a Stalin may be found to conceal a deeper layer of sincerity. 'Ultimately Stalin was a devout Marxist "of semi-Islamic fervour" allowing no friend or family to stand between him and his mission' (Montefiore 2007: 230). All of this is what needs to be uncovered and tested by the phenomenological investigation.

The gender question

Is the phenomenon of radical disagreement gendered? Do men and women argue differently? Or, more critically, is radical disagreement itself identified with male-gendered language? To confront these questions adequately, it is necessary to plunge briefly into what, for some readers, will be the forbidding terminology of 'difference feminism'. Here we find the most direct challenge to gender-blind universalistic claims that fail to understand their own historical contingency.

Best known, perhaps, through Carol Gilligan's critique of Laurence Kohlberg's rationalist-universalist assumptions in developmental ethics and her subsequent advocacy of the idea of ethics as inclusive conversation (1982; 2002), the discursive assault extends to the idea of language as a symbolic (thetic) system that is already gendered through its exclusion of the pre-symbolic (semiotic) other. Oppositional thought itself (including the construction of sexual identities as opposites) is therefore subverted by the 'semiotic transgression of the thetic' when the gender critique exposes this violence in its very heartland (Kristeva 1986). In Freudian terms, this is the pre-oedipal challenge to the whole of phallocentric western philosophy (Irigaray 1992). It is an attempt to liberate repressed voices from outside the symbolic order itself.

From this perspective, it is not hard to see why the phenomenon of radical disagreement is set aside. Radical disagreements, with their superficial juxtaposition of incompatible truth claims, epitomize male-gendered linguistification – dichotomous simplification, adversarial rationalization, competitiveness, separation from the relational, and the ready physiological antagonism characteristic of those who have a low arousal threshold. In short, radical disagreements, and the conflicts interpreted through them, are seen to be contingent phenomena. And, as such, they can only be dispersed by subversion. To take them seriously on their own terms would be to buy into their delusory universality and to perpetuate the intrinsic violence that they represent. The emancipation of the pre-symbolic other – and thereby the freeing up of the whole universe of non-violent human difference – can only be achieved by a radical displacement of the thetic linguistic order that suppresses it. And this includes a wholesale setting aside of the phenomenon of radical disagreement.

The culture question

Something similar results from a radical culture critique. Here the evidence is drawn primarily from anthropological fieldwork, where scholars have debated the significance of the extraordinary variety of conflict understandings and conflict practices found across different societies – particularly pre-industrial and pre-agricultural societies (Fry and Bjorkqvist 1997). In some cases, serious political conflict seems to be entirely absent given relative isolation, a static social structure, ritualized and hierarchical ways of handling difference, and largely unchallenged belief systems. This has led to a critique of most of the assumptions behind western conflict theory and conflict practice (Avruch, Black and Scimecca 1991). From this perspective, it is simply not true that radical disagreement is the universal linguistic manifestation of serious human conflict, nor indeed that it has historically been the prevalent one.

Even in a well-known typology of 'conflict management styles' that is mainly used in western business training and team-building, the assertive response – which invites counter-assertion and thereby generates radical disagreement – is only one of five main responses to conflict, which also include avoidance, submission, compromise and problem solving (Blake and Mouton 1984). The latter four – and others – are found to be more characteristic of conflict practice in non-western cultures, particularly those that place their main emphasis on honour and 'face-saving' (Arab) and those where concern to preserve group relations and social cohesion outweighs desire for individual satisfaction (Japan).

In some of these cases, the suppression or avoidance of in-group conflict may go together with a ruthless treatment of out-groups, which are not seen to belong to the same system of values (Ross 1993). Those beyond the pale are hunted, killed, enslaved, maltreated and excluded with impunity, but again there is no radical disagreement involved in all this because no rival values are seen to be at issue – the other is outside the scope of value. This may remind us of the brutalities of criminality and gang warfare in ghettoized urban communities, or of the kill-or-be-killed mores that prevail in 'cultures of violence' generally (Nordstrom 1994). So here is another set of severe constraints on any assumption that radical disagreement may be a universal aspect of human conflict.

Yet, despite the force of the radical gender and culture critiques, I will persist in seeing the phenomenon of radical disagreement as the chief verbal expression of intense political conflict. Where this is not the case – where there is no intense political conflict of this kind – this book has nothing further to say. These themes will recur in what follows and are summed up in Chapter 9. Radical disagreements encompass thick cultural divergence, deep value incompatibility and uncompromising political confrontation.

In the rest of the prologue, I will introduce the central topic of the book by initiating a comparison between *descriptions* and *examples* of radical disagreement. Readers are invited to decide for themselves whether particular third-party descriptions are adequate to the radical disagreements that they purport to describe.

Definition and description

The editors of a special academic journal issue on 'disagreement and difference' define disagreement – and by extension radical disagreement – as follows:

> First, not all forms of diversity entail conflict; disagreement does. People may display markedly different characteristics without those being in any way rival characteristics; diversity takes the form of disagreement only if people are at odds in some way. Second, disagreement does not encompass every form of conflict but only conflicts of a particular sort: conflicts of belief. Two people may have different and conflicting preferences, but if these are conflicts of *mere* preference – conflicts of brute want or mere taste – it would be odd to describe that conflict as 'disagreement'. The normal subject matter of disagreement is belief, albeit 'belief' in its broadest sense.
>
> (Jones and Carey 2003: 1)

A further distinction is then made in order to identify those beliefs that 'find their way onto the agenda of politics':

> The different and conflicting beliefs that have preoccupied recent political philosophy have been value-beliefs and, more particularly, beliefs that relate to the question of how we should live.'

Disagreements are described as 'conflicts of belief' where the 'conflicting beliefs' are attributed to conflict parties in much the same way as are their 'preferences'.

Others use different language but subscribe to a similar general idea. Here are some descriptions of radical disagreement from the top end of the conflict spectrum taken from well-regarded accounts of the conflicts in question:

> In Northern Ireland the 'uncompromising mantras' uttered by the embattled communities are expressions of 'conflicting perceptions' in which 'the only solution is utter capitulation by one side or the other, as they see it'.
>
> (Ryder and Kearney 2001: 365)

> In Kashmir 'fundamentalist beliefs' and 'hardened attitudes' lead to violence, where all sides in the conflict 'speak their own truth' and spill the blood of 'those of the opposite persuasion'.
>
> (Schofield 1996: 121)

> In Kosovo, the Albanians and Serbs 'not only live in segmented territories, but in segmented realities and segmented time, claiming the monopoly of victim status'.
>
> (Nicolic 2003: 54)

> In Jerusalem, 'Arabs and Jews inhabit different mental worlds, informed by fundamentally different ideological axioms, infected with profound collective suspicions of each other and infused with a mutual dread that has repeatedly exploded into hate-filled aggression'.
>
> (Wasserstrom 2001: xi)

And here is a description from critical political discourse analysis, which also refers to opposed 'ideological beliefs', 'mental representations', 'views about reality', 'discursive representations' and 'discourse worlds':

> This research differs in its attempt to understand this conflict situation [in Northern Ireland] by relying on the different perceptions that may be politically transmitted about one single reality.
>
> (Filardo forthcoming 2010)

Conflicting perceptions, embattled beliefs, hardened attitudes, opposed truths, segmented realities, contrasting mental worlds, antithetic ideological axioms, incompatible ideological beliefs, alternative mental representations, differing views about reality, divergent discursive representations, different discourse worlds – all of these can be seen to come within the same general idea that radical disagreements are conflicts of belief taken 'in its broadest sense'. So I will provisionally call this 'the common description'.

In some understandings, radical disagreements are analysed in terms of opposed arguments and claims (content). In others, radical disagreements are described in terms of the expression of incompatible cultural perspectives or narratives (form). In yet others, radical disagreements are interpreted in terms of psychological projection, or material struggle, or the social construction of knowledges and truths in the service of interest and power (explanation).

Radical disagreement is not peripheral to serious political conflict, but can be seen as its chief linguistic hallmark. This applies at all levels. Even two children squabbling over a toy, for example, appeal to justice and to truth:

|'It's mine.' ; 'I had it first.'|

Indeed, I suggest that it is radical disagreement that most clearly distinguishes serious political conflicts from other forms of contestation, such as sporting encounters, economic competition, or legal disputes. All of these may become serious conflicts if the framework of rules is itself brought into question. This is when emotionally charged radical disagreements erupt.

- A football match is merely a contest, however impassioned, until the referee's action is controversial. Then, as players crowd round and fans become inflamed, the contest becomes a conflict and radical disagreements break out.
- Economic competition, however intense, is deepened into full-scale conflict when accusations of unfair practice are made – radical disagreements over protectionism accompany trade wars.
- A legal case becomes embroiled in conflict when the legitimacy of the court is challenged – radical disagreement between supporters of former leaders and those seen to control the international tribunal or international criminal court before which they are tried comes to involve the whole distinction between criminality and politics.

I end the prologue with another example of radical disagreement in order to test the common description – the idea that radical disagreements are conflicts of belief attributable to conflict parties. I have chosen a simple domestic instance of radical disagreement between two individuals for the sake of clarity.

A family quarrel

|'God is the creator of the universe.'

'God is a figment of the human imagination.'|

This radical disagreement took place between two members of my family. It was a very painful one concerning the future upbringing of children: what should the children be taught from infancy? The disagreement took place many years ago when my wife and I were entertaining what was meant to be a happy family gathering. As host, I went around taking instamatic photos (which underlines how long ago it was). I have a photograph of the disagreement taking place – although at first I did not see that it was a disagreement. The two family members were sitting beside each other on a seat in the garden. It was only when voices were raised angrily and other family members started getting upset that I realized what was happening – and thought that as host I should try to intervene to calm things down. See Figure P.1.

On the right in the illustration is one member of my family who insisted that the children be brought up as Christians. Early teaching would ensure that they remained good Christians for the rest of their lives. This would bring deep fulfilment in this world and eternal salvation in the next. It was the supreme duty of parenthood. On the left in the illustration is another member of my family who was horrified at the thought of the children being brainwashed to believe what he called 'outdated and dangerous mumbo-jumbo'. Let them decide for themselves when they have grown up. With luck, they will by then be sensible enough to reject it.

I tried to mediate the dispute by getting each to acknowledge the sincerity of the other's convictions in the hope of finding space for common ground. The fact that I failed is, I suppose, not surprising given the intransigence of these positions – and the memory of my clumsy and no doubt uncalled for intrusion still causes me some embarrassment. But it is the reason *why* I failed that shocked me then – and shocks me to this day. This was when I first came to appreciate the significance of the phenomenon of linguistic intractability.

In order to clarify the situation, I took an instamatic photograph of the speakers and wrote 'God made humans' in inverted commas next to the image of one speaker, and 'Humans made God' in inverted commas next to the image of the other. The disputants – somewhat reluctantly – agreed that this did represent their disagreement:

|'Humans made God.'

'God made humans.'|

B   A

l'Humans made God' ; 'God made Humans'l

Figure P.1 A family quarrel: the disagreement

These were their statements and each rejected what the other was saying. Incompatible courses of action were being recommended as a result. I then took what I innocently thought was the next logical step in the representation of the disagreement. This is the gist of what I said:

> In other words, this whole disagreement stems from a simple difference of perception. There are some people who, because of their religious convictions, think that God created the world. On the other side are equally sincere people who are just as convinced that God is merely a human construction. Each sees the other's belief as a dangerous and damaging delusion, especially when it concerns the upbringing of children.

I converted the two statements into two cartoon clouds, the first emanating from one head and the second from the other: 'so one of you believes this, and the other believes that'. See Figure P.2.

This time, all hell broke loose.

The first speaker (A) said that this was exactly what was so pernicious about my fashionable 'liberal' views. It was also why my wife's and my own children had not grown up to be Christians to their great cost – unlike the children of my brother and his wife who had brought their children up with proper responsibility. I reduced everything to a matter of opinion without realizing that this is what I was doing. In this way, I simply reinforced the view that she utterly rejected. If I wanted to use the language of belief, then let me at least describe her belief accurately. She believed in the true God, the creator and bringer of life, to whom we pray, and upon whose mercy we depend for our present sustenance and future

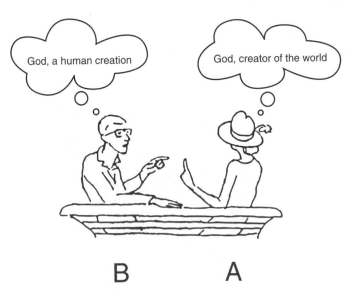

Figure P.2 A family quarrel: the description

fate. The transcendent reality of God could not be represented on the photograph at all – and certainly not in a cloud coming from her own head. God exists first. Then His creatures may or may not come to believe – in that order. God *causes* our belief – if we have ears to hear. See Figure P.3.

At this point, the second speaker (B) became equally vehement. *All of this* was precisely the first speaker's belief, and therefore rightly belonged inside that cloud. To try to include God outside the cloud was not to describe the disagreement at all, but only what the first speaker believed. Nor was the second speaker's own insistence on the need for empirical evidence when discussing this issue an 'equivalent belief ' as I was suggesting in my description. This is what theists were always fatuously trying to pretend. Fundamentalist theists know they are right because of what they have read in a holy book. Nothing can dislodge their belief because it is usually the product of childhood indoctrination, not reason. The results, as we can see in the world, are almost entirely pernicious. That is why children must not be mentally abused by having 'faith' foisted on them before they are capable of making up their own minds. By contrast, what is indicated by empirical reason – namely the extreme improbability of there being a supernatural being of this kind that created the world – is based not on blind faith in a holy book but on a proper unbiased study of the evidence. That is why nearly all eminent scientists are atheists. This evidence is not just personal belief, but the public basis on which the whole of science is constructed – always open to disproof but only as a result of better evidence or a better interpretation. See Figure P.4.

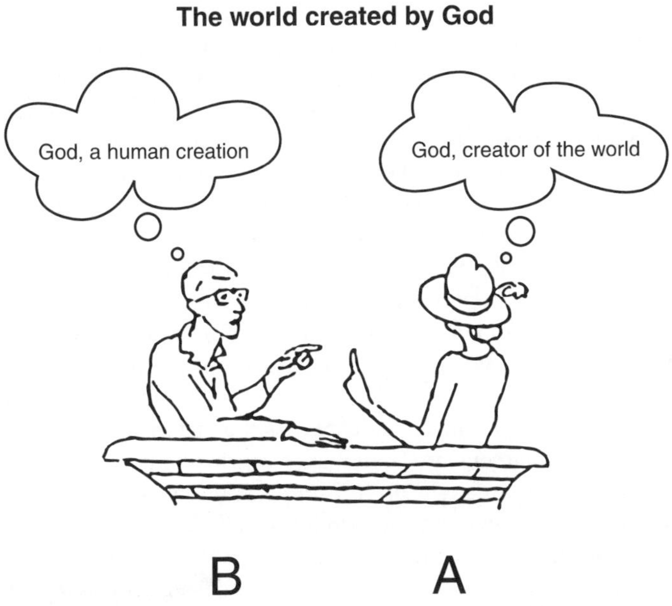

The world created by God

Figure P.3 A family quarrel: disquotation A

The world in which God is a human creation

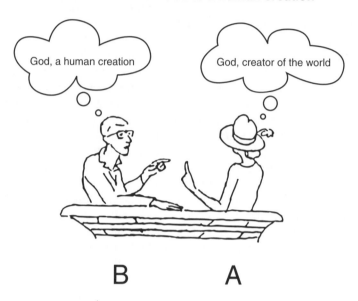

Figure P.4 A family quarrel: disquotation B

I had by now lost control entirely. The first speaker (A) said that this was a complete misunderstanding of the situation, and just represented what the second speaker wrongly believed it to be. Old-fashioned rationalists like him always come up with vulgar caricatures of religious faith that would make a first-year theology student wince. The more they detest religion, the more ill-informed their criticisms of it tend to be. It was this wrong belief that should be in the cloud coming out of the second speaker's head – including his inability to understand that he did not understand. Our faith in the transcendent God of Christianity springs from the example and teaching of His Son, our Saviour Jesus Christ, and from the inspiration and power of love that continuously pours from His Holy Spirit and illuminates the lives of those who turn to Him. To cut children off from this source of truth and joy by bringing them up as miniature rationalists programmed to be unbelievers is a terrible abuse of trust.

What shocked me about this experience was the fact that my own third-party description of the disagreement – in terms of conflicting perspectives or beliefs – was already integrally caught up in it through the prior involvement of the distinctions in terms of which the description was defined. Was it that each mis-understood what the other was saying to the extent that they were talking about different things? But neither was having any of that. They understood all too well what the other was saying – and rejected it. That was the disagreement. And that was why they insisted that the children should not be abused by being brought up wrongly. In the end, they both turned on me and said that I was the one who did not understand by continually supposing that I could include their positions within a third position which corresponded with neither – that I did not take the issue seriously, that I did not realize what it was about and that I failed entirely to grasp its gravity.

Part I

Radical disagreement and intractable conflict

Radical disagreement is located at the intersection of the three great realms of human difference, human discourse and human conflict. Preliminary comments on human difference have been made in the prologue and will be revisited in Chapter 9. Here the focus is on the other two realms. Part I surveys discourse analysis, conflict analysis and conflict resolution in the search for an adequate account of the phenomenon of radical disagreement. This will provide a foundation for the enquiry that follows in Part II.

It hardly seems ten years since Sue Wright, Paul Chilton and Dan Smith were able to call their book *Language and Conflict: A Neglected Relationship* (Wright 1998). The idea that language and conflict has been a neglected relationship may seem strange in view of the fact that it has been axiomatic in discourse analysis that conflict, like all other human behaviours, is from the outset verbalized (Schäffner and Wenden (eds) 1995). In any case, since then quite a lot has been written at the interface of discourse analysis, conflict analysis and conflict resolution (for example, Dédaic and Nelson (eds) 2003; Chilton 2004; Hayward and O'Donnell (eds) forthcoming 2010).

1 Radical disagreement and discourse analysis

Most discourse analysis moves straight from description to explanation in rela-tion to the phenomenon of radical disagreement. It does not recognize the value of investigating examples of radical disagreement on their own terms. It regards this as uncritical. Most of the analysis is conducted by third-party experts, not conflict parties. Little original ethnomethodological fieldwork is undertaken into the phenomenon of radical disagreement.

In the communicative sphere, it is the *clash of discourses* – radical disagreement – that is the chief linguistic form of intense political conflict once conflict parties have formed. This can be seen in the Israeli-Palestinian conflict where the Israeli security discourse, the Palestinian liberation discourse and the international (UN) peacemaking and state-building discourses (among others) all struggle for suprem-acy. Each tries to impose its own language. Each wants to provide the lens through which the conflict is viewed. Some commentators see a combined Israeli-American discourse as the prevailing one, and the Palestinian discourse as the challenger (Pressman 2003). This is certainly how most Palestinians see it:

> An essential prerequisite for seizing the strategic initiative is to shape the nature of the discourse within which the issue of Palestinian independence is discussed. A discourse is a framework of language within which verbal communication takes place. It is the discourse that determines what can and cannot be said within it and how this is to be understood. At the moment, the Palestinian national struggle is nearly always discussed in terms of other people's discourses. This is like playing all football matches on other teams' pitches. It is always an away game – we begin one goal down. Palestinians must refuse to participate on those terms. We must explain and promote our own discourse and make this the primary language within which the Palestinian issue is discussed.
>
> (Palestine Strategy Group 2008: 13)

The clash of discourses reverberates across the entire conflict field. There is no aspect that is immune, from the story of the Jewish influx in the 1920s and 1930s and Arab resistance to it, through to responsibility for the collapse of two-state negotiations in the 1990s and the eruption of violence that followed. There are also vital sub-discursive clashes within Israeli and Palestinian societies that cut across the main discourse formations. Examples of this are the struggle between secular and orthodox discourses within Israeli discourse, and the struggle between national-secular and Islamist discourses within Palestinian discourse. Indeed, Israeli orthodox and Palestinian Islamist discourses in many ways turn out to have more in common with each other than they do with their secular counterparts. Nor are these sub-discourses themselves monolithic. On the contrary, as in chaos theory, the more detailed the investigation into the nature of the radical disagreement in question, the greater the complexity that is found to be replicated at lower levels. It is true that in the furnace of intense political conflict, variety is melted down into the bipolar confrontations that generate radical disagreement, a process much studied in the analysis of conflict polarization and conflict escalation. But enquiry into the resultant radical disagreements equally regularly uncovers a persistent generation of new and ever-varying discrepancies. And these offer a starting point – even in the most intransigent phases of the conflict – for possible future reconfigurations and realignments.

In addition to all this, well-meaning third-party discourses, together with associated actions, are also found not to be immune. This is a fundamental discovery that only the phenomenology of radical disagreement can uncover in detail. In this extract, for example, an inclusive Palestinian strategy group dismisses the 'conflict resolution' assumptions of many external peace promoters:

> Two international discourses in particular are inappropriate for the Palestinian case. Unfortunately these are the usual frameworks adopted by the international community. The first is a peacemaking discourse, which assumes that the problem is one of 'making peace' between two equal partners, both of whom have symmetric interests, needs, values and beliefs. This is the wrong discourse because there are not two equal conflict parties. There is an occupying power and a suppressed and physically scattered people. The second is a state-building discourse, which assumes that the problem is one of 'building a state' along the lines attempted in Cambodia or El Salvador or Mozambique – or even to a certain extent in Afghanistan. This is the wrong discourse because there is no Palestinian state ... The appropriate discourse uses the language, not of peacemaking or statebuilding, but of national self-determination, of liberation, of emancipation from occupation, of individual and collective rights, of international law.
>
> (Palestine Strategy Group 2008: 13–14)

A similar rejection of the third-party international 'peacemaking' discourse is found among Israelis.

Discursive battles – radical disagreements – lie at the heart of the struggle in the most serious political conflicts. This is as true in Northern Ireland or Sri Lanka as it is in Palestine. So it might be supposed that the phenomenon of radical disagreement would be of central concern in discourse analysis, where lines of conflict convulse the discursive field and shifting axes of radical disagreement criss-cross the terrain. The discourse analytic field is large and varied, and so in search of an adequate account of radical disagreement, I will focus on its four most promising sub-fields in this regard: *conversation analysis, informal reasoning analysis, social/psychological constructionist analysis*, and *critical political discourse analysis.*

Conversation analysis

The natural point of embarkation in this search is that part of structural linguistics known as conversation analysis. There are different kinds, but for the analysis of radical disagreement the most useful is the 'ethnomethodological' tradition, where the emphasis is on naturally occurring conversation and on people's own knowledge of the 'tacit rules' and 'commonsense theories' that enable them to take part successfully in conversational exchange.[1]

Two features in particular make conversation analysis a useful launching pad for the study of radical disagreement.

The first feature is the fundamental technique of recording and transcribing natural conversation so that it can be reproduced and analysed in detail. It would be better in many ways for the analysis of radical disagreements if the interchanges that take place face-to-face could be videoed. But since that is beyond the scope of this book, no more will be said about it here.

The second relevant feature is that:

> Conversation, as opposed to monologue, offers the analyst an invaluable analytical resource: as each turn is responded to by a second, we find displayed in that second an *analysis* of the first by its recipient. Such an analysis is thus provided by participants not only for each other but for analysts too.
>
> (Levinson 1983: 320–1)

The study of radical disagreement shares this feature, but goes further. It is not just that each conversational contribution is responded to by a second, but that the second is then itself responded to in turn – and so on. This characteristic affects the role of the analyst, and the whole nature of what is studied.

It might appear that conversation analysis would focus, among other things, on radical disagreement, because this is very much part of 'ordinary language verbal interchange', and there are plenty of 'naturally occurring' examples of radical disagreement in day-to-day speech. But to my knowledge, this has not happened. Conversation analysis has tended to concentrate on minute fragments of conversation taken from the clinical or academic settings where the linguists work Or, in the case of fieldwork pioneers like Harvey Sacks, examples are taken from chance encounters that caught his eye:

> People often ask me why I choose the particular data I choose. Is it some problem that I have in mind that caused me to pick this corpus or this segment?

And I am insistent that I just happened to have it, it became fascinating, and I spent some time on it ... When we start out with a piece of data, the question of what we are going to end up with, what kind of findings it will give, should not be a consideration. We sit down with a piece of data, make a bunch of observations, and see where they will go ...

(1984: 27)

I think that the main reason for this neglect of radical disagreement is that conversation analysis is more concerned with process and procedure than it is with conversational substance. For Labov and Fanshel, for example:

[T]he central problem of discourse analysis is to discover the connexions between utterances ... [and] ... how utterances follow each other in rational, rule-governed manner.

(1977: 299)

Common across much of the field has been a search for ways in which linguistic units (specific illocutionary acts) and combinatorial rules (mutually ordered sequential moves) are used by conversationalists to construct an 'architecture of intersubjectivity' – a shared interactional world publicly observable to the investigating analyst.

There is some interest shown in how speech acts are shaped to minimize 'dispreferred responses' and how they are 'repaired' when this is threatened, and there is also interest in 'saving face' in conversation (Pomerantz 1984). But this interest lies in the *mechanics* of threat and repair, not in the *substance* of the disagreement. The focus, for example, is on 'adjacency pairs' of utterances and on the way 'turn-taking' contributes to coordinated interchange. In speech act theory, the emphasis is on the 'felicity conditions' for successful interchange (Searle 1969: 47). In pragmatics, it is on 'cooperative principles and maxims' (Grice 1975: 46; see also Sperber and Wilson 1986).

The methodological similarities and differences between conversation analysis and the exploration (phenomenology) of radical disagreement can be illustrated by means of an example. See Box 1.1.

Box 1.1 Example of conversation between caller to a radio phone-in show and its host as transcribed in conversation analysis

Source: Hutchby and Wooffitt 1998: 105.

1	Caller:	I think we should (.) er reform the la:w on
2		Sundays here, (0.3) w- I think people should have
3		the choice if they want to do shopping on a
4		Sunday, (0.4) also, that (.) i-if shops want to
5		open on a Sunday th- th-they should be given the
6		choice to do so.

```
 7   Host:     Well as I understand it thee: (.) the la:w a:s
 8             they're discussing it at the moment would allow
 9             shops to open .h for six hour:s, .hh [e:r  ] on a=
10   Caller                                        [Yes.]
11   Host:     =Sunday,
12   Caller:   That's righ[t.
13   Host:                [From:, midday.
14   Caller:   Y[es,
15   Host:      [They wouldn't be allowed to open befo:re that.
16             .hh Erm and you talk about erm, (.) the rights of
17             people to: make a choice as to whether they
18             shop or not, [o:n] a Sunday,=what about .hh the=
19   Caller:                [Yes,]
20   Host:     =people who may not have a choice a:s to whether
21             they would work on a Sunday.
```

In this extract (Hutchby 1992), it can be seen that the main effort in conversation analysis is to record hesitation, breath-taking, interruption and so on (semi-colons record short pauses; round brackets indicate longer pauses, some with timings; square brackets record interruptions; equals signs record that the original speaker carried on across the interruption). In this way, the analyst is able to identify a recurrent mechanism for expressing scepticism through the host's use of the argumentative device 'You say X (lines 16–18) but what about Y (lines 18–21)'. That this is recognized by both conversation partners as a single compound turn, rather than two separate turns, is suggested by the way the host does not wait for a response in line 18 and by an interpretation of the recipient's 'Yes' in line 19 as a 'continuer'. The interest is in the mechanism of conversational interchange (the units and the rules), rather than its content. The focus is on the backstage machinery, not what is happening at the front of the stage.

In marked contrast, the whole interest in the exploration of radical disagreements is in the content – what appears between the bar lines in written notation. The focus is on what is happening publicly on the front of the stage. It is the content (as well as the context) that makes it a radical disagreement.

Below is an example of part of the text in Box 1.1 transcribed as a radical disagreement:

|'I think we should reform the law on Sundays here. I think people should have the choice if they want to do shopping on a Sunday. Also, that, if shops want to open on a Sunday, they should be given the choice to do so.'

'You talk about the rights of people to make a choice as to whether they shop or not on a Sunday. What about the people who may not have a choice as to whether they would work on a Sunday?'|

Radical disagreement analysis does not need the elaborate transcription notations of conversation analysis because its main interest is not in 'the connexions between utterances and how utterances follow each other in rational, rule-governed manner'. In this sense, the study of radical disagreement is more superficial. On the other hand, with reference to the example above, whereas the conversation analyst already has enough information to draw the conclusion given and has no need to question the speakers further, the exploration of the radical disagreement has hardly begun. In fact, it is not yet certain that this *is* a radical disagreement because it is not known whether the host's position is her/his own, nor what recommendations for practical action are being made, nor how important all of this is to the conversation partners. If we, as analysts, want to find out, we will have to ask them. It will not be enough just to observe and analyse their behaviour – even their verbal behaviour. And in turn, our observations must be fed back for comment to the protagonists. We must listen to what they say because our observations are not separate from what is at issue. If we want to learn anything significant, we have to plunge into the disagreement itself.

Informal reasoning analysis

I turn now to the complementary field of informal reasoning analysis – sometimes called 'informal logic' or the wider 'critical thinking' movement. Initiated again in the 1950s and 1960s, this time in reaction to the monopoly of reasoning analysis claimed by formal logic, here we do find a concern with the content of what is said in conversation and with the subset of conversational exchanges that includes argumentation and dispute.[2]

In his seminal, *The Uses of Argument* (1958), for example, Stephen Toulmin mounted a frontal assault on the assumption in logic that formal analytic criteria provide the benchmark for validity in general, and that all inductive processes are by these deductive standards invalid. This would mean that no argument can be both substantial and conclusive, that all arguments produced in defence of challenged assertions or claims in everyday reasoning are unsound, and that we have no good reasons for any of our attendant beliefs. For Toulmin, this result was not only absurd from a practical perspective, but also formally fallacious. Formal analytic criteria were irrelevant to most 'actual arguments', not because they represented a loftiness unattainable in ordinary natural language arguing, but, on the contrary, because the logicians had committed a category mistake – they had conflated at least five distinctions into one, which they then made 'the absolute and essential condition of logical salvation' for all arguments, analytic and non-analytic, forgetting the field-dependence of all such standards:

> I shall argue that formal logicians have misconceived their categories, and reached their conclusions only by a series of mistakes and misunderstandings.
>
> (Toulmin 1958: 146–7)

Instead, Toulmin abandoned the stipulations of formal logic and asked how actual arguments used in our day-to-day lives can be critically assessed ('how people, dumb as they are, actually argue', as Wolfgang Klein less flatteringly put it):

> Suppose, then, that a man has made an assertion and has been challenged for his backing. The question now is: how does he set about producing an argument in defence of the original assertion, and what are the modes of criticism and assessment which are appropriate when we are considering the merits of the argument he presents?

> (Ibid.: 12)

This is clearly of great relevance to the enterprise of investigating radical disagreements. Toulmin set out the distinctions that he had found to be 'of practical importance in the layout and criticism' of putative inductively forceful arguments. He saw these as of universal applicability. Toulmin's original determination of the 'patterns of an argument' – in terms of data, claim, warrant, qualifier, rebuttal, and backing – is no longer applied in detail these days, and most of his examples were fabricated. But contemporary 'real argument' analysis follows in much the same tradition.

Perhaps most clearly presented today in university courses that aim to teach students not taking formal philosophy classes how to reason clearly and how to discriminate critically when confronted with the rhetorical ploys of political and commercial 'persuaders', informal reasoning analysis focuses on inference and the construction and testing of arguments. The aim is to analyse what reasons are being proposed for believing or acting in certain ways and to assess whether or not these reasons should be accepted.

Three features of informal reasoning analysis are worth noting at this point because it is their cumulative effect that reduces most analysts' interest in the specific phenomenon of radical disagreement. The main objects of evaluation in informal reasoning analysis are single extended arguments. Radical disagreements in which such arguments engage each other are not thought to pose distinct or additional difficulties. Indeed, the idea of disagreement is already accommodated in the notion of an argument in the first place – an argument is a system of propositions linked by inference in order to persuade an audience on a controversial issue that a certain conclusion or set of conclusions is true (and that some others are false).

The first feature that militates against interest in radical disagreement relates to the distinction often drawn (although now sometimes controversial) between factual assessment of the *truth of propositions* (premises or conclusions) and logical assessment of the *validity or force of inductive inference*. See Box 1.2.

Box 1.2 Truth and validity

Here are two arguments. In each case are the three propositions (the two premises and the conclusion) *true*? And is the inference from the premises to the conclusion *valid*? In other words, if the premises were true, would the conclusion follow?

Argument (1)

> Premise A   Mourinho managed Chelsea in 2006/7
> Premise B   Benitez managed Liverpool in 2006/7

Therefore

> Conclusion Manchester United won the Premiership in 2006/7

Argument (2)

> Premise A   Manchester United came second in 2006/7
> Premise B   Chelsea won more points than Manchester United in
>   2006/7

Therefore

> Conclusion Chelsea won the Premiership in 2006/7

I think that in argument (1) the three propositions are true but the inference is invalid (the conclusion does not follow from the premises – whatever we may think of the managers in question), whereas in argument (2) the three propositions are false but the inference is valid (the conclusion would follow from the premises were the premises true). Many other combinations are possible.

Factual assessment and logical assessment both contribute to the evaluation of the soundness of an argument – the assessment of whether there are good reasons for accepting the truth of its conclusion(s). But in informal reasoning analysis, it is the latter – logical assessment – that is the main concern. In the factual assessment of the truth of a proposition, a hearer may adopt four stances:

1 acceptance (believing it)
2 rejection (not believing it)
3 abstention
4 indifference.

The second stance, rejection, is not usually seen to introduce special complications. Indeed, relatively little effort is usually expended on the substance of a dispute – in other words, on whether particular premises are true. The main focus of attention is on the logical assessment of the validity or force of the inference. This is seen to be less contaminated by empirical and speaker-related factors, and therefore to be more amenable to clarity of analysis. To this extent, informal reasoning analysis still bears the hallmarks of its origins in the field of formal logic. And to this extent, the phenomenon of radical disagreement, where the substance of the dispute usually turns out to be inseparable from the validity of the reasoning, spills out of its zone of interest – and control.

The second feature to be noted is that in informal reasoning analysis the evaluation of good and bad arguments is usually abstracted from political context so as to preserve the purity of the analytic field. This insulation is effected by drastic restriction of the scope of contextual relevance – for example to the supplying of undeclared assumptions or implicit premises in the reconstruction of arguments to be evaluated (perhaps in accordance with the principle of charity), or to the clarification of connotations or extended designations in cases of vagueness or ambiguity, or to the accommodation of questions of rational persuasiveness for a given audience in the case of additional reasons that may be seen to defeat an otherwise sound argument. But radical disagreements cannot be abstracted from the conflict context in this way, because they are the chief verbal manifestation of the context. Whatever third-party analysts may want, in radical disagreement, conflict parties import political context at every turn. Recommendations, exhortations, justifications, claims, refutations, appeals – these make up the texture of the impassioned exchanges – and are irrevocably contextually defined and politically charged. In radical disagreements, conflict parties continually reach out to background context when they meet an impasse – and the background is as regularly found to be foreground, that is to say, to be already integral to what is at issue.

The third feature that reduces the interest of radical disagreement for informal reasoning analysis relates to the set of core distinctions that constitutes the analytic framework employed and thereby defines the field. In addition to the distinction between validity and truth, are distinctions such as those between:

- formal fallacies (logical mistakes) and substantive fallacies (adoption of mistaken premises);
- rational justification in terms of arguments and pragmatic justification in terms of desirable consequences;
- argumentative errors and rhetorical ploys;
- explanations for why things are so and arguments for why we should believe that things are as they are said to be;
- non-speaker-relative and speaker-relative statements.

Yet radical disagreement can almost be defined as the prior involvement of distinctions such as these when they are invoked by the conflict parties, as here:

|'Israel will prove to be good for the Palestinians and the Arab world in general, because of the model of democracy and free-market economy that it provides ...'

(Dershowitz 2005: 31)

'The very idea of a Jewish-democratic state of Israel is a contradiction in terms ....'|

(Rouhana 2006: 133)

These points will be elaborated further in Part II.

Social-psychological consructionist analysis

The third sub-field of discourse analysis that bears directly on the methodology for studying radical disagreement is the social-psychological constructionist approach. Rooted in the highly technical fields of sociolinguistics and psycholinguistics, constructionist analysis seeks to trace the ways in which language constructs social and psychological reality and relates to cognitive processes such as perception, text-processing and projection. The aim is:

> to develop a research programme in social psychology which takes full account of the dynamic properties of language use.
>
> (Potter 1996: 5)

The focal point is the analysis of 'factual discourse' in relation to contestable 'versions of reality'. This has obvious relevance for a study of radical disagreement:

> Our everyday lives are often disputatious: in everyday conversation we regularly engage in activities such as 'disagreeing', 'arguing', 'contesting', 'accusing', 'defending', 'criticizing' and so on. In short, it is a perfectly normal feature of everyday life that we enter disputes with other people about something that happened, or didn't happen when it should, or the implications and consequences of events. On these occasions people will be using language to warrant their perspective, position or point of view.
>
> (Hutchby and Wooffitt 1998: 203)

It is 'unlikely that each side will agree with each other's interpretation of the facts, even if they are able to agree on what the facts are'. As can be seen, this is a development of the tradition of conversation analysis previously discussed, with a prime emphasis on uncovering the ruses and discursive resources employed by speakers to 'warrant' the objective existence of their referents and to guard against anticipated counter-claims. Apparently neutral factual utterances perform 'delicate interactional work' which the analyst tries to expose as in the example below where the counsel for the defence in a court case (C) is cross-examining the chief prosecution witness, the victim of alleged rape (W):

> C: (referring to a club where the defendant and the victim met) it's where uh(.) uh gi:rls and fellah:s meet isn't it? (0.9)
> W: People go: there.
> C: An during the eve:ning: (0.6) uh: didn't mistuh (name) come over tuh sit with you (0.8)
> W: Sat at our table.
>
> (Drew 1992: 489, quoted Hutchby and Wooffitt 1998: 207–8, adapted)

The rhetorical ploys by which C tries to discredit W, and W's counter-ploys are evident. This is a battle to control the wording of apparently factual statements in order to sway the jury in the desired direction.

Linguistic ploys and counter-ploys of this kind 'lead us to consider the relationship between language and states of affairs or events in the world which are being described'. The upshot of a number of recent studies is to confirm older critiques, which rejected the naivety of unqualified object-talk and truth-talk in favour of the notion of the constitutive role of language in 'social constructions of reality'. Although different analysts reach different specific conclusions, these rhetorical practices are generally seen to be 'externalising devices' through which we create our versions of the world and of the things in the world:

> We experience ourselves as if these things had a concrete existence in the world, but they are all brought into being through language.
>
> (Burr 1995: 58)

Developed originally from Mead's work on symbolic interactionism and extended latterly within an anti-essentialist and post-structural perspective, social-psychological constructionism has roots in both the sociology and the psychology of knowledge, exemplified in early contributions by Berger and Luckmann on the 'social construction of reality' (1966) and Gergen on 'social-psychology as history' (1973). The former (roughly) offered a view of ways in which knowledge is manufactured via processes of linguistic externalization, social objectification into what appear as factual existents, and consequent internalization by future recipients as if these were the deliverances of an independent truth and reality. The latter (roughly) developed the thought that, granted the changes that continually shape human societies, the role of social psychology can only be to give historically conditioned accounts of how things appear at a specific time.

The general outcome has been a severe discrediting of traditional ideas of language, first as sincerely or insincerely expressive of inner attitudes, motivations and cognitions, and second as more or less accurate or inaccurate representations of an independent external world.

From the post-structural constructionist perspective of 'the death of the author', it looks as if to take radical disagreements seriously is to fall into the trap of interpreting spoken or written utterances as manifestations of the 'inner' attitudes and intentions of speakers. The constructionist emphasis is on the performative action-oriented function of language – concrete contextualized linguistic performances from which 'interpretative repertoires' can be collected and compared. Discourse psychologists look for the metaphors, grammatical constructions, figures of speech and tropes used in the construction of accounts for specific purposes – to warrant particular versions of events and to pre-empt or discredit alternatives (Potter and Wetherell 1987; Edwards and Potter 1992; Potter 1996). The author of a piece of text and her/his supposed intentions are in this sense seen to be irrelevant. A text is a manifestation of prevailing discourses.

Similarly, from the constructionist perspective of 'the disappearance of the external world', the project of taking radical disagreement seriously looks equally naive and mistaken. Michael Billig, for example, sees the very nature of discourse as inherently argumentative and 'dilemmatic', since in 'persuasive communication', some counter-alternative is always implicitly, if not explicitly, rejected. This delivers the idea of the speaker as 'rhetorician', and the nature of social-psychological discourse analysis as once again the deconstructing of texts in order to uncover the linguistic devices used to present justifiable and 'reasonable' accounts located within a context of public debate and argument (Billig 1991). Here it might seem that we would find an account of what is happening in radical disagreements when the other, nevertheless, answers back – as it were an analysis of linguistic battles between rhetoricians. But this does not appear to be the case, and once again I think that it is traceable to the constructionist view that there is 'nothing outside the text' and that talk of 'fact', 'truth' or 'reality' is always only reference to alternative versions of events constructed for particular purposes through language (Parker 1992). Why waste time investigating how one set of rhetorical ploys relates to another – together with whatever illusions of externality may go along with this?

In short:

> The idea that there is one version of events that is true (making all others false) is ... in direct opposition to the central idea of social constructionism, i.e. that there exists no 'truth' but only numerous constructions of the world, and which ones receive the stamp of 'truth' depends upon culturally and historically specific factors.
>
> (Burr 1995: 81)

Yet it is precisely characteristic of radical disagreement that conflict parties *do* appeal to truth, reality and justice, and not just to their own 'constructions'. So for analysts to begin with a third-party presumption that there is no 'truth' but only contingent constructions is to beg the main question, and to preclude serious enquiry into the phenomenon being investigated.

Similarly, in terms of methodology, the idea that linguistic practices are 'externalizing' is seen to apply to all social activities, that is to say, to 'all occasions in which people employ the sense-making interpretative procedures which are embodied in the use of natural language'. From this premise, a sweeping conclusion can be reached about social science research in general, and especially about social science research that 'employs people's accounts as investigative resources' – as does the phenomenology of radical disagreement:

> When people are asked to provide reports of their social lives in ethnographic research projects, or when people are required to furnish more formal answers to interview questions about attitudes or opinions, they are not merely using language to reflect some overarching social or psychological reality which is independent of their language. Rather, in the very act of reporting or describing, they are actively building the character of the states of affairs in the world to which they are referring. This raises serious questions about the status of

findings from social science research projects which trade on the assumption that language merely reflects the properties of an independent social world.

(Hutchby and Wooffitt 1998: 228)

The exploration of radical disagreement trades on no such assumption. But nor does it trade on the opposite assumption that when people use language to describe, justify, recommend or refer to how things are or should be in the world, they merely construct the states of affairs that they refer to. To make assumptions of either of these kinds is to prejudge what is being investigated. Whereas, to anticipate Part II, it turns out more often than not that it is these very distinctions that are integral to what is found to be at issue in the disagreement – and that this is the key to linguistic intractability.

Critical political discourse analysis

Finally, I turn to critical political discourse analysis, and in particular to what is sometimes termed Critical Language Study. Here the main focus is on the relationship between language and power. Critical political linguists look back to the early Marxist readings of Volosinov (1930/1973), developed through the work of Pécheux (1975/82) and others influenced by Althusser's writings on ideology in the 1970s, and on to those who have applied mainstream European social theory (Bourdieu; Foucault; Habermas) to a close analysis of texts (Fowler *et al.* 1979; Kress and Hodge 1979; Laclau and Mouffe 1985; Macdonell 1986; Fairclough 1989).

A wide spectrum of approaches is evident here, converging at one end on 'neutral' conceptions of ideology in many ways akin to the ideas looked at in the previous section. But the main challenge to the project of developing a phenomenology of radical disagreement as advocated in this book comes from the other end of the spectrum. Here a 'critical' conception of ideology prevails:

Critical conceptions are those which convey a negative, critical or pejorative sense. Unlike neutral conceptions, critical conceptions imply that the phenomena characterized as ideology or ideological are misleading, illusory or one-sided; and the very characterization of phenomena as ideology carries with it an implicit criticism or condemnation of it.

(Thompson 1990: 53–5)

From a critical perspective, in Thompson's words, 'to study ideology is to study the ways in which meaning serves to establish and sustain relations of domination'. It is concerned with 'the ways in which symbolic forms intersect with relations of power', and ideology is seen as a phenomenon to be exposed, combated and 'if possible, eliminated'. The aim is to uncover traces of the discursive play of unequal power relations in the production, reception and dissemination of texts (and visual images) within the wider nexus of social and economic relations, and thereby, it is hoped, contribute something to the empowerment and emancipation of the dispossessed. So the discursive sites chosen are those most likely to exhibit the exclusionary manipulations of power and the inequalities in communication that play to the disadvantage of the vulnerable. The material analysed includes party political, medical, educational, legal, commercial, bureaucratic, military and other texts, with increasing attention paid to the role of the media. The critical analyst looks to uncover the consciously or unconsciously employed discursive manoeuvres that bolster dominant interests, and to trace these through processes of production and interpretation to their material embodiment in the social and institutional structures that both generate them and are perpetuated by them. So textual analysis is only part of this wider discursive enterprise. At its heart, discourse is seen to be a medium through which ideological struggles generated by wider social and economic forces play themselves out. The critical discourse analyst aims to open this out and explain its workings.

From this perspective, it is not difficult to see why the project of exploring the phenomenon of radical disagreement with the conflict parties appears naive and uncritical. For Michel Pécheux, for example, discourses evolve out of clashes with each other in which the analyst must uncover the way words 'change their meaning' according to the 'positions from which they are used' (positionality) (1975/1982: 111). They take on meanings only within such discursive processes. Words are the effects of material struggle and are deployed as weapons in the wider ideological war. Ideologies are shaped by each other in the crucible of class conflict where 'words may be weapons, explosives or tranquillisers or poisons' and 'certain words struggle amongst themselves as enemies'. As language is commandeered, the fight is transmuted into an antagonism of verbal meanings where contrasting 'vocabulary-syntaxes' may lead the same words in different directions 'depending on the nature of the ideological interests at stake'. There is no universal semantics or 'mother tongue', only 'a seizure of power by a dominant tongue within a political multiplicity' (Deleuze and Guattari 1976: 53). Meanings are not determined by individuals, so no purpose would be served by focusing in the first instance on how individuals interpret and respond to each other's utterances.

Diane Macdonell sums up the decisive reason why critical political discourse analysis does not recognize the legitimacy of the phenomenology of radical disagreement as a research project:

> No other order, no order which took discourses themselves as a starting-point, could even begin to indicate how discourses exist materially.
>
> (1986: 95).

Edward Said argues similarly with reference to the analysis of radical disagreements in asymmetric conflicts such as that between Israelis and Palestinians:

> If there is one thing that deconstructive philosophy has effected it is to have shown definitively that bipolar oppositions always, regularly, constitutively mystify the domination of one of the terms by the other ... [so that] to place the Palestinian and the Israeli sides within the opposition on what appears to

be an equal, opposite and symmetrical footing is also to reduce the claims of the one by elevating the claims of the other.

(1986, quoted in Jabri 1996: 155).

The study of radical disagreement – the exploration of agonistic dialogue or what is contained within bar lines in the written notation – has no quarrel with what Macdonell or Said say in general. What they say in general is no doubt true. What is mistaken, though, is any implication that this applies to the enterprise of the phenomenological exploration of radical disagreement. The key question is: does the study of radical disagreement assume that conflictants appear 'on an equal, opposite and symmetrical footing'? And the answer – as Part II clearly shows – is that it decidedly does not. On the contrary, the argument will be that it is only the phenomenology of radical disagreement – the study of specific examples of radical disagreement – that uncovers the deeply problematic nature of linguistic intractability and in this way contributes a further emancipatory potential that the more didactic traditions of deconstructive philosophy and critical political theory do not provide.

Conclusion

Within the wide field of discourse analysis, language is generally taken to be a signifying system through which material objects and social formations are given meaning. Human discourse is seen as a site of contestation in which competing versions of 'reality' are constructed in the service of interest and power. As a result, disagreement is treated purely instrumentally. At neither end of the spectrum of interpretation – from the idea that nothing exists outside the text, to the idea that texts exist in an already politicized space shaped by real material-discursive struggles – does the phenomenon of radical disagreement itself arouse interest as a possible object of research.

The idea of taking radical disagreement seriously as a phenomenon worth studying in its own right is identified with the outmoded 'idealist' practice of taking the beliefs and attitudes of conversation participants and their own naive self-understandings at face value. For neuroscientists and psychologists, this means ignoring the biological and psychological roots of belief. For critical discourse theory, it does not do justice to intertextuality and is tantamount to an abandonment of the ethical task of unmasking hegemonic exploitation as ideological in the interest of emancipation. Conflict parties in radical disagreements tend to regard their language as transparent – another idea that is anathema to discourse analysts because of its positivist and representationalist assumptions. The either/or binaries, characteristic of radical disagreement, are regarded with equal suspicion and are deconstructed, dismantled or dissolved by sophisticated post-structural analysts before they have time to form.

As a result of all this, there is to my knowledge no sustained ethnographic fieldwork on radical disagreement in conversation analysis, informal reasoning analysis, social-psychological constructionist analysis, or critical political discourse analysis. The sociology, psychology and political economy of radical disagreement move straight from description to explanation without passing through the medium of direct exploration with the conflict parties. In contrast, the phenomenology of radical disagreement is not expert third-party analysis of other people's texts, but a practical investigation, with and by conflict parties, into their own impassioned discursive engagements.

Notes

1 Conversational discourse analysis emerged in the 1950s and 1960s out of the shadow of Saussurean and Chomskyan structural and generative linguistics from which it borrowed some of its original ideas. It has embraced the experimental social psychological analysis of conversation in academic laboratories and psychotherapeutic centres, and the work of linguists in language research schools. It has been built on the insights of philosophers of speech act theory and pragmatics. And it has reached out to adapt the distinctive ethnomethodological innovations pioneered by Harold Garfinkel and his followers at the University of Chicago (Garfinkel 1967; see also Heritage 1984).
2 Other terms used are Monroe Beardsley's original 'practical logic', Marvin Pollner's 'mundane reasoning', as well as 'informal logic', 'practical reasoning', 'the practical study of argument', and so on. See Toulmin 1958; Scriven 1976; Blair and Johnson (eds) 1980. For more recent work, see Fisher 1988, Bowell and Kemp 2002, and the journal *Informal Logic*.

2 Radical disagreement and conflict analysis

A survey of the broad field of conflict analysis shows how and why the phenomenon of radical disagreement is generally discounted. It is regarded as epiphenomenal in contextual analysis, functional in internal analysis, and merely subjective in relational analysis. It is not recorded adequately in complex systemic conflict mapping.

Conflict analysis is over-determined. There are too many theories of conflict. It has been said that more has been written about conflict than about any other subject except love and God. Different conflict theories – often contested – lie at the heart of the biological, sociological, anthropological, political, historical and psychological sciences. Darwin, Nietzsche, Marx and Freud all based their thinking on conflict theories. For Machiavelli, conflict is a result of the human desire for self-preservation and power (the Roman Empire was acquired as a result of successive prudent applications of the principle of 'pre-emptive defence'); for Hobbes, the three 'principal causes of quarrel' in a state of nature are competition for gain, fear of insecurity, and defence of honour; for Hume, the underlying conditions for human conflict are relative resource scarcity and limited altruism; for Rousseau, the 'state of war' is born from 'the social state' itself, and so on.

On the medical analogy, symptoms should first be noted, classified, and interpreted before doctors can move on confidently to prognosis, and – where possible – cure. Diagnosis comes first, but in the case of intense political conflict, the diagnosis is often already found to be affected by what stands in need of treatment. In the search for an adequate account of radical disagreement, the three essential prerequisites for good conflict analysis – data gathering, data classification, and data interpretation – are as often as not part of what is at issue in the dispute.

First, data sets reflect the purposes and mindsets of those collecting them. The Correlates of War (COW) statistics at the University of Michigan, for example, measured battle-related deaths within a classical realist international relations model of conflict (Singer and Small 1972; Singer 1996), whereas the Hamburg University (AKUF) Project produces different figures by relating the onset of war to 'the development of capitalist societies' where conflict is 'a result of the new forms of production, monetarization of the economy and the resulting dissolution of traditional forms of social integration' (Gantzel and Schwinghammer 2000). In contrast to both of these is the University of Uppsala Conflict Data Project, which approaches the analysis more from a conflict resolution perspective. Unlike COW or AKUF, which are 'satisfied once they have identified the actors and the actions', the Uppsala project 'requires that the conflict should have an issue, an incompatibility' (Wallensteen 2002: 24).

The figures produced are also often highly controversial, as anyone who has followed the vicious disputes about numbers of casualties in Iraq since 2003 will know. Here, for example, is the experience of a co-founder of the Iraq Body Count project, John Sloboda, communicated in an email message (2007):

> Since January, a whole army of people have been stirred up by lies, distortions, and outrageous personal libels against me and my colleagues, and we have been bombarded with daily abusive emails basically demanding that we stop our work, and 'confess our crimes'. Journalists who should know better, such as John Pilger, have joined in the attacks on us. Even worse than this, our attackers have written to many of the newspapers and media sources that use our data, telling them that our data are wrong, and that they should stop using our work ... Not only has this deeply damaging campaign actually obstructed the truth about Iraqi casualties from reaching people, it has made the lives of Iraq Body Count personnel hell. We have had to stop almost all of our core work, and give up any possibility of social life, to deal with these constant attacks, and put together the defence which you now see. We have no illusions that this will stop the attacks. In fact it may cause them to redouble. The main purpose in writing the article is to provide the information which shows conclusively (to anyone with an open mind) that the attacks on us are baseless, and that our data continue to provide as reliable and comprehensive a picture of the ongoing civilian death toll as exists.

Radical disagreement reaches deep into the business of conflict data collection.

Second, classification is equally disputed. One example can be found in the Uppsala classification, as published annually in the Stockholm International Peace Research Institute (SIPRI) Yearbook, which distinguishes 'territory conflicts', including interstate wars and ethno-national secessionist wars, from 'government conflicts', including ideological wars to preserve or change the form of government (socialist/capitalist, secular/religious) and economic wars that seek to gain control of government in order to commandeer resources (SIPRI 2008). But in my experience, those caught up in major conflicts, like Kashmir or Darfur, classify them under all four of these categories, depending upon the affiliation of the classifier.

Third, interpretations are themselves found to be part of the conflict. John Whyte's (1990) analysis of disputed interpretations of the Northern Ireland conflict for example, can be replicated in many other cases, such as Sri Lanka and Afghanistan. See Box 2.1.

Box 2.1 Interpretations of the Northern Ireland conflict

1 Britain v. Ireland

'The Irish people form a single nation and the fault for keeping Ireland divided lies with Britain.' (*Nationalist interpretation*)

2 Southern Ireland v. Northern Ireland

'There are two peoples in Ireland who have an equal right to self-determination and the fault for perpetuating the conflict lies with the refusal of nationalists to recognize this.' (*Unionist interpretation*)

3 Protestant v. Catholic within Northern Ireland

'The cause of the conflict lies in the incompatibility between divided communities in Northern Ireland.' (*Third party interpretation*)

4 Capitalist v. worker

'The cause of the conflict lies in an unresolved imperial legacy and the attempt by a governing capitalist class to keep the working class repressed and divided.' (*Marxist interpretation*)

For these three reasons, it might be imagined that the topic of radical disagreement would feature large in conflict analysis from the outset. In order to see whether this is the case, I will simplify a complicated field by pursuing the search within three broad classes of conflict theory (see Figure 2.1):

1 interpretations that look mainly at the *conflict context*;
2 interpretations that focus mainly on the *nature of the conflict parties*;
3 interpretations that mainly emphasize *relations between the conflict parties*.

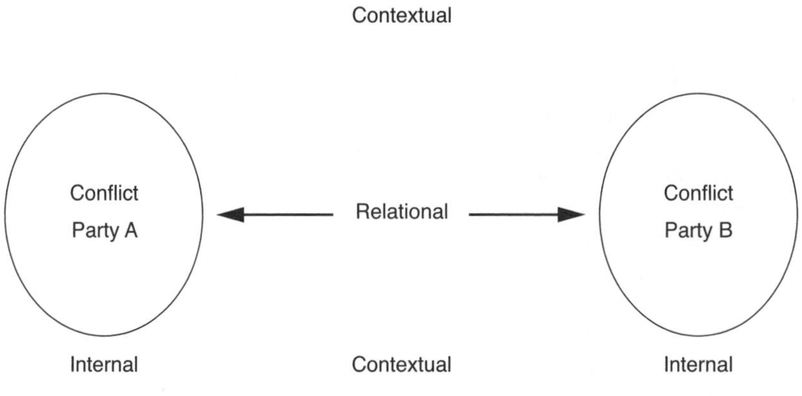

Figure 2.1 Contextual, internal and relational conflict theories

Most theories are hybrid. Frustration-aggression theory, for example, combines resource scarcity (contextual), human nature (internal) and subsequent competitive behaviour (relational) (Dollard *et al.* 1939).

Contextual conflict theories

The scene can be set by David Barash's comment on the causes of war:

> In attempting to assess the causes of any war in general, it is important to distinguish between the announced reasons for its outbreak, which are often excuses concocted as public justification, and the actual, underlying causes, which may not even be accessible to the participants.
>
> (2000: 7)

If this is the case, it is unlikely that much attention will be paid to what the disputants are saying, or in other words, to the phenomenology of radical disagreement.

And so it turns out in predominantly contextual theories, such as Marxist theory or realist international relations theory. Here it is the context that creates or shapes the conflict (the class struggle, the international anarchy). Conflict parties form within this nexus and the roles of individuals, including what they think or say, are consequently severely constrained.

In the Marxist tradition, the previous chapter showed why critical discourse analysis ignores radical disagreement. The role of critical theory is to expose the class-based function of ideology, thereby helping to disarm the power-holders. Work on discourse of this kind

> finds part of its function in its ability to unmask discourses and knowledges, which, from various institutions, and in the face of all the inequality that divides our society (the basic inequality of class, the imposed inequalities of race, gender, religion), claim to speak on behalf of everyone, saying in effect: 'we are all the same: we all speak the same language and share the same knowledge, and have always done so'.
>
> (Macdonell 1986: 7)

The same happens in Marxist conflict analysis in general. For Louis Althusser, for example, ideologies must not be seen as free-floating products of human consciousness. Rather, they exist only in those 'apparatuses' through which the class struggle is politicized – not just governments, but educational systems, churches and the media. Ideological struggle is not a meeting of distinct pre-existing entities for the same reason that classes are not mutually distinct and pre-existent to the class struggle. Ideological state apparatuses provide

> an objective field to contradictions which express ... the effects of the clashes between the capitalist class struggle and the proletarian class struggle, as well as their subordinate forms.
>
> (Althusser 1970/1: 141–2)

Individuals and groups cannot get outside the ideologies that constitute them as those agents who act in terms of such beliefs. A dominant ideology 'interpellates' individuals as subjects through the mechanism of recognition, just as someone who turns in response to a shouted name thereby recognizes that this is who s/he is.

This is the fundamental reason why Marxist conflict analysis does not recognize the phenomenology of radical disagreement – it is seen to embrace an inherently idealist epistemology. In Marxist analysis, on the other hand, the materialist position is genuinely revolutionary, because it is inseparable from the political interests of the workers. 'Philosophies of contradiction' like Marxism need make no claim to impartiality or to 'ultimate truth' in the way that hegemonial liberal epistemologies do because they have never claimed to be disinterested in the first place. That is why it is foolish from a Marxist perspective to think that anything can be learned from the phenomenology of radical disagreements without having first determined the 'material, social, political, ideological and philosophical conditions' that produce 'already existing knowledge' in the first place. In a somewhat watered down version, this is also the burden of Robert Cox's much repeated observation that:

> theory is always *for* someone, and *for* some purpose.

> (1981: 128)

I will argue in Part II that this is to misunderstand the phenomenology of radical disagreement. Of course, theory is always for someone and for some purpose, but who determines who that someone is and what those purposes are? In critical political economy approaches, it is usually the expert analyst who provides the answers because only the analyst understands the overall context that generates domination, exploitation and conflict in the first place. This may well be true. But, naive though it no doubt appears to critical theory, once conflict parties have formed and political struggle has become verbalized, the phenomenology of radical disagreement is not interested in what third parties say *on behalf of* conflict parties, however knowledgeable they may be, but only in what *conflict parties themselves* say, however ignorant from a critical perspective. Only this gives insight into linguistic intractability. And, as will be argued in Part II, it may as a result open up an additional avenue for emancipation that critical theoretic and critical political economy approaches, on their own, do not provide.

Turning to realist international relations theory, a similar disinterest in the phenomenon of radical disagreement is evident. In the *locus classicus* for realist theory, Thucydides' *History of the Peloponnesian War*, it was 'the growth of Athenian power and the fear this caused in Sparta' that 'made war inevitable'. When the Athenian generals demanded that the inhabitants of the small island of Melos join their alliance, they famously dismissed the Melians' 'fine phrases' and appeals to fairness – such as the argument that the Melians merited Athenian forbearance because 'they had never done them any harm'. Appeals to justice are irrelevant between unequal powers:

> By conquering you we shall increase not only the size but the security of our empire … The strong 'do what they have the power to do' and the weak must 'accept what they have to accept'.
>
> (Thucydides 1954: 360–5)

This is usually interpreted as a realist dismissal of the relevance of radical disagreement in the harsh world of action in international politics. I will argue later that this is not the only interpretation. Indeed, I will suggest that the Melian dialogue can just as well be seen to be itself a radical disagreement.

A similar discounting of the significance of 'fine phrases' and the radical disagreements that go with them appears in realist explanation more than two millennia later. For Hans Morgenthau, writing at the onset of the Cold War (in many ways a re-run of Thucydides' war between Athens and Sparta):

> it is a characteristic aspect of all politics, domestic as well as international, that frequently its basic manifestations do not appear as what they actually are – manifestations of a struggle for power. Rather, the element of power as the immediate goal of the policy pursued is explained and justified in ethical, legal or biological terms. That is to say: the true nature of the policy is concealed by ideological justifications and rationalizations.
>
> (1948: 83–4)

The justifications and rationalizations that make up radical disagreements only hide the truth about political conflict. Why do politicians, nevertheless, use such language? Opponents of realism sometimes cite this as evidence against it:

> The strongest argument against Realism's moral scepticism is that states employ a moral language of rights and duties in their relations with each other.
>
> (Brown 1992; see also Frost 1996 and Risse 2004).

Realists respond with two words – hypocrisy and self-deception:

> Hypocrisy is rife in wartime discourse, because it is especially important at such a time to appear to be in the right. It is not only that the moral stakes are high; the hypocrite may not understand that; more crucially, his acts will be judged by other people, who are not hypocrites, and whose judgements will affect their policies towards him.
>
> (Walzer – although not himself a realist – 1977: 20)

> Politicians have an ineradicable tendency to deceive themselves about what they are doing by referring to their policies not in terms of power but in terms of ethical or legal principles … In other words, while all politics is necessarily pursuit of power, ideologies render involvement in the contest for power psychologically and morally acceptable to the actors and their audience.
>
> (Morgenthau 1948: 83–4)

Beneath these psychological arguments lies a more fundamental contextual reason why neo-realism discounts radical disagreement. It is expressed most clearly in structuralist theories of international politics, such as that of Kenneth Waltz. For Waltz, high politics can only be explained at systemic level, where state actors operate in an international anarchy shaped by the numbers of major players and their relative power. Causal explanation is entirely abstracted from unit level 'reductionist' analysis and elevated to this structural level. State behaviour on the international scene (including the behaviour of those individuals in positions of power within it) is pre-adapted to this logic via socialization and competition (Waltz 1979: 18, 74). This introduces a sharp contrast between an anarchic order like the international system, and a hierarchic order such as that imposed within a state if a government is strong enough to lift that polity 'out of nature's realm':

> Nationally, the force of a government is exercised in the name of right and justice. Internationally, the force of a state is employed for the sake of its own protection and advantage. Rebels challenge a government's claim to authority; they question the rightfulness of its rule. Wars among states cannot settle questions of authority and right; they can only determine the allocation of gains and losses among contenders and settle for a time the question of who is the stronger. Nationally, relations of authority are established. Internationally, only relations of strength result.
>
> (Waltz 1979: 112)

That is why for neo-realists it would be a category-mistake to take the phenomenon of radical disagreement seriously at system (international) level.

Some students of war do concern themselves with the motivation and behaviour of human agents, but such concern is mainly to do with decision-making and is again usually identified with 'proximate' causes as distinguished from 'underlying' explanations:

> Whatever may be the underlying causes of international conflict, even if we accept the role of atavistic militarism or of military-industrial complexes or of sociobiological drives or of domestic tensions fuelling it, wars begin with conscious and reasoned decisions based on the calculation, made by *both* parties, that they can achieve more by going to war than by remaining at peace.
>
> (Howard 1984: 22)

Work has focused, for example, on perception and misperception among decision-makers (Jervis 1976), struggles to preserve cognitive consistency (Festinger 1957), and the influence of 'groupthink' particularly under crisis conditions (Janis 1972). In his book, *Perception and Misperception in International Politics*, for instance, Robert Jervis distinguishes the 'psychological milieu' (the world as the actor sees it) from the 'operational milieu' (the world in which the policy will be carried out). The operational milieu includes the three 'non-decision-making levels' of bureaucracy, the state and the international environment. These provide the contextual parameters, because they 'assert the importance of the objective situation or the actor's role'. So, in explaining 'how, why, and when highly intelligent and conscientious statesmen misperceive their environments in specified ways and reach inappropriate decisions', it is in the psychological milieu that agents' errors are located. Radical disagreements are not noticed as significant given the merely subjective nature of the perceptions involved.

In conclusion, it can be seen why contextual conflict analysis discounts radical disagreement as epiphenomenal to the underlying factors that are seen to generate major armed conflict at these levels. My argument later in the book is that this is a mistake. It is an error, for example, for international decision-makers to ignore the linguistic intractability that both accompanies and contributes so powerfully to the intransigence and ferocity of the conflicts with which they grapple. This is not just peripheral. It is central to success or failure in the exercise of power.

Internal conflict theories

Internal interpretations in conflict analysis focus mainly on the nature of the conflict parties. What notice is taken from this perspective of the phenomenon of radical disagreement?

Whereas contextual conflict theories concentrate on the conditioning environment of conflict and dismiss radical disagreements as epiphenomenal, internal conflict theory regards radical disagreement as merely functional for the real drivers of human conflict, which are biological, cultural, social and psychological. We are in the realm of explanation in terms of individual and group psychology, anthropology, and ideas about human nature drawn in many cases ultimately from Darwin and Freud.

Comparative anthropological studies provide a rich source of material for internal conflict analysis. One example is Marc Ross' *The Culture of Conflict*, which compares ethnographic data from ninety pre-industrial societies in an attempt to answer the question: 'Why are some societies more conflictual than others?' (1993). Drawing on what are in some cases by now venerable studies, he asks why among the Yanomamo of southern Venezuela a 'militant ideology and the warfare associated with it are the central reality of daily existence' (Chagnon 1983), whereas the Mbuti pygmies of the Zaire rain forest are 'at peace with themselves and with their environment' (Turnbull 1978). His general answer is that

> the psychocultural dispositions rooted in a society's early socialization experiences [e.g. childrearing] shape the overall level of conflict, while its specific pattern of social organization [e.g. kinship] determines whether the targets of conflict and aggression are located within a society, outside it, or both.
>
> (Ross 1993: 9)

Ross then generalizes this 'culture of conflict theory' to post-industrial societies and finds it precisely (if surprisingly) confirmed in explaining the incidence of protracted conflict in Ireland and the 'relatively low levels of conflict in Norway'.

The main point is how the theoretical presuppositions of anthropological conflict theory of this kind can be seen to discount radical disagreement as, at most, merely functional for the internal drivers of conflict in different societies.

The same applies to other anthropology-based internal conflict theories, and for similar reasons. Sometimes, these have a more psychological than a sociological gloss, as seen here, where, having looked at 'cultural influences on conflict resolution' and offered examples of widely varying practice from culture to culture, the editorial 'final words' of Fry and Bjorkqvist's *Cultural Variation in Conflict Resolution* are:

> We conclude that the source of conflict lies in the minds of people. External, social conflict is a reflection of intrapsychic conflict. External control does not solve the roots of the problem. If we wish a conflict really to disappear, then a change in attitude is needed.
>
> (1997: 252)

Similar results are obtained if attention shifts from the internal nature of conflict parties to human nature in general. Much has been written here about the roots of human aggression (Rapoport 1989; Staub 1989). In the field of conflict analysis, Konrad Lorenz's 'hydraulic' theory (1966) and Robert Adrey's 'territorial imperative' theory of human aggression (1966) were influential in their day. Latterly, animal ethologist, Franz de Waal, offers 'peacemaking among primates' as an instructive model (1989), while Jane Goodall's emphasis is more on the murderous propensities of our genetically nearest cousins, the chimpanzees (1986). In answer to the question, 'why do we believe what we believe?', Andrew Neuberg and Mark Waltman reply by 'uncovering our biological need for meaning, spirituality and truth' (2006).

Behind all this again lies a bitter dispute between those who argue that violence is not rooted in human nature or endemic in human beings, but is a learned behaviour taught by culture and eradicable through socialization, and evolutionary psychologists who reject this as a 'politically correct' travesty and have revived the idea that human mindsets predisposed to violence 'evolved to deal with hostilities in the ancestral past'. The idea that violence and war are learned behaviours was made famous through Margaret Mead's claim that 'warfare is only an invention – not a biological necessity' (1940) as amplified in the 1989 'Seville Statement on Violence' that challenged as 'scientifically incorrect' the idea that war is an evolutionary predisposition in human beings (Groebel *et al.* 1989: xxiii–xvi). Felicity de Zulueta argues similarly that 'humanity is essentially cooperative' and that the roots of destructiveness (dehumanization of the other, narcissistic rage) lie in violations of childrens' affiliative needs as identified in attachment theory (2006: 343).

In sharp contrast, Steven Pinker rejects this 'central dogma of a secular faith', and draws on recent studies of the mind, the brain, genetics and evolution to bridge the gap between culture and biology, in a bid to provide secure physiological foundations for an understanding of human nature (2002). He concludes that human bodies and human minds do show 'direct signs of design for aggression', pointing to:

- male body size, the effects of testosterone, anger and teeth baring, fight-or-flight response of the autonomic nervous system, aggressive acts initiated by circuits in the limbic system;
- the trans-culturally rough-and-tumble behaviour of boys 'which is obviously practice for fighting';
- evidence that the 'most violent age is not adolescence but toddlerhood';
- the 'shockingly high homicide rates of pre-state societies, with 10 to 60 per cent of the men dying at the hands of other men'.

This radical disagreement is ongoing. Here is a fierce counter-critique that dismisses Pinker's 'evolutionary psychology' (EP):

> the claims of EP in the fields of biology, psychology, anthropology, sociology, cultural studies and philosophy are for the most part not merely mistaken, but culturally pernicious … Like the religious fundamentalists, the fundamentalist Darwinians who wish to colonise the social sciences have political as well as cultural objectives … The political agenda of EP is transparently part of a right-wing libertarian attack on collectivity, above all the welfare state.
>
> (Rose and Rose 2001: 3, 125, 8)

On the question of internal conflict theory and radical disagreement, I will leave the last word to Nietzsche, who invokes Darwin to dismiss verbal disagreement as a herd phenomenon located at the most attenuated end of language, itself an attenuation of consciousness, which is in turn 'the last and latest development of the organic and hence what is most unfinished and unstrong' (1974: 84–5). This triple downgrading of the significance of verbal justification and dispute is derived from the idea in evolutionary biology that animal and human action is impelled by unconscious physiological drives: 'Every drive is a type of thirst for power; every one has its perspective, which it wants to force on the other drives as a norm'.

For these perspectives to masquerade as independent deliverances of reason or power-free knowledge is nothing more than a lie. So, to approach them in terms of their own self-articulations would be foolish in the extreme:

> Whatever becomes conscious becomes by the same token shallow, thin, relatively stupid, general, sign, herd signal; all becoming conscious involves a great and thorough corruption, falsification, reduction to superficialities, and generalization … Man, like every living being, thinks continually without knowing it; the thinking that rises to consciousness is only the smallest part of this – the most superficial and worst part – for only this conscious thinking takes the form of words …
>
> (Nietzsche 1974: 298–300)

So much for the project of taking radical disagreement seriously. I reel under the impact of Nietzsche's rhetoric.

Nevertheless, I will argue in Chapter 6 that even from the perspective of internal interpretations of conflict, it is once again a mistake to disregard the phenomenon of radical disagreement. How, for example, is the bitter radical disagreement about innate human violence referred to above accommodated within internal conflict theory? The same applies to Nietzsche. What of the contempt with which Zarathustra dismisses his opponents in the radical disagreements that characterize his tempestuous passage through the world? And who is more polemical than Nietzsche himself?

Relational conflict theories

I turn, finally, to the third broad class of conflict theories – those that focus on relations between conflict parties. This may seem the most likely site for serious exploration of the phenomenon of radial disagreement since the idea that disagreements are conflicts of belief is built into the 'common description' of radical disagreement as exemplified in the prologue.

Relational theories of conflict loom large in my own field of conflict resolution, particularly in the charting of processes of escalation and de-escalation. More will be said about this in the next chapter, so I will be brief here. Conflict relations are generated, for example, by all three dimensions of Johan Galtung's 'conflict triangle' (1996: 72). See Figure 2.2.

Here the *contradiction* refers to the underlying conflict situation, which includes the actual or perceived 'incompatibility of goals' between the conflict parties generated by what Chris Mitchell calls, a 'mis-match between social values and social structure' (1981: 18). In a symmetric conflict, the contradiction is defined by the parties, their interests, and the clash of interests between them. In an asymmetric conflict, it is defined by the parties, their relationship, and the conflict of interests inherent in the relationship.

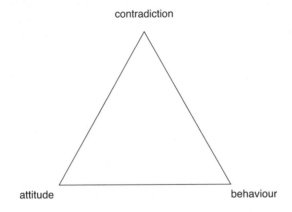

Figure 2.2 The conflict triangle

Attitude includes the parties' perceptions and misperceptions of each other and of themselves. These can be positive or negative, but in violent conflicts parties tend to develop demeaning stereotypes of the other, and attitudes are often influenced by emotions such as fear, anger, bitterness and hatred. Analysts who emphasize these subjective aspects are said to have an *expressive* view of the sources of conflict ('a social conflict exists when two or more parties believe they have incompatible objectives' – Kriesberg 1982: 17).

Behaviour is the third component of the conflict triangle. It can include cooperation or coercion, gestures signifying conciliation or hostility. Violent conflict behaviour is characterized by threats, coercion and destructive attacks. Analysts who emphasize objective aspects such as structural relationships, competing material interests or behaviours are said to have an *instrumental* view of the sources of conflict (there is conflict 'whenever incompatible activities occur ... an action that is incompatible with another action prevents, obstructs, interferes, injures or in some way makes the latter less likely to be effective' – Deutsch 1973: 10).

Galtung argues that all three components have to be present together in a full conflict. A conflict structure without conflict attitudes or behaviour is a latent (or structural) conflict. Galtung sees conflict as a dynamic process in which structure, attitudes and behaviour are constantly changing and influencing one another. As the dynamic develops, it becomes a manifest conflict formation as parties' interests clash or the relationship they are in becomes oppressive. Conflict parties then organize around this structure to pursue their interests. They develop hostile attitudes and conflictual behaviour. And so the conflict formation starts to grow and intensify. As it does so, it may widen (drawing in other parties), deepen, and spread, generating secondary conflicts within the main parties, or among outsiders who get sucked in. Interests, behaviours and attitudes feed off each other in escalating relations of mutual hostility, threat perception, polarized identities, projection of enemy images and fear. This often considerably complicates the task of addressing the original, core conflict. Eventually however, resolving the conflict must involve a set of dynamic changes that involve de-escalation of conflict behaviour, a change in attitudes, and transforming the relationships or clashing interests that are at the core of the conflict structure, perhaps through institutional change.

I call the three sets of relations generated by the conflict triangle:

1 relations of interest
2 relations of belief
3 relations of power.

I will say more about these three relations and the interconnections between them later. Here the main point is that relations of belief – which is seen to include the phenomenon of radical disagreement – are subsumed into the category of 'conflict attitude' in general, together with emotions and desires. And it is emotions and desires that predominate in determining that 'attitudes' are interpreted as subjective attributes of people:

Conflict attitude   Emotive – feelings
                        Conative – wills, desires
                        Cognitive – beliefs

This is the main reason, I think, why the phenomenology of radical disagreement – the exploration of the internal economy of relations of belief – is not usually pursued seriously in relational conflict analysis. Beliefs are seen to be little more than one aspect, among others, of subjective conflict attitudes in general. People 'have' beliefs in much the same way as they 'have' desires or feelings. And subjective attitudes are then, as often as not, themselves further subordinated under what are seen as the more measurable objective dimensions of contradiction (interest) and behaviour (power). Relations of belief are – wrongly in my view – reduced to mere reflexes of relations of interest and relations of power.

Radical disagreement and the mapping of complex conflict systems

I conclude this chapter with a look at conflict mapping. This, too, is seen to be an essential element in conflict analysis as preparation for determining the best ways to act or intervene.

Conflict mapping – for example, of conflict parties, conflict issues, conflict relations and so on – has been characteristic in the field of conflict resolution from the beginning, as summed up in Paul Wehr's, *Conflict Regulation* (1979). This interest has recently been revived in the form of complex or systemic conflict mapping, often by aid and development workers, with a view to understanding the interrelationships between the diverse factors that make up complex conflict situations (Körppen *et al.* 2008).

The challenge of analysing systemic complexity was clearly recognized by the founding theorists of conflict resolution – Lewis Fry Richardson before World War II, and Kenneth Boulding, Quincy Wright, Johan Galtung, Anatol Rapoport, John Burton, and others from the 1950s. They began from the premises that conflict analysis must be multi-level and multi-disciplinary, that the sum is greater than the parts, that positive feedback loops reinforce systemic resistance to change, that interventions have unpredictable outcomes, and that at critical moments there can be sudden and abrupt bifurcations as the set of interlocking systems adjusts to changing environments and eco-landscapes in a process of co-adaptation – these are self-organizing and complex adaptive systems.

For example, Boulding recognized early on (1962: see also Sandole 1999) that systemic complexity is quite consonant with long-term stability, since once a complex system has settled into a pattern, no single stimulus or even collection of stimuli may be sufficient to overcome its constantly reinforced inertia (his modelling was mainly in terms of fluctuating and interpenetrating fields of force drawn from economic theory). In these cases, either the complex must be affected as a whole, or the system must be displaced to another environment which is more benign. Either way, it was recognized that the process of transition would be likely to be less stable, more turbulent, and perhaps potentially more dangerous, than the original more familiar concatenation. Indeed, there was no guarantee that the new equilibrium, if found, would necessarily be more congenial.

Richardson was an expert on mathematical computations on predictability and turbulence in weather systems. Influenced by this, in the first issue of the *Journal of Conflict Resolution* (1957), Boulding and Wright proposed global conflict data centres to alert the international community to the upcoming squalls and storms of international conflict. Burton's thinking was greatly influenced by general systems theory, particularly in the form of the distinction between first and second order learning (Burton 1968; Ramsbotham, Woodhouse and Miall 2005: 43–7).

More recently – over the past twenty years – the conflict analytic field has been enriched by a further transfer of complex system ideas from the natural to the social sciences, with inputs from sociology, political theory, social psychology, organizational theory and other disciplinary areas influenced by cognate ideas (Hendrick 2009). This has not been without controversy (Rosenau and Earnest 2006). There is no one overarching approach, but – as may be fitting given the topic – a hybrid coming-together of different transdisciplinary frameworks. The main question for this chapter is how the phenomenon of radical disagreement is modelled in complex conflict systemic analyses of this kind. The most usual way this is done is in terms of 'mental models' and the roles they are seen to play in perpetuating intractable conflict. These are the conceptual frames or cognitive structures, largely unconscious, that shape our tacit knowledge and beliefs and adapt us to conform to prevailing social norms – what Lakoff and Johnson have called 'the metaphors we live by' (1980).

David Stroh has said that 'systemic thinking is mental models made visible'. Norbert Ropers (2008 in Körppen *et al.* (eds): 13), building on the work of Oliver Wils *et al.* (2006), takes thinking in mental models as one of the defining 'characteristics of "systemic thinking"':

> *Thinking in (mental) models yet acknowledging perspective-dependency:* Accepting that all analytical models are a reduction of the complex reality (and are necessarily perspective-dependent) and are therefore only ever a tool and not 'the reality' as such.

This idea recurs, albeit not in name, in attempts to accommodate 'beliefs, feelings, and behaviors' in the dynamical-systems approach (Coleman *et al.* 2008: 6). 'Mental models' are included as distinct elements in systems perspective maps (Woodrow 2006). Mental models are identified with 'widely-held beliefs and norms' in systemic conflict analysis maps within the 'attitude' dimension of the SAT model of peacebuilding (Ricigliano 2008: 2). 'Mind maps', encompassing stakeholder and evaluator perceptions and interpretations, are used for testing resonances and exploring collective dialogue in the emergent evaluations of large-scale system action research (Burns 2006: 189).

The key question is how this relates to radical disagreement. For example, how does the phenomenon of radical disagreement appear in the systemic mapping of mental models in a context of intense and intractable political conflict?

The following observations may suggest why the idea of *conflicting mental models*, as currently exemplified in systemic conflict analysis maps, seems to me to be not yet adequate to capturing the role played by the phenomenon of radical disagreement in generating and sustaining linguistic intractability. See Figures 2.3 and 2.4.

1   In some systems perspective maps, mental models are represented by 'belief clouds'. Here the content of the cloud is a statement by a conflict party (e.g. 'we must protect what we have'). Occasionally, a contradictory statement by another conflict party may also be included in a thought bubble elsewhere on the map. But even this is not yet a radical disagreement because it misses the systemic nature of the whole, which can only be represented by the appearance in written notation of the radical disagreement itself, in this case, with reference to conflict in Burundi:

|'We must protect what we have.'

'We are the majority. We deserve more.'|

(Woodrow 2006: 8)

This is what stands in need of phenomenological exploration with the conflict parties.

2   An alternative way in which radical disagreement is indicated in systems perspective maps is through third-party description (e.g. 'mutual perceptions of victimhood' or 'competing narratives'). Here the assumption is that the descriptive terms 'perceptions', 'narratives', 'beliefs', 'constructions', 'projections', 'rationalizations' and so on are adequate to the task in hand, that is, they are independent of what is in question in the radical disagreements thus described. But this is often to beg the question at issue, as demonstrated later in this book. Conflict parties in intense political conflicts do not accept that their claims, recommendations and arguments are 'mere' mental models, perceptions, narratives, beliefs, etc. This again is integral to linguistic intractability.

3   Most of the elements included in the systems perspective map are presented as unproblematic, that is to say, as unconnected with the phenomenon of radical disagreement. But further phenomenological investigation usually shows that some of these, too, are radically contested (e.g. 'human rights violations' or 'venality, criminality and corruption'), or that what is referred to lies at the epicentre of the political radical disagreement itself (e.g. 'the final status of Kosovo').

4   Where does emotion or motive/desire appear in systems perspective maps? These again usually appear unproblematically (e.g. 'fear and hatred' or 'determination to prevail at all costs'). But this does not capture the way affective

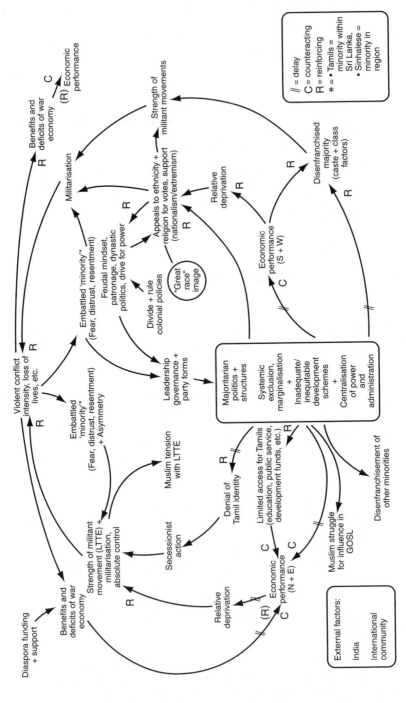

Figure 2.3 Conflict in Sri Lanka: a systems perspective

Source: Ropers 2008: 26–7.

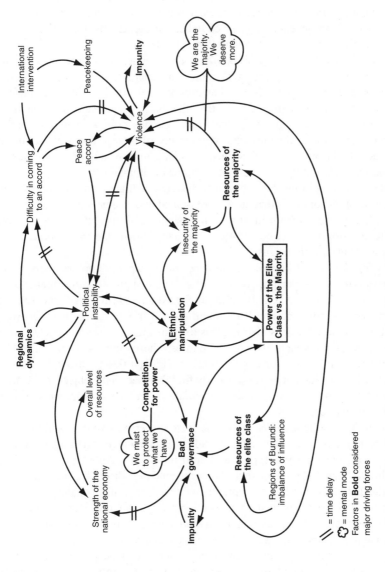

Figure 2.4 Understanding the Burundi conflict: a systems perspective

Source: Woodrow 2006: 8 – a participatory workshop product.

Factors within the image:

International intervention

Peacekeeping

Impunity

We are the majority. We deserve more.

Difficulty in coming to an accord

Peace accord

Violence

Resources of the majority

Insecurity of the majority

Regional dynamics

Political instability

Ethnic manipulation

Power of the Elite Class vs. the Majority

Overall level of resources

Strength of the national economy

Competition for power

We must to protect what we have

Bad governace

Resources of the elite class

Regions of Burundi: imbalance of influence

Impunity

‖ = time delay

❀ = mental mode

Factors in **Bold** considered major driving forces

and conative aspects are inseparable from cognitive aspects in the explosion of radical disagreement in intense conflict situations. In radical disagreement, for example, the *emotion* of indignation and the *will* to rectify injustice infuses and is infused by what is *referred to* as the outrage in question. This is what then comes to constitute a key element in the substance of the resultant phenomenon of radical disagreement when it is itself contested. It is what is only revealed in the phenomenology of radical disagreement (the exploration of agonistic dialogue) as outlined in Part II below.

5   And what of the dynamics of conflict? This is essential to systemic analysis. Yet it cannot be easily represented on two-dimensional systems perspective maps, except via a static array of arrows between fixed points. The phenomenon of radical disagreement, on the other hand, is dramatically dynamic in every sense. It emerges with sudden force at any point – including conflict transformation workshops (the only feature of intense political conflict to appear in this way) – and the speed at which spirals of linguistic contestation consequently ramify and proliferate can be breathtaking.

6   The various shifting axes of radical disagreement are also difficult to map. One example of this is that the axes of radical disagreement *within* compound conflict parties, often critical both to systems analysis and to systemic conflict transformation, as noted below, are to my knowledge, rarely indicated on systems perspective maps.

7   As for third-party interventions, these usually appear unobtrusively in the corner of systems perspective maps (e.g. 'regional players', 'the international community', 'the UN'). This masks crucial axes of radical disagreement *among* interveners (for example, Russia and the US in the Middle East Quartet).

8   More importantly, this also ignores axes of radical disagreement *between* third-party interveners and conflict parties. These often transmute in sudden reversals during the course of the conflict. Third parties, for example, who are initially welcomed, may subsequently find themselves the objects of hostility of perhaps most, or even all, the immediate stakeholders. Interveners become conflict parties.

9   Then there is the involvement of the systems perspective map and the mapmakers themselves. Here axes of radical disagreement often again emerge *between* third-party mappers and conflict parties. An example of this is illustrated in Chapter 6, when the 'peacemaking' discourse implicit in the third-party map produced by international analysts is itself challenged by one or more of the protagonists. This is often a key to linguistic intractability.

10   Finally, there is radical disagreement *among* third-party analysts that also does not appear on the map. With reference to the enterprise of conflict transformation, for example, systems analysis may claim to look deeper than complexity analysts into what underlies such complexity, or may refute purely constructivist approaches. Conversely, critical analysts may see a failure in conflict transformation to take proper account of power imbalance and positionality in its analysis. Or Foucauldian analysts may identify the peacebuilding norms of conflict transformation as covertly hegemonic despite protestations of context

sensitivity. Or culture analysts may see conflict transformation as limited by assumptions implicit in the languages and associated mental frameworks in which the conflict mapping is articulated. Or gender analysts may castigate conflict transformation as gender-blind.

I will return to the subject of complex systemic mapping in Chapter 4. There I will acknowledge its importance in the methodology for studying radical disagreement. It is a significant advance on previous conflict mapping techniques, and has proved its usefulness in preparing the ground for well-informed and more effective aid and development, as well as conflict resolution, interventions. Nevertheless, I hope that this brief critique has established why, at a certain point, the phenomenology of radical disagreement has to move beyond it.

Conclusion

A survey of the broad and diverse conflict analysis field shows once again that the phenomenon of radical disagreement is not generally seen to be significant or worth studying in its own right. It is dismissed as epiphenomenal in contextual analysis, functional for deeper drivers of conflict in internal analysis, and merely subjective in relational analysis. It is not fully accommodated in complex systems analysis. Yet this is the main verbal manifestation of intense political conflict. It is the key to linguistic intractability. Perhaps more is made of it in the field of conflict resolution, where, after all, intense political conflict and intractability constitute the chief challenges. This is the topic of Chapter 3.

3   Radical disagreement and
conflict resolution

*Conflict resolution identifies radical disagreement with destructive conflict and the
terminus of genuine dialogue. As a result, the aim of conflict resolution from the
outset is to by-pass or transform radical disagreement, not to learn from it.*

All cultures have their own ways of understanding and handling internal and
external conflict. These vary widely. But the formal field of conflict resolution
has been mainly a western venture despite the original influence of Buddhist
and Hindu traditions. Strenuous efforts have recently been made to weave wider
cultural dimensions – including Islamic dimensions – into the fabric of conflict
resolution, and important centres have been set up all over the world. Nevertheless,
the literature is still predominantly North American and European. Conflict resolution is taken here as the generic name for the enterprise which encompasses
conflict settlement at one end of the spectrum, and conflict transformation at the
other. Conflict settlement means peacemaking between conflict parties in order to
avoid direct violence. Conflict transformation means the deeper long-term project
of overcoming underlying structural violence and cultural violence and transforming identities and relations.[1]

Although this western bias is a continuing weakness in the field, from the
perspective of studying radical disagreement it may be an advantage. Edward
Hall distinguished high-context communication cultures in which most of the
information is transmitted implicitly through context and comparatively little
is conveyed directly through verbal messages, from low-context communication cultures in which most of the information is transmitted through explicit
linguistic codes (1976: 91). He identified the former with languages like Arabic
and Chinese, and the latter with languages like German, English and French.
Perhaps synaptic pathways in the brain are programmed differently as these
languages and their associated cultural mores are learned. The subject-predicate
grammar of English, for example, creates a fixed world of objects and attributes,
and encourages stark logical dichotomies (true/false, right/wrong), exclusive
categories, and adversarial relationships. So the preponderance of European
languages in the formal conflict resolution field should mean that the topic of
radical disagreement – where information is explicitly exchanged through direct
coded messages, and where sharp antagonisms and antitheses are most abruptly

expressed – becomes a focal point for linguistic analysis. This chapter is an enquiry into what the conflict resolution field says about the phenomenon of radical disagreement. For this reason, what follows will be confined to the communicative sphere. For a broader survey of the field, see Ramsbotham, Woodhouse and Miall (2005).

Conflict resolution is a multidisciplinary, multilevel study of human conflict that began professionally in the 1950s and for most practitioners is both analytic and normative. Accurate analysis is the foundation. The normative aim is most simply expressed as the overcoming of violence. Johan Galtung famously distinguished direct violence (children are killed), structural violence (children die as a result of poverty and malnutrition) and cultural violence (whatever blinds people to direct and structural violence or makes them think that these are good things) (Galtung 1996). There are complex interconnections. Structural violence (injustice, exclusion, inequality) and cultural violence (prejudice, ignorance, discrimination) lead to direct violence; direct violence reinforces and perpetuates structural and cultural violence; and so on. The normative aim of conflict resolution is not to overcome conflict. Conflict cannot be overcome – it is an unavoidable feature of social development. And conflict should not be overcome; in combating an unjust situation, there may need to be more conflict before this can be achieved. The aim, rather, is to transform actually or potentially violent conflict into non-violent forms of social struggle and social change.

The early work of Morton Deutsch can serve to set the scene. Drawing on the pioneering insights of Mary Parker Follett in labour relations (1940), Kurt Lewin in social psychology (1935), von Neumann and Morgenstern in game theory (1944) and others, Deutsch distinguished destructive conflict from constructive conflict, suggesting that the former was to be avoided, but the latter was a necessary and valuable aspect of human creativity (1949, 1973). The aim of constructive conflict resolution is to transform destructive conflict into constructive conflict. The main difference between destructive and constructive conflict, in addition to their damaging or benign consequences, lies in the contrast between *competition*, in which parties' goals are negatively interdependent, and *cooperation*, where they are positively interdependent.

Where does radical disagreement fit in? Deutsch identifies constructive conflict with 'constructive controversy' and destructive conflict with 'competitive debate'. Radical disagreement is included in competitive debate:

> The major difference ... between constructive controversy and competitive debate is that in the former people discuss their differences with the objective of clarifying them and attempting to find a solution that integrates the best thoughts that emerge during the discussion, no matter who articulates them. There is no winner and no loser; both win if during the controversy each party comes to deeper insights and enriched views of the matter that is initially in controversy ... By contrast, in competitive contests or debates there is usually a winner and a loser. The party judged to have 'the best' ideas, skills, knowledge, and so on, typically wins, while the other, who is judged to be less good,

loses. Competition evaluates and ranks people based on their capacity for a particular task, rather than integrating various contributions.

(2000: 28)

Deutsch's ideas can be illustrated by a well-known model that has been influential in conflict resolution almost from the beginning. It represents gains and losses for two competing parties locked in a competitive conflict. See Figure 3.1.

A-C-B is the constant sum line (often, misleadingly, called the zero-sum line because one person's gain is another's loss). All positions along it add up to a constant number – in this case 1. At position A, party X wins (1) and party Y loses (0). At position B, party X loses (0) and party Y wins (1). At position C, they each get half (½,½). Conflict settlement or bargaining, where a fixed asset or scarce resource is divided by mutual agreement, appears along this line in various proportions. The win–lose line, for example, can be seen to reflect the proportion of the territory of historic Palestine under the sole sovereignty of the State of Israel and the proportion possibly to be included in a future Palestinian state. Since 1949, the State of Israel has held 78 per cent of mandate Palestine, with Israeli settlements encroaching further on the remaining 22 per cent (Gaza and the West Bank) since 1967.

D-C-E is the non-constant sum line. Here the conflict parties may find that they both lose (lose–lose) or both win (win–win). Along the D-C-E line, lose–lose does not necessarily mean the worst outcome for either party, just that both end up worse off than they would have been had another strategy or course of action been adopted. And win–win does not mean an ideal solution, but that both are better off than they would have been otherwise. Constructive conflict resolution searches for creative outcomes along this line, warning that the great majority of protracted destructive conflicts end up in disastrous lose–lose outcomes, so that it is in the vital interest of all parties to find a way out of the 'prisoner's dilemma' trap. In the case

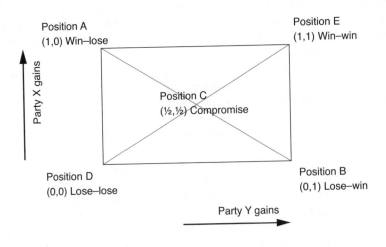

Figure 3.1 Win–lose, lose–lose, win–win

of the Israeli-Palestinian conflict, for example, the argument is that, although the Palestinians have so far come off much worse than the (Jewish) Israelis, even the Israelis are worse off than they would have been had they reached an agreement earlier. Evidently, this is all part of the ongoing conflict – and lies at the heart of the associated radical disagreements.

In prisoner's dilemma, two prisoners pursuing individual self-interest (to max-imize their own gain) and impeccable logic (each knows that the other is doing the same) are nevertheless driven to make choices that end in a lose–lose outcome that is not in their individual self-interest. Given the rules of the game, the dilemma is inescapable. They can never reach the elusive win–win outcome in which both will be better off. There is no way out in single one-off encounters, See Figure 3.2.

In prisoner's dilemma it can be seen that, whatever choice the other may make, each player considered singly gains a higher pay-off by choosing to defect. If the other cooperates, defection earns 3 points rather than 2. If the other defects, defec-tion earns 1 point rather than 0. So the only rational course for both of them is to defect if they want the highest pay-off. But if they do this, they both end up with only 1 point. This is not even the highest mutual pay-off. They could each have had 2 if they had both cooperated. In this case, win–win is (2,2) and lose–lose is (1,1). So self-interest and inescapable logic have led to the lose–lose outcome. What if they could have communicated? Even then, at the point of decision, how could each guarantee that the other would not defect, tempted by the 3 point (win–lose) prize and driven by the same logic? They are still trapped.

Prisoner's dilemma has generated an enormous and often highly technical literat-ure. One way out of the trap was famously demonstrated by Robert Axelrod (1984)

Prisoner's dilemma is a non-zero-sum game for rational self-interested players. Two prisoners accused of a crime are each given two choices: to cooperate with each other (remain silent) or to defect (inform on the other). The choices are made in ignorance of what the other will do – they are kept in separate cells. The possible pay-offs are given here with prisoner A's pay-off first and prisoner B's pay-off second within each bracket. The higher the pay-off the better: 3 means release, 2 means a short sentence, 1 means a life sentence, 0 means execution.

	Prisoner B	
	Cooperate	Defect
Cooperate	(2,2)	(0,3)
Prisoner A		
Defect	(3,0)	(1,1)

Figure 3.2 Prisoner's dilemma pay-off matrix

when he set up a computer programme for iterated prisoner's dilemma games and invited strategies prepared to compete against each other. The conflict resolution theorist, Anatol Rapaport, submitted 'tit-for-tat' that begins by cooperating despite the risk of initial loss, then copies what the other does thereafter. Given certain starting conditions, tit-for-tat beats more 'selfish' strategies that persist in competitive (defect) moves. It is initially generous (it begins cooperatively), responds toughly to aggression (it retaliates), but is forgiving (it reverts to cooperation when the other does) and is generally predictable. There have been many other variations of play in some of which tit-for-tat does not do so well. The 'shadow of the future' – the fact of continuing future relationships – determines that there can be an 'evolution of cooperation' even for competitive self-interested players, as illustrated in the nuclear weapon and anti-ballistic missile treaties between the USSR and the USA.

The important point is that tit-for-tat beats more competitive strategies, not in an altruistic sense, but because it makes the greatest gains in terms of accumulated pay-offs in its own self-interest. 'Generosity' and 'forgiveness', defined strategically, eventually win. As Richard Dawkins put it in *The Selfish Gene*, 'nice guys come first' (1989: 202–3).

But even tit-for-tat can be locked into mutually destructive conflict if the other persists in competitive play, as happens in intractable conflicts, where mutual suspicion (lack of trust) and the security dilemma (your defence is factored into my worst-case planning as offensive threat and vice-versa), as well as ideological commitment and the self-interest of intransigent parties in the continuation of the conflict, perpetuate mutual retaliation. Another way of springing the trap, therefore, is to follow the conflict resolution route and to change the players' perceptions and calculations of gain – and eventually relationship – by reframing the conflict as a shared problem. All key stakeholders must be persuaded that existing strategies lead to a lose–lose impasse and that preferable alternatives are available and will be to their advantage. Remaining irreconcilable spoilers must simply be defeated. Perceived 'pay-off' rules can be altered in ways such as these:

- by increasing scarce resources (enlarging the cake);
- by offering bold gestures on less important issues in order to reduce tension and build trust (logrolling and 'graduated reciprocal' strategies),
- by creating new options not included in the original demands (brainstorming);
- by looking for 'superordinate goals' such as mutual economic gains that neither party can achieve on its own – e.g. joint membership of the EU (superordination);
- by compensating those prepared to make concessions (compensation);
- by increasing the penalties for those who are not (penalization).

Deutsch sums up the theory of constructive conflict resolution as follows:

> In brief, the theory equates a constructive process of conflict resolution with an effective cooperative problem-solving process in which the conflict is the

mutual problem to be resolved cooperatively. It also equates a destructive process of conflict resolution with a competitive process in which the conflict parties are involved in a competition or struggle to determine who wins and who loses; often the outcome of a struggle is a loss for both parties ... At the heart of this process is reframing the conflict as a mutual problem to be resolved (or solved) through joint cooperative efforts.

(Deutsch 2000: 30–1)

Radical disagreement is identified here with destructive conflict and lose–lose outcomes – and ultimately with violence. It is seen as a superficial feature of conflict from which nothing further can be learned. The aim of conflict resolution is to loosen the knot of misunderstanding. Radical disagreement ties the knot tighter. It reinforces the entrapment of conflict parties. In radical disagreement, substantive issues are surrounded by a penumbra of emotion that chokes off constructive communication and reduces verbal exchanges to a 'conversation of the deaf'. Conflict parties blame each other, justify themselves, and endlessly repeat inherited mantras of hate. Radical disagreement is seen to be an unproductive dead-end. It is all too familiar. It is a terminus to dialogue. From the outset, therefore, Deutsch's advice is not to focus on radical disagreement, because there is no point in doing so, but, on the contrary, to look in the opposite direction:

Place the disagreements in perspective by identifying common ground and common interests. When there is disagreement, address the issues and refrain from making personal attacks. When there is disagreement, seek to understand the other's views from his or her perspective; try to feel what it would be like if you were on the other side ... Reasonable people understand that their own judgment as well as the judgment of others may be fallible.

(Ibid.: 32, 35)

But what happens when reasonable people do not, or cannot, behave like this? What happens when the radical disagreements persist? This is not a rare event. It is the norm in the intractable conflicts with which radical disagreement is chiefly associated, such as those in Sri Lanka or Kosovo or Georgia or Tibet or the Middle East. These are the conflicts that defy settlement and transformation for years, if not decades. 'Competitive debate' continues to fuel intractable conflict despite the best efforts of those who seek to dispel it. What happens when conflict resolution fails?

Is there really no more to say about radical disagreement from a conflict resolution perspective? It is worth investigating further by looking at the four best-known communicative approaches: *negotiation and mediation, interactive problem solving, dialogic conflict resolution* and *discursive conflict transformation*.

A good idea of the range of methodologies and approaches available can be found on Heidi and Guy Burgess' website *Beyond Intractability: A Free Knowledge Base on More Constructive Approaches to Destructive Conflict* (http://www.beyondintractability.org).

Negotiation and mediation

Since the 1970s, a number of systematic analyses and comparative studies of successful and unsuccessful negotiation approaches and styles have become available. The same has been true in the mediation field (Ramsbotham, Woodhouse and Miall 2005: 159–84). These studies cover negotiation of different kinds and at different levels (commercial, family, neighbourhood, community, through to international diplomacy) and mediation of various sorts (official, unofficial, with or without 'muscle', good offices, facilitation by individuals, by local representatives, by state officials and international organizations). Attention is paid to the nature of the conflict (actors, issues, evolving power relations), the nature of third-party interveners (status, capacity, roles), the process of negotiation (venue, timing, phases, complementarity of activities) and the skill-sets required (clarity and consistency of analysis, trust building, active listening, communication and persuasion skills). Efforts are made to evaluate and compare results in different situations in order to find out what works and what does not work.

This section takes the examples of *alternative dispute resolution* at domestic level and *interest-based negotiation* at international level as the most likely venues for insight into the internal economy of radical disagreement and the nature of linguistic intractability.

Alternative dispute resolution

Alternative Dispute Resolution aims to settle industrial, commercial, racial, neighbour, divorce, and other disputes, short of recourse to the courts – and extends to victim-offender mediation and restorative justice. The purpose is to shift the focus away from dead-end adversarial argument about 'delusory facts' (truth, falsehood, right, wrong) – in other words away from radical disagreement – and on to productive exploration of how to accommodate the different interpretations, perceptions and feelings that are the 'real issues'. I will take Andrew Floyer Acland's book, *Resolving Disputes Without Going to Court*, as exemplary here:

> [I]t is the tangle of material interests, emotions, prejudices, vanities, past experiences, personal insecurities and immediate feelings that drive disputes and make them so hard to resolve: these are the *real* issues. People are not motivated by *facts*: they are motivated by their *perceptions* of the facts, their *interpretations* of the facts, their *feelings* about the facts.
>
> (Floyer Acland 1995: 57 original italics)

Radical disagreement is identified with the adversarial approach that alternative dispute resolution seeks to avoid:

> [I]f the establishment of right and wrong, truth and falsehood, is important, then the adversarial process is a very good way to achieve it. But in many other situations there is a misunderstanding, a failure of communication, a clash of

values, a collision of equally valid interests. In these the problem is not that people are right or wrong, but that they are *different*; they want different things and are headed in different directions.

(Ibid.: 10)

In advising mediators how to handle such disputes, Floyer Acland offers a nine-stage process of which the first four stages bear on the phenomenon of radical disagreement. So perhaps some insight will be given here into the inner workings and nature of linguistic intractability.

Stage one is preparation. Here intransigent disagreements or disagreements over principle are ruled out as unsuitable because in these cases:

> there is no motivation for you or the other side to settle short of a trial; perhaps because you want to fight, or you are seeking public vindication, or you are just too angry even to meet …; a fundamental point of rights or principle is involved, and it needs to be proclaimed with the full majesty of the law.

(Ibid.: 76)

If mediation is to go ahead, 'conceptual preparation' means understanding that 'the adversarial assumption is ingrained and mediation involves encouraging a fresh "mind-set" – new attitudes and approaches to a problem'. The key requirement as communicated to the disputants is:

> Go into your mediation thinking: '*Let us invest time and effort in the possibility of agreement before we devote our energies and resources to disagreement*'. See if you can get the other side to adopt a similar attitude.

(Ibid.: 78 original italics)

Stage two is the setting up of the mediation. This involves pre-negotiations, choice of mediator and venue.

Then comes *stage three*, the 'opening moves', which include the mediator's introduction:

> As I think your advisers will have already explained, mediation is not like going to court, and my job is not to tell you who is right and wrong here. My task is to help you work out an agreement which suits you.

(Ibid.: 100–1)

Disagreement tends to focus on the past, whereas alternative dispute resolution tries from the beginning to look to the future. Participants are advised that opening statements should confine themselves to the positive, to the specifics of what is wanted and why, and to what can be offered in order to attain it. The disputing parties are permitted to react negatively to each other's opening statements, but only if this is couched reflexively in terms of their own reactions:

Describe how strongly you feel about what has been said by talking about your *feelings* and *reactions*; avoid accusations. Talking about your feelings and reactions is legitimate: they will listen to them. If you describe and judge *their* behaviour, they will stop listening and start thinking why you are wrong.

(Ibid.: 110 original italics)

In *stage four* – 'putting your case' – the main focus is on communication, with an emphasis on 'common causes of communications failures', including the simplifications and generalizations necessary for linguistic communication when experience has become too 'deep' or 'complex' or 'emotionally charged' to be conveyed otherwise. This then becomes a cause for misunderstanding (113–16). In order to influence others, the advice is to listen attentively, welcoming new information, being open to persuasion, and trying to respect others 'even when – perhaps *especially* when – you disagree with them'.

In summing up the 'way to success', participants are advised that disputes are easier to resolve if you:

- start by outlining the issues;
- explain what you need to achieve and why;
- ask others what they want;
- encourage appropriate allocation of responsibility;
- address the issues objectively;
- respect the other side;
- look for common ground and build on areas of agreement.

In contrast, the dispute will be harder to resolve if you:

- start with *your* solution and insist that it is the only one;
- make extravagant claims and ignore the interests of others;
- tell people only what you want;
- blame the other side for everything;
- personalize the issues;
- insult the other side;
- concentrate on differences and polarize the issues.

(Ibid.: 123).

I will not comment on the other five stages of alternative dispute mediation which move on to the generation of alternative outcomes, to the drafting of proposals, and to the breaking of anticipated deadlocks.

It can be seen that in this account of alternative dispute resolution, for entirely understandable reasons, radical disagreement is presented as the antithesis of what is required. As such it is proscribed from the very beginning. No further attention is paid to it, so there is no more to be learned about it here.

But what if, to borrow Floyer-Acland's language, the 'establishment of right and wrong, truth and falsehood' *is* important? Or there is no motivation for you or the other side to settle because you *do* want to fight or are 'seeking public vindication' or are 'just too angry even to meet'? Or a 'fundamental point of rights or principle' *is* involved and 'needs to be proclaimed'? And what if, as investigators, this is what we want to study? What if we want to explore what is said in these circumstances, and to discover what role this plays in generating the intensity and intransigence of the conflicts in question?

In that case, we will have to look elsewhere.

Interest-based negotiation

In the *Harvard Negotiation Project*, Roger Fisher, William Ury and their colleagues have attempted to move away from traditional competitive 'distributional bargaining' and to follow the earlier lead of Mary Parker Follett in the direction of the 'mutual gains' seen to be offered by 'integrative bargaining' (Fisher, Ury and Patton 1981/1991). As originally presented, this *interest-based negotiation* approach is encapsulated in a number of maxims for negotiators:

* Separate the people from the problem and try to build good working relationships.
* Facilitate communication and build trust by listening to each other rather than by telling each other what to do.
* Focus on underlying interests and core concerns, not demands and superficial positions: this includes concealed interests as well as those yet to be realized.
* Avoid zero-sum traps by brainstorming and exploring creative options without commitment to see if legitimate interests on both or all sides can be accommodated.
* Use objective criteria for evaluating and prioritizing options in terms of effectiveness and fairness.
* Anticipate possible obstacles.
* Work out how to overcome the obstacles, including the drafting of clear and attainable commitments.

The aim is to define, and if possible expand, the zone of possible agreement, and to increase its attraction in comparison with the best alternatives to a negotiated agreement as perceived by the negotiating partners individually. It also means assessing the likelihood of the worst alternatives materializing if no agreement is reached. A recent reworking of this process lays stress on 'using emotions as you negotiate' (Fisher and Shapiro 2005/7).

Perhaps the best place to see how the phenomenon of radical disagreement fits in here is *Beyond Machiavelli*, where Roger Fisher offers a 'tool-box' for negotiators seeking agreed settlements to a range of intractable international conflicts (Fisher *et al.* 1994: 17). Negotiators are offered help in clarifying their own goals and in understanding the perceptions and choices confronting their opposite numbers in order to learn how best to influence them in the preferred direction. This is an exercise in positive conflict management, not an attempt to 'solve' individual conflicts.

In the process, insights into the nature of serious political disagreement are given, such as how 'people almost always see their own perceptions as legitimate' (1994: 27), or how divergent mutual perceptions of the same message are easily generated – Fisher gives the example of the intended message of the US bombing of North Vietnam and the very different way it was received in Hanoi (1994: 46). But the reason for making these points is to contrast the pitfalls of unproductive radical disagreement (personal antagonism, dogmatic positional inflexibility) with the productive process of engaging with non-personal and non-positional 'continuing differences' and 'conflicting views' – the constructive controversies that it is the main aim of principled negotiation to encourage:

> Coping well with conflict … tends to strengthen a working relationship and to improve the ability of parties to deal with future differences … Every tool is intended to ask questions or to stimulate better questions. Better questions are not about who is right and who is wrong, or about one-shot solutions, but about the process for dealing with conflicting views about right and wrong, and for dealing with the inevitable changes that lie ahead.
>
> (Fisher *et al.* 1994: 143–4).

What is the upshot of this for the handling of radical disagreement? Advice is given to negotiators from three perspectives: their own, that of the other, and that of a third party.

From their 'own perspective', protagonists are advised to 'look forward with a purpose' to preferred goals, not backward at past resentments. They are asked to set aside their own ideas about the rights and wrongs of the situation, and to substitute a process in which differences are bracketed, detached from the question of outcomes, and subordinated to the joint search for the best ways of dealing with the conflict. In particular 'What do I think is the best goal?' should be substituted by 'How shall you and I best proceed when each of us has different ideas about what ought to happen?'

From the perspective of 'the other', the advice is to 'step into their shoes' and explore their perceptions, since:

> in each situation the key to the dispute is not objective truth but what is going on in the heads of the parties … the better we understand the way people see things, the better we will be able to change them.
>
> (Ibid.: 20, 28).

Here judgements about the world are to be translated into perceptions 'in the heads of the parties', and factual statements or normative recommendations into perspectives or expressions of feeling. This takes precedence over what the parties are in fact saying. In the case of listening to a Palestinian, for example, although we are advised to 'phrase the perceptions in the voice of the person we are trying to understand', we are warned that 'this does not mean writing a point in precisely the way they might express it'. For example 'Israelis are Zionists, and Zionists are racists' is personal and offensive, and should therefore be translated into a statement, not about what Israelis *are*, but about how Israeli actions *appear* to a Palestinian to be:

> In general, it is more useful to draft statements that describe feelings and the impact of what others do than to draft statements that judge or describe others.
>   Understanding the perception of Palestinians that Israel discriminates against Arabs will help us understand why Palestinians judge Zionists to be racists, even if we do not agree with either the perception or the judgment.
>
> (Ibid.: 27–8)

From a 'third-party' viewpoint, the critical move comes with the advice to 'look behind statements for underlying interests' (1994: 35–6). Negotiators should set aside superficial position statements that simply freeze the situation (the radical disagreement). Instead, the focus should be on the concealed and often unrealized 'true interests' or core concerns that lie beneath these positions and lead to their adoption in the first place. These are more likely to overlap and to offer wider scope for policy choice.

What is the upshot of these three excellent pieces of advice for negotiators? Undoubtedly, they greatly increase chances of an agreed settlement if the advice is mutually followed. But what happens when this fails?

This can be illustrated through the advice given by Fisher to negotiators in the Sikh secessionist conflict with the Indian government in the 1980s. Here is Fisher's advice to negotiators, and in particular, to the Sikhs:

> One way to contrast such differing priorities is to write out in parallel columns statements of positions that identify the dispute. These phrases record what each side is actually saying. Then, looking down first at their side and next at our own, we can write out phrases that suggest underlying reasons for our different positions.
>
> (1994: 39)

Positions record 'what each side is actually saying', in other words, the radical disagreement. Consider this example:

|'Sikhs require an independent nation.'

'India must remain unified.'|

Contained in this are claims, assertions and recommendations for action, supported by a wealth of historical argument and appeals to principle, in short, the characteristic features that make up radical disagreement.

But Fisher advises that all of this should be set aside as superficial and obstructive. Rather, the focus from the beginning should be on the interests that are the 'underlying reasons for our different positions':

> Many people become so locked into a position that they forget the very inter-
> ests that led them to take that position in the first place.
>
> (Ibid.: 36)

Interests are deeper than positions because they explain *why* these subjective perceptions have been adopted and clung to. In the case of the Sikhs, for example,
attention must shift away from the superficial position statement:

> 'Sikhs require an independent nation.'

and must focus instead on the more profound *substantive, symbolic* and *domestic
political* interests that have generated it. What are these interests? Fisher suggests
that they include:

- A substantive interest in 'political representation, local control and prosperity
  for farms', protection from atrocities, and the 'ability to practice [the] Sikh
  religion in peace';
- A symbolic interest in the 'protection of minority Sikh rights' and a 'Hindu
  apology for past violence';
- A domestic political interest that 'Sikhs regain confidence in the Indian
  government'.

> (Fisher *et al.* 1994: 40)

What is the upshot of this translation? The upshot is that the Sikh demand for
national independence and a sovereign Sikh state, the core of the radical disagreement, has disappeared from view. The *process* of interest-based negotiation has
predetermined the *outcome*.

   Is this a good thing? Before responding to this question, let us first consider
another example of radical disagreement about secession from India, this time
from an earlier period. The year is 1947, on the eve of Indian independence. The
issue is Muslim separatism rather than Sikh separatism. Jinnah is speaking to an
ecstatic crowd of Muslim supporters. Nehru is articulating a response overwhelm-
ingly endorsed by the Indian Congress:

> |'There are two nations on this sub-continent. This is the underlying fact that
> must shape the future creation of Pakistan. Only the truly Islamic platform of
> the Muslim League is acceptable to the Muslim nation' (Jinnah);

> 'Geography and mountains and the sea fashioned India as she is, and no human
> agency can change that shape or come in the way of her final destiny. Once
> present passions subside, the false doctrine of two nations will be discredited
> and discarded by all.' (Nehru)|
>
> (quoted in Schofield 1996: 291ff)

The outcomes in these two cases were opposite. The Sikh bid for an independent state – Khalistan – failed. The Muslim bid – Pakistan – succeeded. Was this good or bad? For the huge numbers who lost their lives and livelihoods in the break-up of India in 1947, the outcome was catastrophic. The consequences have reverberated ever since – not least in Kashmir. But the answer to the question can be seen to be an integral part of the continuing radical disagreement. Jinnah and Nehru decidedly *did not* 'draft statements that describe feelings and the impact of what others do' and explicitly *did* 'draft statements that judge and describe others'. Their successors still do the same. That is what makes this a radical disagreement. We may prefer that this did not happen. We may wish that there were no radical disagreements. But when there *are* radical disagreements, it can be seen to be integral to their linguistic intractability that the distinction between positions and interests is part of what is caught up in them.

Radical disagreement and interactive problem solving

Morton Deutsch, as seen above, sees problem solving as central in conflict resolution and identifies the heart of the process as one of reframing adversarial win–lose competition (so often degenerating into lose–lose) into 'a mutual problem to be resolved ... through joint cooperative efforts'. This is what Ronald Fisher (1997: 163–4) calls 'interactive conflict resolution'.[2] Problem solving is seen to overlap with negotiation but to go beyond its focus on 'issues' and 'interests':

> Proponents of [interactive conflict resolution] generally assume that conflict at all levels is a combination of objective and subjective factors. Sources are to be found in both realistic differences in interests over resources that generate goal incompatibilities, as well as in differing perceptions of motivations and behaviors. Conflicts based in value differences or that threaten basic needs are not expressed in substantive issues amenable to negotiation, but involve preferences and requirements of living that will not be compromised, and must be given expression in some satisfactory fashion. Escalation does not simply involve the realistic application of threats, sanctions, and actions of increasing magnitude, but elicits subjective elements that come to drive the conflict more than the substantive issues. Hatred between two ethnic groups coveting the same land, which escalates to reciprocal massacres, cannot be understood or managed by simply dealing with tangible issues. In short, [interactive conflict resolution] assumes that the phenomenological side of conflict must be considered as it is expressed in the perceptions, emotions, interactions and social institutions of the parties.

This looks very promising since we might suppose that the phenomenological side of serious human conflicts must include the inner economy of the radical disagreements that are the most prominent linguistic manifestation of those conflicts. But the sharp contrast drawn here between objective 'realistic differences in interests' and subjective 'differing perceptions' may already suggest that this will not be followed up. And, indeed, it eventually turns out that there can be no place for concern with contradictory arguments and claims when the only alternatives are said to be non-cognitive 'realistic' objectivity on the one hand, and purely psychological 'phenomenological' subjectivity on the other. So it is that the competing justifications that make up the substance of radical disagreement are not found among the conflicting interests and goal incompatibilities that constitute the former, nor among the perceptions, emotions, interactions and social institutions included under the latter. Ronald Fisher is himself a psychologist, so perhaps this is not surprising. The phenomenology of radical disagreement as understood in this book slips away between the two.

John Burton and needs theory

This can be exemplified in John Burton's 'needs theory', invoked by Ronald Fisher:

> In the 1980s a general theory emerged which could be applied to all social levels and in all cultures. Its focus was the way in which social and economic structures frustrate basic human needs, such as the needs for recognition and identity, leading to protest and frustration responses. This explanation of conflict provided the basis of policies to [prevent] violence and anti-social behaviours generally. Rather than coercive compliance measures, there could be analytical problem-solving processes that reveal the sources of problems in relationships, leading to possible reconciliation.
>
> (Burton 1997: xv)

The failure of existing structures and institutions – notably the prevailing state system at both domestic and international levels – to satisfy basic human needs like those of identity, security, development and political access, is seen to be the underlying cause of 'deep-rooted conflicts' of all kinds:

> The conclusion to which we are coming is that seemingly different and separate social problems, from street violence to industrial frictions, to ethnic and international conflicts, are symptoms of the same cause: institutional denial of needs of recognition and identity, and the sense of security provided when they are satisfied, despite losses though violent conflict.
>
> (Burton 1997: 38)

Unlike disputes over competing interests, which can be settled through bargaining and compromise, conflicts rooted in denial of fundamental human needs are onto-logical (inherent in human beings as such) and non-negotiable. This makes them intractable, and apparently irrational, from any perspective that fails to satisfy the underlying needs that generate them.

The only adequate solution for Burton, therefore, is to use analytic problem-solving techniques to uncover the deep nature of the unsatisfied needs of the conflict parties, and, in the light of this, to devise appropriate means to satisfy them. The optimistic nature of Burtonian ideas lies in the crucial (and controversial) claim that ontological human needs are generic across cultures and are always, by their very nature, mutually satisfiable (non zero-sum). Unlike interests, security needs and identity needs, for example, are not scarce resources. On the contrary, the security and identity needs of one party can only be finally assured to the extent that the security and identity needs of other parties are equally satisfied. See Figure 3.3.

Jay Rothman's ARIA method of conflict engagement

Here is an example of Burtonian thinking applied to the Israeli-Palestinian conflict over Jerusalem from the problem-solving workshop run by Jay Rothman referred to earlier in the prologue:

> You do not have to convince the other side to agree with you about your needs but only persuade them that you are indeed greatly motivated in this conflict by the pursuit or defense of them.
>
> (Rothman 1992: 19)

So, for example, it is not territorial claims, still less the land itself – in this case Jerusalem – that constitute the substance of what is at issue. These are only manifestations of what lies deeper:

> It is by 'looking beneath the territory itself to the meanings that each side attaches to it' that the roots of the conflict can be discerned and 'common ground can be found'.
>
> (Ibid.)

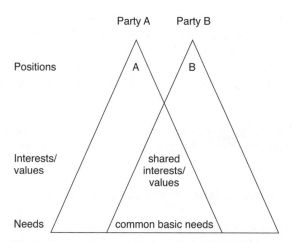

Figure 3.3 Positions, interests/values and needs

Source: Floyer Acland 1995: 50.

Underneath adversarial positions (mutually incompatible claims to sovereignty), overlapping but still often contested interests (competition for resources or political control), or even partially clashing values (Jewish/Muslim rivalry for holy lands) lie shared basic human needs (for security, identity, autonomy, development). Once the conflicting parties have been taken to this level of insight and understanding, sole ownership of 'the territory itself' (Jerusalem) is seen to be less significant and the conflict can be resolved.

This is an inspiring programme for resolving 'identity-based conflicts' and has attained a considerable measure of success (Rothman 1997). Rothman's ARIA methodology aims to move participants away from negative confrontation and towards 'constructive engagement and creative problem solving'. His approach 'allows participants to surface their Antagonism, find shared Resonance, Invent creative options, and plan Action'.

Unlike most conflict resolution specialists, Rothman does begin, in the Antagonism phase, by focusing explicitly on radical disagreement (positional dialogue or adversarial debate):

> One of the problems with previous human relations, activist and problem-solving dialogue efforts between Jews and Arabs is that they have largely been held among the already 'converted' ... Setting forth mutually exclusive positions, where each side vents its anger and articulates its own truth, can set broad parameters of the conflict and enable participants in dialogue to articulate the most common attitudes of their constituencies and/or get their own frustrations off their chests. In terms of searching for an adequate analysis and a full definition of a problem, positional statements help get the process started; the problem is when it also ends there.
>
> (Ibid.: 31)

The main idea of the adversarial stage of the conflict engagement training methodology is to encourage participants to make these 'normal' adversarial frameworks explicit. Otherwise, the assumptions and tacit understandings that constitute them cannot be contrasted with anything else and further progress is impossible. So trainers wait until the dead end of adversarial arguing becomes manifest:

> Such adversarial/positional dialogue would continue until the point at which discussions appear that they might break down altogether.
>
> (Ibid.: 170)

Trainers can then read the last rites on radical disagreement:

> You have now experienced a very familiar, and I am sure you will all agree, a rather unconstructive approach to dialogue. Each of you stated your position, each of you suggested why the other side is wrong or to blame for the conflict. Few of you listened to anyone else, and, frankly, very little, if anything, new

was learned. This is the normal approach that all of you have experienced perhaps every time you have discussed the situation with someone who holds a very different perspective than your own. I invite you now to experiment with a new way.

(Ibid.: 170)

The ARIA method contrasts the pseudo-communication of radical disagreement (positional debating) with the genuine communication offered by the mutual and reflexive analysis of underlying attitudes and emotions, the generation of creative options, and the formulation and implementation of agreed outcomes:

> Moving from positional debating to real communication requires a lot of ana-
> lysis of underlying motivations, hopes, fears of each other, especially in deeply
> rooted intercommunal conflicts.

(Ibid.: 171)

If participants, nevertheless, subsequently fall back into adversarial mode, facilitators are quick to step in:

PARTICIPANT: 'You say Jerusalem is your unity, but this is only ...'
FACILITATOR: 'Wait a minute, it sounds as if you are about to score a point. That's
            positional debate; here we want questions for clarification, for
            understanding, for analytic empathy. In a minute, I will ask you to
            role-play the other side and express their values and core concerns
            as you have heard them. So you should now gather information and
            insight to help you.'

(Ibid.: 175)

But what if, despite this, the radical disagreement continues? What if the disputants refuse to accept the 'subjectivity' of the facts they appeal to and persist in their 'objective' claims? What if they will not relinquish their real territorial rights or translate them into subjective 'meanings' symmetrically attached to their territory and therefore detachable from it, as facilitators want? What if they refute these distinctions? What if they accept that basic human needs may indeed underlie the conflict, but insist that in the present stage of regional and world politics it is precisely and only full sovereignty that can guarantee them? What if their appeal is to the bitter experience of history and to the harsh realities of contemporary power play?

This is exactly what does happen in radical disagreement, but in response the trainers reiterate their philosophy:

> You are still stuck in an illusory adversarial monologue of disbelief, mistrust
> and animosity that condemns you to repeat the mistakes of the past and pre-
> vents you from reaching the underlying human hopes, fears, and values behind
> the newspaper headlines of unbridgeable positions. Only when you come to

realise that at the deepest levels you are both alike in needs and motivations will a new opening for peace and therefore for true security be promoted.

(Rothman 1992 adapted from the original)

So, even when care is taken to note the fact of radical disagreement, the phenomenon is regarded as a negative dead end and it is assumed that nothing of value can be learned from it. Radical disagreement is not seen as genuine communication or real dialogue. It stands in the way of constructive engagement and needs to be overcome as soon as possible if progress is to be made.

But in ongoing intractable conflicts, the result of this, in my experience, can be that at the critical point it is the facilitators and trainers who find themselves involved in radical disagreement with the conflict parties – as I did in the example of the family quarrel described at the end of the prologue. That is the point at which the phenomenology, epistemology and praxis of radical disagreement begins.

Psychodynamic workshops

Vamik Volkan set up the Center for the Study of Mind and Human Interaction (CSMHI) at the University of Maryland with the following purpose:

> We remain constantly alert for those conscious and, more importantly, unconscious psychological factors which may render political processes unworkable and even malignant. We have found that large groups are profoundly influenced by such factors as ethnic or national pride, and by mental representations of historical grievances and triumphs which are transmitted, with their accompanying defenses and adaptations, from generation to generation. Underlying these factors is a need to belong to a large group and to have a cohesive group identity. Such factors function as 'unseen powers' in relationships between groups. CSMHI's aim is to shed light on these unseen powers, and to relate our findings to official decision makers so that they may deal with real world issues in a more adaptive way.
>
> (Volkan and Harris: 170–1, quoted in Fisher 1997)

Here human needs for belonging and identity are not seen to be as benign as in Burtonian theory. A psycho-social 'need to have enemies', for example, is recognized as one of the main 'unseen powers' that bedevil attempts at conflict resolution (Volkan 1988). Above all, concealed and hidden meanings are regarded as more significant than overt and surface ones because they are drivers of behaviour that are not under the conscious control of actors. Psychoanalytic defence mechanisms, such as introjection, externalization, projection and identification are deployed to protect protagonists from 'perceived psychological danger' (Volkan 1990). Relevant psychotherapeutic concepts include:

(1) the awareness that events have more than one meaning and that sometimes a hidden meaning is more important than a surface one; (2) that all

interactions, whether they take the form of overt or concealed actions, verbal or non-verbal statements, formal or informal gatherings, are meaningful and analyzable; (3) that the initiation of a process in which problems become the 'shared problems' of opposing parties is more essential than the formulation of 'logical' or 'quick' answers; and (4) that the creation of an atmosphere in which the expression of emotions is acceptable can lead to the recognition of underlying resistances to change.

(Volkan and Harris 1992: 24)

The phenomenon of radical disagreement is associated with what is overt, conscious and lies on the 'surface'. This is contrasted with those things that are hidden, unconscious and 'underlying'. So there is little motive for paying attention to the former, when it is the latter – the 'unseen powers' – that are far more potent in driving the dynamics of violent conflict.

Public decision conflict resolution

What Franklin Dukes terms 'the public conflict resolution field' uses problem-solving approaches to address the foundations of democratic politics (1996). Beginning in ethnic/racial dispute resolution in the United States, then expanding into environmental disputes and other areas requiring public decision-making, such as education, health and economic development, public conflict resolution is seen by Dukes, not only as a means for reaching agreement over specific issues, but also as a way of raising public consciousness and increasing popular participation in decisions affecting the community:

Increasingly the practical need to gain agreement among divergent interests who have a stake in public decisions, who share limited power, and who have very different goals, has led to new kinds of decision-making forums.

(Dukes 1996: 1)

Transformative public conflict resolution

encompasses more than a theory of resolving disputes. Such thinking is contributing to an evolution in the understanding of what conflict means, when conflict is valuable, where it is destructive, and how it can be transformed ... It is becoming part of the reconception of how democratic institutions and communities may be sustained.

(Ibid.: 7)

Dukes welcomes conflict as the 'basis for social change' in a democratic society and encourages the productive dialogue associated with it. But he distinguishes this from adversarial debate (radical disagreement):

Just stimulating people to challenge and contest status quo conformities

> ... is likely to do little more than provoke disagreement and controversy, increase polarization, and ultimately end in win–lose, impasse, compromise, or chaos.
>
> (Blake and Mouton 1970: 421, quoted Dukes 1996: 165)

Radical disagreement is associated with 'rancorous personal debate' and is identified with the worst features of 'the Anglo-American adversary system' that is seen to distort so much of public discourse:

> We all know the characteristics of an all-out, knock-down, drag-out debate. Opponents line up against one another to seek (or invent) the weaknesses in others' statements. Nobody ever admits wrong or uncertainty. Everyone begins with the answer and defends that answer against all attack.
>
> (Dukes 1996: 69)

> This system encourages speaking and penalizes listening ... The goal of adversarial proceedings is not to develop understanding, not to find constructive solutions, and not even to discover the truth. The goal of speech in these situations is to win. Indeed, in adversarial systems ... speech is another species of aggression and power.
>
> (Ibid.: 130)

The programme of transformative public conflict resolution is creative and effective. But once again the phenomenon of radical disagreement is identified with what the programme seeks to overcome and is not thought to be worth investigating in its own right.

Dialogic conflict resolution

Ronald Fisher explains how dialogic conflict resolution approaches differ from the problem-solving processes looked at in the previous section:

> Unlike the more focused forms of interactive conflict resolution, such as problem-solving workshops, dialogue interventions tend to involve not influential, informal representatives of the parties, but simply ordinary members of the antagonistic groups. Furthermore, dialogue is primarily directed toward increased understanding and trust among the participants with some eventual positive effects on public opinion, rather than the creation of alternative solutions to the conflict.
>
> (Fisher 1997: 121)

The aim is to improve communication, sensitivity, critical self-awareness and mutual understanding between individuals and groups, the lack of which is seen to be a key ingredient in generating the social milieu in which violent conflict breeds.

An idea of the wide spectrum of dialogic techniques for handling conflict and effecting non-violent social change (which overlaps with problem solving) can be found in the Pioneers of Change Associates 2006 survey, *Mapping Dialogue* (www.pioneersofchange.net).[3] For all the variety among the different approaches, the survey finds 'clear common patterns':

> They focus on enabling open communication, honest speaking, and genuine listening. They allow people to take responsibility for their own learning and ideas. They contain a safe space or container for people to surface their assumptions, to question their previous judgments and worldviews, and to change the way they think. They generate new ideas and solutions that are beyond what anyone had thought before. They create a different level of understanding of people and problems.
>
> (Pioneers of Change Associates 2006: 6)

And a clear contrast is once again drawn between true dialogue and mere debate (radical disagreement):

> The most common dictionary definition of a dialogue is simply as a conversation between two or more people. In the field of dialogue practitioners, however, it is given a much deeper and more distinct meaning. David Bohm went back to the source of the word, deriving from the Greek root of 'dia' which means 'through' and 'logos' which is 'the word' or 'meaning', and therefore saw dialogue as meaning flowing through us. Elements of this deeper understanding of the word include an emphasis on questions, inquiry, co-creation, and listening, the uncovering of one's own assumptions and those of others, a suspension of judgment and a collective search for truth. Bill Isaacs calls a dialogue a conversation 'with a center, not sides'.
>
> (Ibid.: 10)

In contrast, 'a debate is a discussion usually focussed around two opposing sides, and held with the object of one side winning. The winner is the one with the best articulations, ideas and arguments'.

In view of this variety, what follows will be selective and will focus on recent developments in dialogic approaches at both individual and group levels influenced by the philosophy of Hans-Georg Gadamer, with a particular emphasis at group level on intercultural dialogue. The Gadamerian approach ultimately sees dialogue as a 'fusion of horizons' across cultural and historical differences. It is called 'hermeneutic dialogue' because it draws a parallel between a conversation and the interpretation of texts. For Gadamer, interpreting a text is seen as a form of *conversation* between object and interpreter. In conflict resolution, it works the other way. A dialogue or conversation is seen as a mutual *interpretation of texts*.

Interpersonal dialogue

Dialogic approaches in interpersonal conflict resolution draw mainly from the communication, psychology and active listening literatures. Recent developments point beyond the original psychotherapeutic idea of 'projective' sympathy and empathy in which the aim was to 'enter the private perceptual world of the other and become thoroughly at home in it' (Rogers 1980: 142). Instead, the focus has shifted to the concept of 'relational' empathy in which a more dynamic and productive process is envisaged, whereby, in intense interpersonal exchange that is as much affective as cognitive, participants together generate shared new meaning sometimes referred to as a 'third culture' (Broome 1993). This approach reflects Gadamer's insistence that in the field of interpretation it is 'a hermeneutical necessity always to go beyond mere reconstruction' in reaching understanding:

> This placing of ourselves is not the empathy of one individual for another, nor is it the application to another person of our own criteria, but it always involves the attainment of a higher universality that overcomes, not only our own particularity, but also that of the other.
>
> (Gadamer 1975: 272)

Heavy demands are thereby made on participants, who are expected to be able to recognize that they can never escape the universal reach of their own prejudice and that the attempted 'fusion of horizons' or relational empathy will always be the creation of something that did not exist before (a third culture), and an on-going project, never a completed programme. They are asked to 'decentre' their own identities to the point where – in the words of Stewart and Thomas – instead of seeking 'certainty, closure and control', they welcome the tension between 'irreconcilable horizons' and adopt a 'playfulness' and open-mindedness appropriate to encounter with new experience or the ultimately unabsorbable 'other' (Stewart and Thomas 2005: 198).

These 'dialogic attitudes' are seen by Benjamin Broome as integral to the conflict resolution enterprise:

> The third culture can only develop through interaction in which participants are willing to open themselves to new meanings, to engage in genuine dialogue, and to constantly respond to the new demands emanating from the situation. The emergence of this third culture is the essence of relational empathy and is essential for successful conflict resolution.
>
> (Broome 1993: 104)

There are echoes here of the Rortyan idea of self-distance and irony as hallmarks of open liberal societies (1988), and of Chris Brown's identification of irreverence, humour, recognition of one's own absurdity, and the giving up of aspirations to ground our values in 'some ultimate sense of what is true or false', as what most distinguishes our prevailing Western version of modernity from the unattractive 'fundamentalisms' that challenge it (2002). Rorty admits the unavoidable 'ethnocentricity' involved in his attempt to combine the distance of irony with full commitment to the values thereby safeguarded. Brown similarly tempers his advocacy of irony ('distancing oneself and one's beliefs') by insisting that this must not 'undermine one's basic values' which one must hold 'wholeheartedly'. He acknowledges that this is a 'terribly difficult' balance to strike.

It can be seen that these required 'dialogic attitudes' are far removed from those that characterize radical disagreements. Indeed, in some versions they are diametrically opposed to them. The whole enterprise of fostering relational empathy of this kind is premised on the exclusion of radical disagreement.

Inter-group dialogue

A similar set of ideas can be found in the field of inter-group or inter-communal dialogue. An idea of the range of enterprises loosely grouped under the dialogic heading can be given by noting the activities of the Community Relations Council in Northern Ireland, which has included:

- mutual understanding work ('to increase dialogue and reduce ignorance, suspicion and prejudice');
- anti-sectarian and anti-intimidation work ('to transfer improved understanding into structural changes');
- cultural traditions work ('to affirm and develop cultural confidence that is not exclusive');
- political options work ('to facilitate political discussion within and between communities, including developing agreed principles of justice and rights');
- conflict resolution work ('to develop skills and knowledge which will increase possibilities for greater social and political cooperation').

(Fitzduff 1989)

Here, in the wake of the dramatic and unexpected events of the first decade of the new millennium, the related enterprises of comparative religious ethics and inter-religious dialogue will be taken as an example. The coincidence of the United Nations 2001 *Year Of Dialogue Between Civilizations* with the catastrophe of 11 September projected this to the top of the international agenda.

In response to the events of September 2001, for example, Bikhu Parekh rejected the US government's militaristic and 'punitive' reaction which he saw as counter-productive and morally equivalent to the terrorism it purported to oppose, and advocated 'intercultural dialogue' between Western and non-Western (in this case particularly Muslim) societies with a view to uncovering the deeper sources of grievance and perceived injustice behind the attack:

The point of the dialogue is to deepen mutual understanding, to expand sympathy and imagination, to exchange not only arguments but also sensibilities, to take a critical look at oneself, to build up mutual trust, and to arrive at a more just and balanced view of both the contentious issues and the world in general.

(Parekh 2002: 274)

In order to 'get to the heart of the deepest disagreements' between Western and Muslim societies, Parekh offered two composite 'opening statements' adapted from 'the utterances of intellectuals and political leaders' on both sides. He described these as 'partisan, extreme, polemical, hurtful and sometimes deeply offensive'. We are standing on the outer perimeter of the domain to be explored in this book. But Parekh himself does not want to move further into this terrain. On the contrary, he immediately turns in the opposite direction. The sole purpose of taking note of the disagreement for him, as for others in the dialogic tradition, is thereby to establish the 'discursive framework' within which the 'badly needed dialogue' can take place (2002: 281).

The vision behind the proposed dialogue is of an infinitely subtle series of mutually reinforcing exchanges at various levels in different locations around the world, with a view to building 'better intercultural understanding' and 'a broadly agreed view of the past' in order to expedite eventual 'mutually acceptable compromise' on substantive issues. Continuing radical disagreement of the kind represented in the opening statements would disrupt communication and threaten this programme. 'Deep differences' need to be 'admitted', but must not be allowed to 'get out of control' to the point where they might prevent the building of consensus towards the desired ultimate goal – the creation of a 'shared global perspective' (2002: 282).

Each society also needs to be critical of itself:

A society unable to engage in a critical dialogue with itself and tolerate disagreement is unable to engage in a meaningful dialogue with others.

(Parekh 2002: 276)

Comparative religious ethics

In the field of comparative religious ethics, it is illuminating to continue the Gadamerian theme by looking at what Sumner Twiss rather ponderously calls the 'hermeneutical-dialogical paradigm'. He contrasts this with the 'formalist paradigm' which is focused on the study of 'ourselves (and others)', and the 'historical' paradigm which is focused on the study of 'others (and ourselves)'. The 'hermeneutic-dialogical' paradigm, which Twiss favours, studies 'others and ourselves as equals'.[4] At the core of the hermeneutical-dialogical paradigm is the goal of constructing a 'common moral world' between divergent traditions, which involves a dialectic of mutual translation and receptivity through continual dialogue in a constructive effort to answer the shared question: how should we live together? (Twiss 1993). This involves 'normative appropriation' (fusion of horizons) between insider-participants of the kind mentioned above, and with similar implications.

Inter-religious dialogue

It is also worth noting the related but distinct enterprise of inter-religious dialogue, such as the 1993 Parliament of the World's Religions that attempted to frame a shared 'global ethic'. Recent efforts have been made to bring comparative religious ethics and inter-religious dialogue together (Twiss and Grelle eds 2000). The central purpose of the kind of dialogue envisaged in the 1993 parliament was not to create new shared meaning, but to confirm that

> there is already a consensus among the religions which can be the basis for a global ethic – a minimum fundamental consensus concerning binding values, irrevocable standards, and fundamental moral attitudes.
>
> (Küng and Kuschel 1993: 18)

The substance of the 1993 global ethic was seen to lie in the common demand that 'every human being must be treated humanely' supported by underlying principles of universal beneficence, human rights, and the negative and positive versions of the Golden Rule. On this admittedly somewhat 'western' conceptual foundation, four 'irrevocable directives' or 'broad guidelines for human behaviour' were seen to be generated (Küng and Kuschel 1993: 24–34):

1 'commitment to a culture of non-violence and respect for life';
2 'commitment to a culture of solidarity and a just economic order';
3 'commitment to a culture of tolerance and a life of truthfulness';
4 'commitment to a culture of equal rights and partnership between men and women'.

The success of the enterprise depended once again on the 'bracketing out' of serious disagreement, but this time by the simple mechanism of omission, on the assumption that whatever was left could then be said to constitute the desired global religious consensus.

Traces of the bracketing process are evident throughout. In terms of management, for example, the filtering out of disagreement was controlled by Hans Küng, whose draft *Declaration* (based on prior consultations) was not subsequently altered during the week-long meeting of the Parliament, except that its title was changed to *Toward A Global Ethic (An Initial Declaration)*. Similar signs of positive management appear in Küng's edited, *Yes To A Global Ethic* (1996), which collected expressions of support from religious and political leaders. In terms of participation, certain discordant voices were self-eliminating ('even at the planning stage, evangelical and fundamentalist church groups refused to collaborate with the Parliament' (Küng and Kuschel 1993: 95)). On matters of substance, some divergent views could be accommodated by ambiguous wording (the pacifist commitment to 'a culture of non-violence' was glossed so that 'those who hold political power' need only 'commit themselves to the most non-violent, peaceful solutions possible'); others by abstract language which delivered formal unanimity but at the cost, in some eyes, of allowing pernicious interpretations to lurk unchallenged. Sallie King detected an 'is/ought struggle' in the text between what was already common religious teaching and what was not but should be ('surely no one could seriously propose' that the commitment to equal rights for men and women 'accurately reflects' an ethic that 'already exists within the religious teachings of the world' (King 2000: 132). As a final resort, deeply recalcitrant issues could simply be omitted, including – to the surprise of some – specific references to God.

As for Küng himself – in a way reminiscent of the different liberal dialogic tradition seen above which wants to combine irony with commitment – a chapter on 'the God of the non-Christian religions' in his book *Does God Exist?* aims to 'recognize, respect and appreciate the truth of other conceptions of God', but at the same time 'without relativizing the Christian faith in the true God':

> Does God exist? We are putting all our cards on the table here. The answer will be: 'Yes, God exists'.
>
> (Küng 1978/80: xxiii)

What does this mean? And above all, what does it mean in a context of radical disagreement when real choices have to be made between incompatible commitments and outcomes in the shared public world? An idea can be gained from Küng's response to the claims of the tolerant, reformed Hinduism of Sarvepalli Radhakrishnan. This is dismissed as 'a specifically Hindu tolerance' based on the authority of the Vedanta and thus a thinly disguised exclusivity every bit as absolute as that of 'the prophetic religions' (Judaism, Christianity and Islam):

> Conquest as it were by embrace in so far as it seeks not to exclude but to include all other religions.
>
> (Ibid.: 608)

To the question, 'Who is God?', Küng replies unequivocally that the true God is the Triune God of the Roman Catholic Christian faith who alone has full salvific authority and reality. I think that, regardless of a global ethical consensus, in situations of intractable interfaith doctrinal conflict, it is clear whose side Küng is on.

Is dialogue for mutual understanding always appropriate?

In light of the above, and before moving on to the final section of this chapter, it is worth asking whether the enterprise of expanding the scope for inclusive dialogue work, along the lines suggested by Biku Parekh and others, is always appropriate. Its aim is to sideline or transform radical disagreement. But what if radical disagreements nevertheless persist? *Should* we be prepared to participate in this kind of dialogue and 'safe spaces' work if we are ourselves party to a radical disagreement? And *can* we do so if we are not? My answer in both cases is 'no'.

In the first instance, where we are ourselves a party to the conflict, suppose that what the other says is patently absurd, morally repugnant or murderous – a blatant manipulation of the facts to build support for an unacceptable political programme. Should we pretend to engage in 'deepening mutual understanding', as Parekh recommends, or aim to 'take a critical look at ourselves' and 'expand' our 'sympathy and imagination' with a view to enriching our comprehension of the other's arguments? I do not think so. The question is, rather, should we give the other a platform for spreading such hateful ideas at all?

Faced, for example, with an assertion such as this by David Irving:

> 74 000 Jews died of natural causes in the work camps and the rest were hidden in reception camps after the war and later taken to Palestine, where they live today under new identities.
>
> (*Times Online*: February 22 2006)

my own response is to want to minimize its political impact and to refute it outright – along the lines painstakingly undertaken by critics such as Deborah Lipstadt or Richard Evans:

> Clearly ... the work of the 'revisionists' who deny that Auschwitz ever happened at all, is simply wrong ... Auschwitz was not a discourse.
>
> (Evans 1997 quoted in Wheen 2004: 97)

The fact that holocaust denial is rife in parts of Europe and across the Middle East does not alter this. So far as I am concerned, to 'understand' why some people believe such patent untruths is simply to find explanations for why the other holds such false beliefs. For me to pretend otherwise in this case would be a sham.

The same applies generally. Here is an example where outrage is expressed at the murder of the Rev Julie Nicholson's daughter, Jenny, by Mohammad Siddique Khan on the Edgware train on 7 July 2005:

> There are few human words that can adequately express what we feel about people who indiscriminately carry out apparent acts of senseless violence against innocent civilian populations and, unbelievably, do so in the name of God. Such delusion, such evil, is impossible for us to begin to comprehend.
>
> (*Guardian*: September 4 2005)

Julie Nicholson herself eventually gave up her own ministry because she could not forgive the perpetrator:

> No parent should reasonably expect to outlive their children. I rage that a human being could choose to take another human being's life. I rage that someone should do this in the name of a God. I find that utterly offensive. We have heard a lot in the media about things causing certain groups of people offence and I would say that I am hugely offended that someone should take my daughter in the name of a religion or a God.
>
> (Ibid.)

In a case like this, where we are ourselves a party to radical disagreement, the aim of dialogue with the other, if it takes place at all, can only be to show the other, or the other's potential supporters and sympathizers, why s/he is factually mistaken, morally wrong or insincere.

And what of radical disagreements in which we are not immediate conflict parties? Here again, if we take radical disagreement seriously, my conclusion is that we cannot encompass it within the usual canons of dialogue and safe spaces work. A common rule in dialogue work, for example, is that each should listen to the other with mutual respect so that differences can be tolerated, if not celebrated. But we can see how, in radical disagreements, such conceptual/emotional space does not exist. To insist on dialogic rules of this kind is to exclude radical disagreement. However uncomfortable it may be for liberals (among whom I include myself) to accept this, we simply do not respect what the other says – or the other as sayer of it – in such circumstances. (The idea that we may nevertheless respect the other's *right* to say it will be considered later).

There is no room in the rules of dialogue, for example, to accommodate this radical disagreement between the governor of South Dakota, Mike Rounds, and his chief Democrat opponent, Steve Hildebrand:

| 'Abortion is murder. God creates human life and it is blasphemous for any of God's creatures to take it away. It is an unforgiveable sin. The State of South Dakota is right to ban it by law absolutely.'

'They've gone too far. They're essentially saying that if your daughter gets raped, she has no choice but to have the criminal's baby. This is entirely inhumane and morally deeply wrong. It is un-Christian. It must be immediately reversed.' |

(*USA Today*: 7 March 2006)

To insist that the purpose of dialogue as encapsulated in its regulatory framework is to 'increase understanding and trust among participants' is to assume that more understanding will lead to more trust. It omits the possibility that more interchange will deepen mistrust, or that more understanding will make it even clearer to participants why they hate each other. Here is Jerry Falwell on the cause of the events of 11 September 2001:

The attack on the Twin Towers was God's wrath against the pagans and the abortionists and the feminists and the gays and the lesbians and the American Civil Liberties Union and People for the American Way – against all those who try to secularise America.

(quoted in Wheen 2004: 183–4)

In the case of radical disagreement about the de-legalization of abortion in South Dakota, or attempts to reverse Wade versus Roe in the US Supreme Court, the recommendations for action are starkly incompatible. Either the law is imposed, or it is revoked. That is what makes this a radical disagreement. The rules of dialogue as defined in many conflict resolution approaches exclude radical disagreement from the outset.

Radical disagreement and discursive conflict transformation

In the communicative sphere, two features in particular have led to criticism of mainstream negotiation, problem solving and dialogue approaches as described above, and have generated new thinking. These features are the *complexity of conflict* and the fact of *asymmetric conflict*. Some identify these responses with a move from conflict resolution to conflict transformation. John Paul Lederach and Norbert Ropers will be taken as exemplars of the first, and Vivienne Jabri of the second. But first a comment on the recent work of one of the founders of the field, who now also adopts the transformationist language – Johan Galtung. How is the phenomenon of radical disagreement treated in these examples?

At the heart of Galtung's TRANSCEND methodology (2000; 2004) lies an adaptation of the *win–lose, lose–lose, win–win* model looked at in Figure 3.1. This is interpreted as a model of conflict outcomes. In constant-sum (zero-sum) conflicts, one or other party prevails (either–or) or there is some form of compromise (part–part). In non-constant-sum conflicts, neither party gets what it wants (neither–nor: negative transcendence) or both parties get what they want (both–and: positive transcendence). Galtung's main adaptation is to identify the lose–lose outcome with negative transcendence; it can sometimes be better than the win–lose alternatives.

Faced with the 'two nations, one territory' problem in Palestine, for example, Galtung notes five possible outcomes, of which negative transcendence (neither–nor) would be better than the two win–lose (either–or) alternatives:

1 one Israeli state (Palestinians out) Either–Or (A);
2 one Palestinian state (Israelis out) Either–Or (B);
3 a two-state solution (Israel and Palestine) Part–Part;
4 a third party takes over (UN protectorate) Neither–Nor;
5 two nations enter symmetrically in one state Both–And.

In general, the either–or outcomes are seen as the worst, and the both–and positive transcendence outcome as the best – where available:

> Positive transcendence [is] the key to transformation in the TRANSCEND method.
>
> (Galtung 2004: 13).

Much of this is already familiar, including the identification of either–or outcomes with 'constraining debate' (radical disagreement) and the both–and outcome with 'creative dialogue' (constructive controversy):

> A debate is a fight with verbal, not physical weapons (in French *battre* = beat). The victory usually goes to he who can catch the other in more contradictions … A dialogue, *dia logos*, through the word, by using words, is something quite different. There is no competition to win a battle of words. The parties are working together to find a solution to a problem.
>
> (Ibid.: 38)

In Gadamerian vein, the aim of dialogue is once again 'to get under the skin of each other in a questioning way, not in the drilling way of a debate', and to search for a fusion of horizons:

> Imagine now that instead of debating, trying to defeat each other with words, they had used their eloquence in a dialogue, with the aim of finding how their contradictions could be transcended and their perspectives combined in a higher unity.
>
> (Ibid.: 57)

Galtung does at times recommend identifying the 'axioms of faith' associated with radical disagreement, but this is only in order to

> start touching them, tinkering with them, shaking them, inserting the word 'not', negating them so that everything becomes more flexible.
>
> (Ibid.: 80)

No further interest is taken in the phenomenon of radical disagreement in the TRANSCEND method.

John Paul Lederach and Norbert Ropers: acknowledging complexity and overcoming binary logic

In his book, *Solving Tough Problems* (2007), Adam Kahane identifies three types of complexity, each of which requires a different remedy. Dynamic complexity refers to the fact that links between cause and effect are non-linear and are individually unpredictable. This requires a systemic approach. Social complexity refers to the fact that there are conflicting views about the problem. This requires a participative approach. Generative complexity refers to the fact that former solutions are no longer succeeding. This requires a creative approach.

John-Paul Lederach, who offered trenchant criticisms of universalist cultural assumptions behind western mediation methods in the 1980s and developed innovative reconceptualizations of peacebuilding in the 1990s, has now also stuck his colours firmly to the transformationist mast (2003, 2005). Within the communicative sphere, Lederach is severely critical of reductive either–or frames of reference (radical disagreement), and strongly in favour of acknowledging the complex webs of interactions that make up the real (lived) world and of nurturing what he calls 'the moral imagination' in learning how to navigate and transform them (2005: 172–3).

Lederach does advocate seeking 'constructive engagement with those people and things we least understand and most fear', in other words, he encourages dialogue that includes 'political and ideological enemies' (2005: 177). So it might be thought that this points towards taking radical disagreement seriously. But his all-embracing critique of either/or and espousal of both/and thinking precludes Lederach from doing this. He does not see anything worth investigating in radical disagreements. In fact, in the end, he seems not to think that there are such things as radical disagreements at all:

> *Develop the capacity to pose the energies of conflict as dilemmas*: I tend to link two ideas with the phrase 'and at the same time'. This is not just a quirk in my writing; it has become part of my way of thinking and formulating perspective. It reflects my effort to shift my thinking from an either/or to a both/and frame of reference. This is what I would call the art and discipline of posing conflicts as dilemmas ... The decisions we faced seemed to pose outright contradictions as framed by the people involved and even by ourselves as practitioners ... When we changed our way of framing questions to 'both and', our thinking shifted. We learned to recognize the legitimacy of different, but not incompatible, goals and energies within the conflict setting ... When we embrace dilemmas and paradoxes, there is the possibility that in conflict we are not dealing with outright incompatibilities. Rather, we are faced with recognizing and responding to different but interdependent aspects of a complex situation. We are not able to handle complexity well if we understand our choices in rigid either/or or contradictory terms. Complexity requires that we develop the capacity to identify the key energies in a situation and hold them up together as *interdependent goals* ... The capacity to live with apparent contradictions and paradoxes lies at the heart of conflict transformation.
>
> (Lederach 2004: 51–3)

The idea of a transformative shift to living with paradox is inspiring. But there *are* radical disagreements. They *are* couched in 'rigid contradictory terms'. And this *is* how the conflict is 'framed by the people involved'. In the unredeemed world we live in, radical disagreements continue as defining features of the most intense and protracted political conflicts. So what are we to make of those who nevertheless persist in posing conflicts, not as dilemmas, but as contradictions? These are the conflict parties. Is there nothing further to learn from what they say?

Norbert Ropers carries the idea of dilemmatic thinking further by invoking the four-fold (plus) traditional Buddhist *tetralemma* in his analysis of the linguistic aspect of the Sinhala–Tamil conflict in Sri Lanka (2008).

This conflict, recently dramatically 'transformed' – but not ended – by force of arms through government military victory, has pitted the secessionist (mainly Hindu) Liberation Tigers of Tamil Eelam (LTTE) and others against the anti-secessionist (mainly Buddhist) Sinhala-dominated Government of Sri Lanka (GoSL).

From 1983, there was almost continuous war, interrupted by the 2002 peace process, until the collapse of the rebels in 2009.

Ropers uses the tetralemma to map out what he calls 'mental models' in the Sri Lankan conflict. Mental models include those interpretations and beliefs that motivate and drive agents to act as they do in the conflict, not only the main conflict parties but also involved third parties. The primary discourses of both Sinhala and Tamil mainstream parties are seen to be made up of potent religious-historical national narratives fired by claims to original settlement, inherited grievance and shared destiny:

> All parties have developed their own narratives or 'mental models' of the conflict, as well as options and possibilities of conflict resolution. These narratives and models have had tremendous impact on the way parties communicate and interact with each other. They often develop a life of their own and are deeply ingrained in the attitudes and behaviour of the respective collectives.
>
> (Ropers 2008: 17)

Whereas a dilemma confronts two apparently incompatible alternatives, a tetralemma envisages four alternative stances on any controversial issue:

Position A;   *Position B*;

Neither position A nor position B;   *Both position A and position B*.

The third century Buddhist philosopher, Nagarjuna, pointed to a further transcendent stance outside these four alternatives expressed by the 'double negation':

Not any of these but also not that.

This is reminiscent of Judaeo-Christian negative theology, and later Sufi Islamic mysticism. It is in the apophatic tradition where the ineffability of God cannot be put into words.

Ropers uses the tetralemma to map out the interpretations and beliefs that make up the mental models driving the Sri Lankan conflict. See Box 3.1.

It is evident that the phenomenon of radical disagreement is not represented on the conceptual map at all because radical disagreement is not a position, but a relation. It is polylogical, not monological. Radical disagreement appears when the two rejected positions (A and B) are not treated separately, or transcended, but are presented together in all their raw mutual antagonism as here:

> |'This blessed land will forever cherish, protect and value the fruits of the brave and courageous operation conducted by the Sri Lankan Security Forces to bring liberation to the people of the East, who for more than two decades were held hostage by the forces of vicious and violent terrorism.'
>
> (M. Rajapaska, President of Sri Lanka 19 July 2007)

Box 3.1 The tetralemma applied to the Sinhala–Tamil conflict in Sri Lanka

Source: Ropers 2008: 29.

Position A

Unitary state or moderate
devolution only

Position B

High level autonomy or
separate state

Neither A nor B

Power sharing is not the key issue:
more important are genuine democracy,
development, good local governance etc.

Both A and B

Compromise – genuine
power sharing, federalism etc.

Position A is that of the government and majority of Sinhala mainstream parties.
Position B is that of Tamil nationalist parties, particularly the LTTE.
Neither A nor B represents the position of a number of civil society groups, who
argue that the 'real problems' are not to do with the question of power-sharing
among the various political elites, but with other unsatisfied needs.
Both A and B represents the position of international peacemakers
(e.g. Norway, the UN) – for example, a 'federal structure within a united Sri Lanka'
(the formula agreed between the LTTE and the Government of Sri Lanka in the
December 2002 negotiations in Oslo).

Ropers also suggests possibilities for a further stance outside the frame,
corresponding to Nagarjuna's 'none of these but not that' – 'avoid any of the
solutions; emphasise other dimensions of mutual engagement; or go to war'.

'We are at a crossroads in our freedom struggle. Our journey has been long
and arduous, and crowded with difficult phases. We are facing challenges and
unexpected turns that no other freedom movement had to face. The Sri Lankan
government has split the Tamil homeland, set up military camps, bound it with
barbed wire, and has converted it into a site of collective torture.'|
(V. Pirapaharan, prominent Tamil Tiger Leader 27 November 2006)

Ropers hopes to use the tetralemma to transcend binary thinking:

The tetralemma 'is a tool that has the potential of overcoming the binary logic
of these two sets of attitudes and fears'.

(Ropers 2008: 17)

This is a noble venture and it may well succeed. It is certainly greatly needed in
the aftermath of the Sri Lankan government's military victory, if peace is to be
consolidated, and the passions that may fuel renewed revolt assuaged. But radical disagreement, such as the example given above, is not taken note of in the
tetralemma. The argument in Part II of this book is that it would be a good idea to
supplement the tetralemma with serious exploration of the radical disagreements

that constitute the core of the linguistic intractability when conflict parties refuse to give up their embattled positions. Quite simply, there is no other recourse in the communicative sphere in times of maximum conflict intractability.

Vivienne Jabri: establishing the critical foundations for a discourse of peace

The second main basis for a transformationist critique is the fact of asymmetric conflict. Asymmetric conflicts are those in which conflict parties are unequal in power, either quantitatively (e.g. strong vs weak states) or qualitatively (e.g. state vs non-state actors) or both. In these circumstances, the conflict resolution aim of converting win–lose competition into an exercise in cooperative problem solving is seen to reinforce the position of the powerful – a *normalization* and *pacification* that plays into the hands of those who want to preserve the *status quo*. Negotiation, problem solving and dialogue, without a wider transformational agenda for addressing the structural, institutional and discursive nature of the asymmetry, are seen as uncritical and counter-productive (a similar critique comes from proponents of non-violent direct action (Dudouet 2006)).

Here is Edward Said's criticism of attempts at cooperative negotiation, problem solving and dialogue in the Israeli-Palestinian conflict:

> There is still a military occupation, people are still being killed, imprisoned and denied their rights on a daily basis. The main prerogatives for us Arabs and Palestinians are therefore clear. One: we must struggle to end the occupation. Two: we must struggle even harder to develop our own independent institutions and organizations until we are on a relatively equal footing with the Israelis. Then we can begin to talk seriously about cooperation. In the meantime cooperation can all too easily shade into collaboration with Israeli policy.
>
> (Said 1995: 37)

Problem-solving workshops operate with 'reasonable people, with reasonable goals such as peaceful coexistence' rather than with those fighting for existential justice. Nadim Rouhana and S. Körper argue that problem-solving workshops cover over the ways in which differential advantages and disadvantages for 'higher power groups' and 'lower power groups' contradict facilitators' basic assumptions about communicative symmetry (1996). Deiniol Jones mounts a sustained critique of the Israeli-Palestinian Oslo Accords along similar lines; given the asymmetry between the two sides, it perpetuated rather than transformed the conflict (1999).

For these reasons, many have turned to critical theory in general, and to Jürgen Habermas' discourse ethics in particular, for a transformative communicative approach that will address asymmetry.

Jay Rothman, for example, appeals to Habermas in the integrative stage of the ARIA method because Habermas' critical epistemology 'seeks to transform reality, such as the international system, by approaching it with a normative view as to what it ought to become':

Critical theory both critiques and attempts to transform the status quo ... [It] is concerned with distinguishing those social meanings that are ideologically based or socially conditioned, and therefore in principle open to transformation, from those that are based on invariant laws that must be discovered and can at best be reordered. These laws, which Habermas (1979) calls *transcendental* criteria of truth, may be discovered in an 'ideal speech' situation in which conditions of perfect freedom and lack of coercion exist such that agents in discussion may converge on 'common opinions'.

(Rothman 1992: 72)

I will say more about Habermas' ideas in Chapter 6. But three moves make this an attractive option for systemic conflict transformation:

1   the uncovering of existing power-saturated discourses and exposure of the ruses that make them seem 'natural' (along the lines described in Chapter 1 of this book);
2   disengagement from this terrain and a shift to second-order critical analysis;
3   reconstruction of a new discourse free from power on a different basis – the ideal speech situation where 'agents in discussion may converge on common opinions'.

This is exemplified in Vivienne Jabri's *Discourses on Violence* (1996).

Jabri begins by rejecting 'uncritical approaches to conflict resolution' that ignore asymmetry and fail to appreciate the discursive and institutional origins of exclusion and war that perpetuate violence:

The facilitation process is represented as being conducted by outsiders, uninvolved observers whose interpretations of the conflict are excluded from the communicative process. Interpretation is, however, centrally involved in the process of facilitation, in its assumption of what constitutes the core set of grievances, the identity of the 'parties' in conflict, and the premise that facilitation as a process may be extracted from the wider structural asymmetries of the conflict.

(Jabri 1996: 155)

In her response, Jabri looks to Habermas' discourse ethics for the foundation of a 'discourse on peace' to replace the 'discourses on violence'. Her argument roughly follows the three moves indicated above.

First, she identifies just war and the language of exclusive identity as dominant discourses that legitimize the continuity of war through repertoires of meaning linked to the state system and drawn upon by strategically situated agents:

[s]trategic and normative (just war) discourses on war share a number of assumptions and indeed constitute together the structuring language of war.

(Jabri 1996: 106–7)

Jabri recognizes language as the site for the interplay of power and contestation:

> Language is a central component in the production and reproduction of societies. Language is also a mechanism of control in highly administered social systems. It constitutes the public domain of political discourse and is the medium through which identity is constructed. Moreover, it is the medium through which contestations become manifest.
>
> (Ibid.: 133)

Since language is both a mechanism of control and the medium through which contestations become manifest, it might be supposed that Jabri would express interest in radical disagreement – about whether, for example, particular wars are just or unjust, or about whether just war criteria are applicable in general (pacifist and realist critiques). But she does not do this for two main reasons. First, actors within the system 'may rationalise their conduct and be able to articulate discursively the reasons for their choice of violence in time of conflict', but this does not mean that they are 'aware of the implications of their conduct' (1996: 91). Actors' utterances are therefore already largely conditioned by unarticulated structures that determine their discourse, so there is no point taking what they say seriously at face value. Second, to enter the just war debate ourselves, even as critics, is already to play by the rules that need to be challenged and therefore to become complicit in the continuities that they thereby perpetuate. Readers will be familiar with this reason for not taking radical disagreement seriously from Chapter 2.

Jabri's second move is to vacate the existing power-saturated public arena entirely. This is done by invoking second-order critical thinking that can analyse and expose it from the outside and point to alternatives:

> In recognising the constructive element of language, discourse analysis goes some way towards contributing to an understanding of conflict as exclusionist discourse reifying a singular way of knowing.
>
> (Jabri 1996: 140)

Otherwise, the 'existing self-interpretation of groups' would be allowed

> a kind of normative inviolability, an ontological defence mechanism against the interrogation of the truth of fundamental beliefs and the justice of operative norms and values.
>
> (Ibid.: 163)

And counter-discourses would be given no space to mount a critique:

> The symbolic orders and interpretative schemes upon which identity is based constitute 'public' or political space. The transformative capacity of counter-discourses must also be located in the public space. It is the domination of this space which generates hegemonic discourses based on exclusionist

ideologies which are used to legitimate the onset of war and the manipulation of information in time of war. Structures of domination point to the existence of asymmetrical access to public space such that the counter-discourses generated by social movements opposed to war are marginalised or rendered invisible. Public space is, therefore, a place of contestation and conflict – it is a space which must be understood if we are to uncover the processes which lead to its control and manipulation as well as those involved in the emergence of dissident voices and counter-discourses.

(Ibid.: 158–9)

But once again, Jabri shows no interest in radical disagreements associated with contestations and conflicts that manifest the emergence of dissent from within the arena of prevailing discourse. The appeal is entirely away from first-order analysis seen to be confined to agents' articulations of their own conduct, and in the direction of second-order analyses conducted by third-party social scientists, who

study aspects of the constitution of social life which cannot be grasped through concepts and tacit forms of mutual knowledge to which agents have access in their day-to-day lives ... Second order analyses, therefore, involve a language or discourse that is situated within the domain of the social sciences.

(Ibid.: 177)

Finally, having vacated the existing power-saturated discourse of war, and invoked the independent stance of critical theory, Jabri is able to make the third move by constructing 'emancipatory, critical approaches to conflict resolution which recognise difference and diversity' along Habermasian lines:

In seeking to situate peace in discourse the suggestion being put forward is that the condition of peace incorporates a process of unhindered communicative action which involves *participation* and *difference* ... For Habermas, emancipation is achieved through uncovering the forces which generate distorted communication and through a discursive process which incorporates critical self-reflection and understanding.

(Ibid.: 161–3)

But what does Jabri say about radical disagreements, first, *within* discourse ethics as competing validity claims are challenged and contested, and, second, from *outside* discourse ethics when the whole basis on which it is set up is rejected?

On the first eventuality, the field of discourse ethics is by its nature argumentative, as claim meets counter-claim in the pure atmosphere of the 'ideal speech situation', to be adjudicated by 'force of argument' alone in inter-subjective communication free from distortion by coercion or power asymmetry. So what happens when conflict parties nevertheless fail to reach agreement?

Individuals and groups involved in social relations do not always reach rational consensus. Where disagreement occurs, a variety of options are available. Groups and individuals may adopt strategic behaviour where actors may seek to influence communicative interaction through, for example, the direct manipulation of information on their intentions or the shared external world. Groups may also break off communication and resort to violence ... A process situated in discursive ethics, however, rejects these options and enters a dialogic relationship of free objection and justification.

(Jabri 1996: 165)

It can be seen that Jabri envisages only three alternatives when 'disagreement occurs'. Two of these, strategic manipulation and resort to violence, do not concern conversational interchange, while the third is a return to the pure depoliticized space of Habermasian communicative action. None of these alternatives relate to ongoing radical disagreement.

On the second eventuality – an external challenge to the presuppositions of discourse ethics itself – Jabri acknowledges that:

Discourse ethics as process is a locale of emancipation from the constraints of tradition, prejudice and myth. However, some of the most pervasive conflicts of late modernity concern issues of religious belief which preclude a questioning of norms, where the text and image considered sacred are not allowed into an intersubjective space of equal interpretation and contestation. This defines a situation where it is not merely inter-subjective consent as an outcome of discourse that is the problem. This is, in fact, a condition which does not allow the occurrence of discourse and precludes any possibility of an emergent dialogic relationship.

(Ibid.: 166–7)

This has, indeed, been characteristic of 'some of the most pervasive conflicts of late modernity'. How does Jabri respond? She follows Seyla Benhabib (1992) in expanding Habermas' framework to include 'moral substance' as well as 'process' in the discursive ethical realm:

To incorporate concrete issues of lived experience into the framework of communicative ethics renders it more responsive to the challenges of contextualised social relations. While the process contains universal constitutive rules framing communicative action, it concedes that it must take place within conditions of value differentiation and heterogeneity. A peace located in discourse ethics must therefore recognise difference as a formative component of subjectivity.

(Ibid.: 167)

Portentous issues of religious belief are defined as mere concrete issues of lived experience, and are thereby reincorporated into the universal constitutive rules that they reject. So it is that the radical disagreement – if it is taken seriously at all – can already be seen to involve the procedural framework that purports to accommodate it. This is why the conflict is intractable. But in the end, I think, Jabri does not recognize agonistic dialogue as a genuine form of dialogue at all. The language of inclusion is extended to distinguish between

> discourse that 'incorporates a process of unhindered communicative action which involves *participation* and *difference*' and 'pseudodialogues' that 'incorporate dogma, rhetoric and ideology' and the wish to impose 'an unshiftable opinion' rather than participate in 'a common search'.
>
> (Jabri 1996: 161, quoting Chanteur 1992: 232)

Jabri absorbs the protests that fuel intractable conflict back into 'a discursive ethics, which not only incorporates difference but celebrates such agency' (1996: 185). The anarchic voice of radical disagreement is silenced in the uniformity of celebration. The discursive conflict transformation programme is innovatory and potent. But it does not recognize the challenge of radical disagreement or offer remedies when the clash of discourses threatens to burst its framework asunder.

Conclusion

In conclusion, I find that for all its different guises, the conflict resolution and conflict transformation tradition remains, to this day, broadly true to Morton Deutsch's original distinction between destructive and constructive conflict. Although there are exceptions that will be particularly helpful when it comes to the question of methodology in Chapter 4 (for example 'constructive controversy', 'constructive confrontation', 'deep democracy', 'constructive management of disagreement'), in general, I think that radical disagreements are still identified with destructive conflict and are seen as the terminus of genuine dialogue. The aim from the outset is to overcome or transform radical disagreements, not to study or learn from them.

Can this be all that there is to be said about radical disagreement, the chief linguistic manifestation of intractable human conflict? I do not think so. But in the light of what has been seen in Part I, the task in Part II is to bracket objections from discourse analysis, conflict analysis and conflict resolution so as to be able to focus clearly and steadily on the phenomenon of radical disagreement itself in order to find out.

Notes

1 Some time ago, John Burton caricatured conflict settlement in order to contrast it with the deeper process of conflict resolution. Now it is fashionable to caricature conflict resolution in contrast to conflict transformation. There are three reasons for keeping conflict resolution as the generic term for what remains a single field: first, that it was the original term, second, that it is still the most widely used term among analysts and practitioners, and third, because it is the term that is most familiar in the media and among the general public.

2 Other terms include John Burton's 'controlled communication' and 'analytic problem solving' approaches, Leonard Doob's 'human relations workshops', Herbert Kelman's 'interactive problem solving', Edward Azar's 'problem solving fora' and Fisher's own 'third party consultation' (see also Mitchell and Banks 1996).

3 The survey covers approaches such as Appreciative Inquiry, Change Lab, Deep Democracy, Future Search, Open Space, Scenario Planning, Sustained Dialogue, World Café, Bohmian Dialogue, Learning Journeys, etc.

4 The formalist paradigm is rooted in the confidence of positivist universalism. The historical paradigm recalls the 'methodological hermeneutics' of Schleiermacher and Dilthey and is reminiscent of the approaches from projective psychology noted above. There is also a fourth paradigm, the 'comparative methods and theory paradigm', which studies 'how we ought to study others and ourselves'.

Part II

Radical disagreement and the transformation of violent conflict

How the acknowledgement, exploration, understanding and management of radical disagreement can help to transform intractable conflicts even when attempts at conflict resolution fail.

In Part I, the search for an adequate account of radical disagreement in discourse analysis and conflict analysis proved disappointing. One reason for this is the way the topic is characterized in the social, political and historical sciences in the first place. Analysis moves directly from description to explanation, and therefore does not linger over what has already not only been explained, but explained away. Nor do most conflict resolution specialists treat the phenomenon of radical disagreement with any greater respect. The central distinction between constructive and destructive conflict identifies radical disagreement with the latter and consigns it from the outset to what must be overcome, not learnt from.

Nevertheless, despite such discouragement, these objections are bracketed in Part II and a full-scale enquiry is launched into what is, after all, the chief verbal expression of the most serious and intractable political conflicts. It is an enquiry into the war of words itself, not in the sense of conscious verbal propaganda and manipulation, but in the deeper sense of the impassioned conflict of belief and truth for sole possession of the one discursive field.

At the heart of the linguistic intractability lies *agonistic dialogue* – dialogue between enemies – that part of radical disagreement in which adversaries respond directly to each other's utterances, whether or not in the first instance through intermediaries.[1] Agonistic dialogue is an admittedly unruly borderland of human dialogue, a 'wild west', where many of the 'federal rules' that govern polite conversation and orderly verbal exchange do not run. But it is still a form of dialogue and has its own procedures, which can be studied and explored.

Beyond radical disagreement, lies Max Weber's polytheism of inarticulately struggling 'gods and demons', or Matthew Arnold's dark chaotic plain 'where ignorant armies clash by night', or the non-speaking attempts at mutual annihilation in H.G.Wells' *War of the Worlds*. Beyond this again lies the 'silence of the oppressed', the vast epochs of the inarticulate victims of subjugation and exclusion. Acknowledgement has already been made in the Preface that this is the pre-history of radical disagreement. These are not radical disagreements because they are speechless. It is only on the far side of radical disagreement that the final boundary of human dialogue is reached.

Note

1   This is not quite the same as Chantal Mouffe's idea of agonism. In Mouffe's conception of *agonistic pluralism*, the raw antagonism and violence characteristic of human society in general (the 'political') is domesticated and tamed within the democratic *agon* so that 'enemies' become 'adversaries' who thereby gain a respect for each other as well as for the democratic 'rules of the game' that define the space of democratic 'politics' (1999: 755). Whereas what I call *agonistic dialogue* is precisely verbal exchange between enemies, it still includes the antagonistic. Agonistic dialogue is the dialogue of intense political struggle in general without trying to distinguish yet between domesticated and undomesticated varieties.

4 Methodology

Studying agonistic dialogue

Methodologies from discourse analysis, conflict resolution, and systemic conflict analysis are learnt from, but then developed beyond the limit where they are usually broken off. A methodology for studying radical disagreement results, which can guide the phenomenology, epistemology and praxis of radical disagreement that follows.

Methodologies associated with the fields of study looked at in Part I provide the starting points for exploring, understanding and managing agonistic dialogue. But in each case, a boundary is reached where discourse and conflict analysts turn back and those who want to take the phenomenon of radical disagreement seriously must press on over a terrain that is much less clearly mapped. The first part of this chapter identifies where those boundaries are. The second part outlines a methodology for carrying the enquiry forward into the less familiar territory that lies beyond.

Lessons and limits from discourse analysis, conflict resolution and systemic conflict analysis

Identifying the methodological boundaries of discourse analysis

From *conversation analysis (CA)*, comes a methodology for recording and analysing conversational exchanges described in Chapter 1. But the study of agonistic dialogue goes beyond this. The emphasis in the study of agonistic dialogue is not just on process, but also on content. And because of the nature of this content, there is no need to 'disrupt' daily conversational practice in order to expose its mechanisms, as was characteristic in early CA ethnomethodology. The disruption is already inherent. Agonistic dialogue is a fierce, but often experienced, discontinuity in day-to-day conversational practice.

The role of third-party facilitators is also different. Whereas in conversation analysis, the commentator draws independent conclusions from what are usually fragments of conversation, in the study of agonistic dialogue, it is the conversation parties who do the analysis. Any third-party contributions are fed into the contested field – and are as often as not found to be already part of what is at issue.

There are two empirical problems with this extension of CA methodology, and one substantial challenge.

The first problem is that direct communication between conflict parties breaks down in intense political confrontation. Conversation is reduced to an exchange of insults, where neither is prepared to listen to what the other is saying. This is the 'dialogue of the deaf'. Here there is, indeed, a role for third parties in helping to surmount this block and eliciting continuing interchange. But in my experience, it is much easier to overcome this hiatus than might be supposed. Most conflict parties, confronted with the other's utterances, react spontaneously in their readiness to explain why what the other says is factually mistaken, morally wrong, or personally insincere. The response is immediate and emphatic.

The second problem is that, particularly in face-to-face exchanges, the dialogue develops at lightning speed and with startling and unpredictable shifts of direction. There are repeated expressions of exasperation or disgust, and explosions of emotion. How can all this be analysed? William Harvey practiced vivisection in order to slow down the motions of the heart so that he could follow them – and in the process killed the object of study. The methodology for studying radical disagreement is not quite so drastic. But it too sometimes has to slow down the subject of analysis without destroying it. Fortunately, as will be seen, there are ways in which this can be done. As for expressions of emotion, these are the hallmarks of radical disagreement. They must be expected. As is elaborated in Chapter 5, it is the fusion of the emotive, the conative (desire, will) and the cognitive that lies at the heart of linguistic intractability.

The substantial challenge is what to do when it is not in the perceived interest of conflict parties – particularly powerful conflict parties – to develop and explore radical disagreement. This applies to both internal and external hegemons. Here we reach a key issue that will become a major preoccupation in Chapters 7 and 8. Again, there are many ways in which this can be managed.

From *informal reasoning analysis* comes a methodology for analysing and evaluating 'real arguments'. Here, the content of what is said is indeed taken seriously. And the methodology for aligning arguments, and for distinguishing different functions of speech acts and different truth claims of propositions (referential, directive, expressive etc.) is evidently highly relevant in the analysis of agonistic dialogue. More will be said about this in Chapter 5, where such distinctions are found to be themselves involved.

But where does the boundary lie beyond which informal reasoning analysis will not take us?

To pinpoint this, here is an example of an argument and the way it is analysed and evaluated in the 'critical thinking movement'.

Alec Fisher subjects US Secretary of Defense, Caspar Weinberger's, 1982 *Open Letter to NATO Allies* in defence of US nuclear deterrent policy to critical analysis and evaluation. His aim in doing this is pedagogic – to teach students how to handle 'real arguments' better (1988:48–69). Here are some brief extracts from Weinberger's letter (Fisher analyses the whole letter):

I am increasingly concerned with news accounts that portray this Administration as planning to wage protracted nuclear war, or seeking to acquire a nuclear 'war-fighting' capability. This is completely inaccurate, and these stories misrepresent the Administration's policies to the American public and to our Allies and adversaries abroad ... It is the first and foremost goal of this Administration to take every step to ensure that nuclear weapons are never used again, for we do not believe there could be any 'winners' in a nuclear war ... The policy of deterrence is difficult for some to grasp because it is based on a paradox. But this is quite simple: to make the cost of a nuclear war much higher than any possible 'benefit' to the country starting it. If the Soviets know in advance that a nuclear attack on the United States could and would bring swift nuclear retaliation, they would never attack in the first place. They would be 'deterred' from ever beginning a nuclear war ... That is exactly why we must have a capability for a survivable and endurable response ... The purpose of US policy remains to prevent aggression through an effective policy of deterrence, the very goal which prompted the formation of the North Atlantic Alliance, an alliance which is as vital today as it was the day it was formed

Fisher analyses Weinberger's argument by identifying and numbering its propositions and working out the logic of their interconnections. See Figure 4.1 for the abstract argument structure that emerges, linking the numbered premises (not given here) and interim conclusions to the main conclusion (C).

Fisher takes Weinberger's main conclusion (C) to be the statement:

'we must have a capability for a survivable and endurable response.'

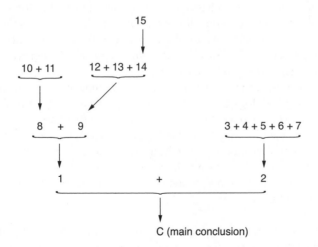

Figure 4.1 Analysis of the argument structure of the 1982 Weinberger Open Letter

and says that this 'appears to flatly contradict' Weinberger's initial 'insistence' that 'we are not seeking to acquire a nuclear "war-fighting" *capability*' (1988:65) (Fisher's italics).

Because real-life arguments are often vague, ambiguous and incomplete, in making such an analysis, Fisher supplies the deficiencies by use of what he calls the 'assertibility question'. He puts himself into the shoes of the arguer and asks:

> What arguments or evidence would justify me in asserting the conclusion? (What would I have to know or believe in to be justified in accepting it?)

He makes the argument as strong as it can be (the principle of charity).

He also uses the assertibility question when it comes to the question of evaluation because 'obviously, the kind of answer given is different in different contexts' (Toulmin's 'field-dependence of standards').

Two points identify the boundary where the methodology of informal reasoning analysis and evaluation stops and the methodology of radical disagreement analysis and exploration begins.

First, there is the status of the assertibility question itself. Fisher insists that it does not refer to truth conditionality ('what would have to be true or false for the conclusion to be true or false?'), but only to justified assertion ('what arguments or evidence would justify me in asserting the conclusion?'). He then – as can be seen – identifies justified assertion ('what arguments or evidence would justify me in asserting the conclusion?') with subject-dependent belief ('what would I have to know or believe in to be justified in accepting it?'). But this is exactly the point where the exploration of agonistic dialogue parts company with informal reasoning analysis. In agonistic dialogue conflict parties do talk about truth conditions and do not translate everything that is said into the language of subject-dependent belief. That is what makes these exchanges radical disagreements. So, for a third-party analyst to dismiss truth conditionality at the outset, in the testing of sound arguing, is to beg what is in question in radical disagreement. Watertight distinctions, such as that between truth and validity, break down in agonistic dialogue and are found to be part of what is disputed (see Chapter 5).

Second, it can be seen that Fisher is analysing arguments, not radical disagreements. In the methodology for analysing and exploring agonistic dialogue, it is not the third party who conducts the analysis, but the conflict parties. In this case, a fitting object of enquiry might be what happens when Weinberger's argument is rejected by antinuclear protesters and he answers back. In fact, although Fisher's purpose is pedagogic rather than political, there is already an embryonic radical disagreement between Weinberger and Fisher that can be written as follows (word omissions are not indicated):

> |'I am increasingly concerned with news accounts that portray this Administration as seeking to acquire a nuclear 'war-fighting' capability. This is completely inaccurate. If the Soviets know in advance that a nuclear attack on the United States could and would bring swift nuclear retaliation,

they would never attack in the first place. That is exactly why we must have a capability for a survivable and endurable response.'

'In this argument Weinberger's main conclusion – "we must have a capability for a survivable and endurable response" – appears to flatly contradict his initial 'insistence' that "we are not seeking to acquire a nuclear war-fighting capability".'|

Because the speakers are not directly responding to each other's arguments, because there is a long time-lag, and because the contemporary political context is missing, we cannot yet say that this is a radical disagreement – the exchange would have to be developed in order to find out. Above all, Weinberger would have to reply in turn to Fisher's critique. So far, in quoting Weinberger, Fisher omits the original inverted commas around the term 'war-fighting' and puts the word 'capability' into italics for the sake of his own argument. He says that Weinberger's main conclusion 'appears' to contradict his initial proposition. The radical disagreement is embryonic. But it already marks out clearly the territory that must be entered if informal reasoning analysis is to develop into an exploration of agonistic dialogue. It is this radical disagreement – the radical disagreement between the communicative actor with political power explaining why he is right to act as he does, and the communicative actor who draws on the whole of informal reasoning analysis in refuting him – that will be the object of exploration in Chapter 5. It is already evident why in this case informal reasoning analysis is part of what is at issue.

From *critical political discourse analysis*, come methodologies for detecting the play of power and contestation across texts and across the wider discourses that contain them – particularly those through which the powerful protect their privilege and the marginalized and oppressed are excluded (Howarth 1998; Howarth, Norval and Stavrakakis (eds) 2000). This is highly relevant to the analysis of radical disagreement in asymmetric conflicts. But again, I will try to specify the point at which the analysis of agonistic dialogue, having learnt from critical language study, has to break away. I will use the example of a BBC Radio 3 interview given by Margaret Thatcher on 13 December 1985, and of a critical discourse analysis of it by Norman Fairclough (1989).

Here is an extract from the interview:

I believe that government should be very strong to do those things which only government can do [on defence, on law and order, on upholding the value of the currency by sound finance, on creating the framework for a good education system and social security]. And at that point you have to say 'over to people'. People are inventive and creative, so you expect PEOPLE to create thriving industries, thriving services. Yes, you expect people, each and every one from whatever their background, to have a chance to rise to whatever level their own abilities can take them. Yes, you expect people, of all sorts of backgrounds and almost whatever their income level, to be able to have a chance of owning some property – tremendously important the ownership of property, of a house where you can bring up your children, gives you some independence, a stake in the future ... I wouldn't call this populist. I would say that many of the things which I've said strike a chord in the hearts of ordinary people. Why? Because they're British, because their character IS independent, because they DON'T like to be shoved around, because they ARE prepared to take responsibility, because they DO expect to be loyal to their friends and loyal allies – that's why you call it populist. I say it strikes a chord in the hearts of people I know, because it struck a chord in my heart many, many years ago.

(Thatcher 1985 in Fairclough 1989: 174–5, repunctuated)

For Fairclough, the task of critical discourse analysis is to determine

the relationship between texts, processes, and their social conditions, both the immediate conditions of the situational context and the more remote conditions of institutional and social structures.

(Fairclough 1989: 26)

This methodology is made up of three interrelated stages. Textual analysis is a description of the formal properties of the text (semantics). Process analysis is an interpretation of the production and reception of the text (pragmatics). Context analysis is an explanation of the social conditions that generate it and which it reinforces (socio-political nexus). The critical analyst is engaged in description, interpretation and explanation.

The play of discursive power operates across and between these different levels and generates 'ideological power, the power to project one's practices as universal and "common sense"' (Fairclough 1989: 33). The 'discourse worlds' of political actors are legitimized via linguistic tropes (metonyms, metaphors, modality indicators) produced by and reproducing ideological formations (Chilton 2004: 154). Texts do not just contain verbal elements, but also 'visuals' – facial expression, movement, gesture, tone of voice. All of these need to be analysed. They are embedded in discursive practices and orders of discourse that determine how they are constituted or produced, who can articulate them, and what the constraints are which dictate how they are received. These are in turn structured by wider contextual social and institutional orders:

[Critical language study] ought to conceptualise language as a form of social practice, what I have called discourse, and that correspondingly it ought to stress both the determination of discourse by social structures, and the effects of discourse upon society through its reproduction of social structures ... People are not generally aware of determinations and effects at these levels, and [critical language study] is therefore a matter of helping people to become conscious of opaque causes and consequences of their own discourse.

(Fairclough 1989: 41–2)

Applying this to Margaret Thatcher's 1985 BBC3 interview, Fairclough sees the granting of the interview as an attempt by the forces of revived conservatism to 'naturalise' its continuing economic and political dominance through a shift from the traditional remote authoritarianism of the past, to a new ideological posture that identifies it with the robust 'commonsense' values and interests of ordinary British people.

At the first (descriptive) stage, the analyst applies critical linguistic techniques to disclose the interviewee's manipulation of her text via choice of words ('we', 'the British people'), grammar (simple 'no-nonsense' phrasing) and so on.

At the second (interpretative) stage, the analyst's task is to 'reconstruct Margaret Thatcher's production process'. Fairclough's aim is to 'reconstruct the interpretative processes of members of the audience' in order to see how her discursive moves are received. He concludes that the 'unacknowledged strategic purpose' of the interviewee is not to 'be herself' at all, but to use the opportunity to get her message across and make a politically favourable impact on the public. In short her aim is

> to *construct* an image of herself, of her audience, and of their relationship, which accords with her strategic purpose.
>
> (Fairclough 1989: 190, original italics)

At the third (explanation) stage, the analyst accounts for the nature, production and interpretation of the text by outlining the wider social-institutional setting from which these are derived and to which they in turn contribute:

> In accordance with the concerns of the stage of explanation ... we now need to look at [Margaret Thatcher's] discourse as an element in social processes at the institutional and societal levels, and to show how it is ideologically determined by, and ideologically determinative of, power relations and power struggle at these levels.
>
> (Ibid.: 192)

Fairclough relates the text and its production/interpretation to the underlying class struggle ('the class struggle between the capitalist class, or the dominant bloc it constitutes, and the working class and its allies') that can be seen to play across it. The social theory appealed to is then made explicit:

> The view of Thatcherism I shall present owes most to the political analysis associated with the Communist Party journal *Marxism Today*.
>
> (Ibid.: 176)

This is the boundary where the methodology for analysing and exploring agonistic dialogue breaks away from the methodology employed in critical language analysis. This is not because, in this case, Fairclough is partisan in his critique of the discourse of Thatcherism. There is no requirement that participants in the exploration of agonistic dialogue should be – or could be – in some way non-partisan. As Fairclough says:

> I should stress that the interpretation of British society which I give is not a neutral one – there are none – but one which reflects my own experience, values and political commitments.
>
> (Fairclough 1989: 32)

Nor, a fortiori, is it because there is anything inadequate in Fairclough's analysis as such.

The reason why the methodology for a phenomenology of radical disagreement has to break away at this point is because critical language study of this kind does not study radical disagreement at all. It has no interest in it and regards it as superficial and naive – even when it sees political language itself as a site for continuous contestation. Its focus is entirely on analysing ways in which discourses within wider social settings produce, maintain and change relations of power that perpetuate dominance and disadvantage through inequalities of communication. Its self-confessedly didactic purpose is to 'help people to become conscious' of 'what they are not generally aware of'. Its topic is to expose the hidden workings of ideology in the manufacture of consent. The struggles for power located in language that it recognizes have nothing to do with the form of radical disagreement, but are defined in advance through prior critical third-party understanding of the social and institutional class relations that generate them. This is the reason why a phenomenology of radical disagreement will get no further guidance from critical linguistics.

The topic for the phenomenology of radical disagreement is what happens (what is said) in the radical disagreement itself – in this case the (embryonic) radical disagreement between Margaret Thatcher and Norman Fairclough. This will be explored further in Chapter 5.

Identifying the methodological boundaries of conflict resolution

Chapter 3 offered an analysis of the mainstream conflict resolution field in an attempt to clarify how and why the phenomenon of radical disagreement has aroused such relatively little interest. Most of the negotiation, mediation, problem solving, dialogic and discursive approaches that were looked at in Chapter 3 provide rich methodological resources for launching such an investigation. So, we do well to follow in the footsteps of those such as Bikhu Parekh, who juxtaposes opposed Islamic and Western perspectives before developing his theme of positive 'dialogue between civilisations'; or Gavriel Saloman and others, who launch their enterprise of 'co-existence education' in the Middle East with an analysis of conflicting Israeli and Arab histories; or David Holloway and Brian Lennon's Community Dialogue, Belfast, which is prepared to risk confrontation in its encouragement of 'rehumanising' cross-cultural exchange; or Franklin Dukes in his willingness to encourage the articulation and analysis of 'valuable' conceptual conflict and 'productive dialogue' within the enterprise of 'public conflict resolution'; or problem solving workshop methodologies, including those pioneered by Herb Kelman, that include an initial presentation of opposed views within the wider problem solving process; or, more generally, the preparatory mutual listening and mutual respect phases that are common across a range of family, neighbourhood and community mediation methodologies.

But, as Chapter 3 also suggests, most of these approaches turn away at exactly the point where a study of agonistic dialogue most needs to press on, although there are some conflict resolution specialists who do take the topic of verbal controversy seriously in their attempts to expedite cooperative decision-making in the public arena, or to mitigate the destructive consequences of intractable conflict.

The aim of David and Roger Johnson's constructive controversy, for example, is to elicit intellectual conflict on the Jeffersonian principle that 'difference of opinion leads to enquiry, and enquiry to truth'. But it turns out in the end that there is no room for radical disagreement within the process of constructive controversy:

> In well-structured controversies, participants make an initial judgment, present their conclusions to other group members, are challenged with opposing views, grow uncertain about the correctness of their views, actively search for new information and understanding, incorporate others' perspectives and reasoning into their thinking, and reach a new set of conclusions. This process significantly increases the quality of decision making and problem solving, the quality of relationships, and improvements in psychological health.
>
> (Johnson and Johnson 2000: 84)

Radical disagreement does not behave like this. It is not 'well-structured'. Something similar applies to other variants on this theme with which I am familiar. In Barbara Bradford's imaginative 'managing disagreement constructively' programme, for example, there is no room for taking the phenomenon of radical disagreement seriously in any of her nine alternatives (Bradford 2004).

The aim of Myrna Lewis' *Deep Democracy* (http://www.deep-democracy.net) deliberately encourages dissent in order to allow minorities to express and spread the 'no' and to challenge majority democracy. Facilitators 'turn up the volume' and amplify disagreement and the group may, as a result, decide to 'go into conflict'. Participants 'own their own side' rather than trying to begin by understanding the other. This is helpful, although the emphasis is on the growth and deepening of relationships, not the winning of battles, and the whole process is strongly monitored and controlled by the facilitators.

Perhaps the nearest conflict resolution approach to the phenomenology, epistemology and praxis of radical disagreement is provided by Guy and Heidi Burgess' Constructive Confrontation (1996; 1997). Constructive confrontation does not aim immediately to resolve intractable conflicts. Rather, it takes full note of power relations, and encourages intra-coalition consensus building. 'Constructive confrontation advisers' are seen as advocates as well as facilitators. All of this is highly relevant. But, as will be noted further in Chapter 8, when it

can be compared with the approach exemplified in Chapter 7, the incremental procedural approach at the centre of constructive confrontation is often found to be
itself at issue in the kinds of intractable conflict looked at in this book.

Identifying the methodological boundaries of systemic conflict analysis

Chapter 2 indicated how the phenomenon of radical disagreement does not show
up on complex systems theory maps of conflict. The idea of 'mental models' as
applied there does not capture what is most characteristic in radical disagreement.

The same happens in other attempts at cognitive mapping. For example, useful
methodologies are developed in the 'conceptual mapping' approach. Here the mapping of belief structures looks for 'nodes', where key concepts cluster, and 'arcs',
which link concepts, in order to produce a visual representation of conceptual
patterns that lie behind particular arguments and belief systems. This illuminates
Quine and Ullian's 'web of belief' – the observation that belief-systems are like
spider webs with some beliefs central to our conceptions of the world and some
more peripheral, so that we are more ready to give up or adapt the latter than the
former (1970). Radical disagreement is, unsurprisingly, found to radiate out from
incompatibilities between core beliefs. But, having reached this point, the phenomenology of radical disagreement has to move on, because its topic is what happens
when those incompatibilities confront each other and struggle to control the whole
of conceptual space. As in a gravitational battle, the entire framework of cognitive
mapping is then found to be affected – the familiar landmarks slide.

An applied methodology for studying agonistic dialogue

Having been carried as far as is possible by the methodologies looked at up to
this point, it is time to attempt to move beyond them and to enter the relatively
uncharted landscape that lies ahead.

Mapping the axes of radical disagreement in complex conflicts

The journey begins by mapping the axes of radical disagreement – embedded in
the wider conflict system – that were neglected in the 'systems perspective' maps
looked at in Chapter 2. This may look daunting, but, having gained a rough initial
view of the conflict system as a whole in terms of interlocking conflict complexes,
the focus of the enquiry is then narrowed down to particular conflict formations,
and then down again to the exploration of specific examples.

Mapping axes of radical disagreement across different conflict complexes

The total conflict system is made up of different overlapping conflict complexes
(for example, the Afghanistan–Pakistan conflict complex or the Middle East
conflict complex). Conflict complexes are in turn constituted by nested conflict

formations. The Middle East conflict, for example, is a nested complex of ever-wider conflict formations: a Jewish Israeli-Arab Israeli conflict formation; an Israeli-Palestinian conflict formation; an Arab-Israeli conflict formation (which includes unresolved Israel–Lebanon and Israel–Syria conflicts); the wider Middle East conflict formation including Turkey and Iran – and so on up to the level of the international community that involves the Quartet (EU, Russia, UN, US). Readers can easily think of other axes of radical disagreement that criss-cross this set of nested conflict formations, such as those that traverse the Palestinian and Jewish diaspora, or the Egypt–Iran and Saudi–Iran conflict confrontations.

The different conflict formations prima facie define conflict parties and third parties. In the Israeli-Palestinian conflict formation, for example, the 22 Arab States are third parties. In the Arab-Israeli conflict formation, on the other hand, they are conflict parties, and so on. In the associated radical disagreements, as noted in Chapter 6, these distinctions are found to break down.

Evidently, the totality of shifting axes of radical disagreement within and across conflict formations and conflict complexes within the whole conflict system is too much for any one analyst to manage. But it is nevertheless important to keep the existence of such a background in mind, even though this book, given its size, does not develop or exemplify it.

Mapping axes of radical disagreement in particular conflict formations

having chosen a particular conflict formation – for example, the Israeli-Palestinian conflict formation – the methodology suggests the following structure for the investigation:

- mapping axes of radical disagreement within the conflict parties;
- mapping axes of radical disagreement between the conflict parties;
- mapping axes of radical disagreement between third parties and conflict parties (there are also axes of radical disagreement within and among third parties).

A full example of this level of enquiry is given in Chapter 7 in relation to the Israeli-Palestinian conflict formation. This example will also show that it is not difficult to conduct the enquiry across different levels of conflict formation simultaneously (e.g. Israeli-Palestinian and Arab-Israeli).

Within this framework, the investigation can then focus down to a phenomenological exploration of the *specific examples* of radical disagreement thus identified.

Phenomenological exploration of specific examples of radical disagreement

In each case, the phenomenology of radical disagreement comprises five aspects:

1 acknowledging that there is radical disagreement;
2 clearing up immediate misunderstanding;

3 aligning arguments in order to promote discursive engagement;
4 uncovering the moments of radical disagreeing (e.g. recommendation, justification, refutation, explanation, description, revision, exploration, action);
5 exploring the resulting radical disagreement.

The first three of these aspects might be called 'prerequisites' and will be commented on here. The fourth and fifth aspects constitute the phenomenology itself
and will be presented with examples in Chapter 5.

Acknowledging that there is radical disagreement

This is often the key to the whole enterprise. Acknowledgement of radical disagreement is culturally conditioned and varies from group to group and person
to person. But it is evident when manifestations of radical disagreement erupt,
mainly because of the super-charged emotional intensity that not only accompanies
intractability, but also, as Chapter 5 shows, actively constitutes it. Here are three
examples from the Israeli-Palestinian conflict – two at intra-party level and one
at inter-party level.

In the context described in Chapter 7, an inclusive Jewish Israeli group exploring
internal radical disagreement seemed to be proceeding quietly. However, during
the Shabbat, when the main business was suspended, a radical disagreement unexpectedly ignited over the authority to interpret the religious text that had just been
read. Engagement was instantaneous and passionate. This was the conflict that had
apparently been discussed earlier. Now it was real. Everything else was at once
eclipsed and the meeting was finally able to move on to the heart of the issue.

An inclusive Palestinian group, meeting in Jordan in the search for a national
strategy to end occupation, was allotting different contextual factors to three categories – positive for the Palestinian cause, negative for the Palestinian cause,
neither positive nor negative for the Palestinian cause. Someone mentioned
'Islamization'. The discussion froze. The shock-wave was palpable. A short silence
of very high tension followed. Reassuring voices made suggestions. The topic was
put in a special category on the bottom left-hand part of the board. The meeting
would come back to it later.

An attempt by third-party facilitators to test three conflict resolution methodologies with a small number of Israelis and Palestinians in a safe university
environment in Europe was progressing gently. Facilitators were asking participants what they would like the situation to be in five years' time. The idea
was to follow this up by analysis of what was blocking these outcomes, so that
discussion could focus on how to remove the blockages or circumvent the barri-
ers. Participants wrote down their future aspirations and these were pinned on the
board. After some minutes, an Israeli hand went up:

> Some of these may be other peoples' hopes, but they are not mine. They are
> my worst nightmares.

The atmosphere was at once electric. High emotion was expressed. Facilitators were dismayed and tried to continue – they said that they had anticipated this and were coming on to discuss it tomorrow. But they had not anticipated it. The meeting was thrown into disarray. This was the sudden detonation of the conflict itself in the middle of the workshop.

To acknowledge that there is radical disagreement is a significant step in being able to explore and understand it.

Clearing up immediate misunderstanding

Acknowledgement on its own is not enough. For discourses to engage substantially, there is a need for unnecessary misunderstandings to be cleared up. Some have suggested, as John Locke famously does here, that once misunderstandings are sorted out, the disagreement will disappear:

> I was once in a Meeting of very learned and ingenious Physicians, where by chance there arose a Question, whether any Liquor passed through the Filaments of the Nerves. The Debate having been managed a good while, by a variety of Arguments on both sides, I (who had been used to suspect, that the greatest part of Disputes were more about the signification of Words, than a real difference in the Conceptions of Things) desired that before they went any further in this Dispute, they would first examine, and establish amongst them, what the word *Liquor* signified.

When they did this, they found

> the signification of that Word, was not so settled and certain, as they had all imagined; but that each of them made it a sign of a different complex *Idea*.
> (Locke 1690/1975: III.ix,16).

Perhaps the best known example of verbal misunderstanding of this kind was Krushchev's outburst in the UN Security Council, 'We will bury you!' This was widely interpreted in the West as a threat of nuclear annihilation, but (I gather) is better translated from the Russian as, 'We will outlast you!' – a less dramatic repetition of the usual Marxist prediction that capitalism would founder due to its own internal contradictions. The problem of communication across languages and cultures in conflict situations is much studied (Augsburger 1992; Cohen 1991; Gulliver 1979). It extends to deep differences between the cultures in which the languages are embedded.

But in the case of intractable political conflict and radical disagreement, the situation often turns out to be the opposite of that described by John Locke. The phenomenology of radical disagreement shows again and again that it is only when initial misunderstandings have been cleared up – including linguistic and cultural differences – that the deeper levels of misunderstanding are revealed. It is when conflict parties speak *the same language* that the deepest differences that generate linguistic intractability appear. And, as Chapter 5 again shows, this includes the question whether there has been misunderstanding in the first place. It is the distinction between Locke's 'signification of Words' and 'a real difference in the Conceptions of Things' that is found to be part of what is in dispute.

Aligning arguments in order to promote discursive engagement

A third essential element in the methodology for studying agonistic dialogue is the alignment of arguments. To begin with, as often as not, conflict parties miss each other entirely and are appealing to different things. This may be as far as the agonistic dialogue goes. It is the job of argument alignment to ensure – so far as is possible – that there is discursive engagement across the full spectrum of the dispute. This is commented upon further in Chapter 5.

In my book, *Choices: Nuclear and Non-Nuclear Defence Options* (Ramsbotham 1987), for example, the purpose was to align arguments and promote full discursive engagement across the spectrum of issues involved in the nuclear weapon debate, at a time when public exchanges had become sloganized and discourses largely failed to meet. In the book, I tested levels of polarization by analysing the debate into forty main sub-issues and twenty recommendations for nuclear and non-nuclear defence options and interviewed nineteen prominent spokespersons to elicit detailed responses across the whole gamut of questions.[1] One of them was US Secretary of Defense, Caspar Weinberger, whose Open Letter to NATO has been considered above. I will comment further on this work in Chapter 5.

Note

1 Interviewees were: Peter Carrington, Michael Carver, Leonard Cheshire, Denzil Davies, John Finnis, Lawrence Freedman, Richard Harries, Michael Howard, Rebecca Johnson, Anthony Kenny, Bruce Kent, Yuri Lebedev, Robert McNamara, James O'Connell, David Owen, James Schlesinger, Edward Thompson, Caspar Weinberger, George Younger.

5 Phenomenology

Exploring agonistic dialogue

In exploring the phenomenon of radical disagreement with conflict parties, the investigation begins by uncovering the moments of radical disagreeing – what conflict parties say in the very process of engaging in agonistic dialogue. Through this, the enquiry is able to move on to an exploration of the resulting radical disagreement itself, and thereby to gain new insight into the nature of linguistic intractability.

The argument in this book has reached the point where the phenomenology of radical disagreement – the exploration of the agonistic dialogue that lies at the core of linguistic intractability – can be directly undertaken. The contention is that it is in this way that the *lacunae* in the complex systemic mapping of conflicting mental models identified at the end of Chapter 2 can best be filled. All ten of the analytic deficiencies noted there can be addressed in this way, beginning with a tracing of the patterns of competing discourses embedded in the dynamic *conflict system* as a whole. As described in Chapter 4, and exemplified in Chapter 7, each of the evolving axes of radical disagreement within the chosen *conflict formation* can then be identified and explored, including those that emerge within conflict parties, between conflict parties, and between third parties and conflict parties. These need to be mapped, investigated and understood if properly informed interventions are to be undertaken. Given the critical role that the phenomenon of radical disagreement plays in conflict intractability, this is vital information for all those who seek positive systemic transformation. This will be carried further in Chapter 7.

Chapter 4 showed how in the case of individual *examples* of radical disagreement pin-pointed in this way, the methodology moves on to investigate five overlapping aspects:

1 acknowledging that there is radical disagreement;
2 clearing up immediate misunderstanding;
3 aligning arguments in order to promote engagement;
4 uncovering the moments of radical disagreeing (e.g. recommendation, justification, refutation, explanation, description, revision, exploration, action);
5 exploring the resulting radical disagreement.

The first three aspects are 'prerequisites' and have already been commented upon in the previous chapter. The fourth and fifth aspects are the subject of this chapter and constitute the phenomenology of radical disagreement itself.

Uncovering the moments of radical disagreeing is an investigation into what conflict parties say in the process of radical disagreement. The arbiters are the *individual conflict parties* as the process of agonistic dialogue unfolds.

This thereby introduces the phenomenological exploration of the resulting radical disagreement itself. It is now no longer up to conflict parties individually – or third parties – to pronounce. It is the *agonistic dialogue*, as it were, that speaks for itself. This yields the main phenomenological insights into the heart of linguistic intractability.

Uncovering the moments of radical disagreeing

The methodology used in uncovering the moments of radical disagreeing is both simple and effective. It is to ask conflict parties themselves to explain what they are saying in the process of agonistic dialogue. This seems superficial and unproductive from a critical perspective, but is exactly the topic that most requires investigation. It is the gateway into the territory that a phenomenological enquiry wants to explore.

To illustrate this, I will use my own investigations carried out over the past 20 years with hundreds of participants from all over the world. These are *simulations* of radical disagreements, which, as a result, 'slow down' the lightning speed of raw political agonistic dialogue and enable what would otherwise move too quickly to be examined. The scenarios vary, but in this case, I use a simulation of radical disagreement over whether atom bombs should have been dropped on Japan in August 1945. The fiction is that participators – usually 20 to 50 – are in the plane carrying the bomb. Whether it is dropped will depend on the decision that they make. Although this is indeed a fiction, what happened historically, from take-off to arrival over the city, is recounted in detail, interspersed with the evolving stages of the radical disagreement. Above all, the participants argue genuinely from their own convictions. This generates remarkable tension and the results can be dramatic. It certainly gives participants insight into the nature of radical disagreement.

In what follows, I give brief samples of the evolving radical disagreement together with comments based on what participants have said. Each case is different. There is no claim that the nature and order of the specific 'moments of radical disagreeing' given here always, or even usually, recur. But I think that what follows is representative. Readers can carry out similar experiments for themselves to test these results. This is an empirical experiment that anyone can do. The only requirements are that the participants' arguments must be their own, that the simulation must be an accurate historical re-enactment up to the point of decision, that those who participate must recommend mutually incompatible actions, that a point of decision must eventually be reached, and that the participants must mind what the outcome is. A full simulation is complex, subtle and unpredictable. Here I will keep the examples as simple as possible, and the comments as brief as possible, without forfeiting the main points.

In this case, the simulation was based on the flight of the three planes that left Tinian island on the 2,500 mile round trip to drop the second atom bomb on Japan on the early morning of 9 August 1945.

|'Drop the bomb.'

'Do not drop the bomb.'|

The flight crews assembled at 0200 on 9 August 1945. USAF Chaplain, Charles Downey, said prayers on the tarmac for the success of the flight.

Under the moment of recommendation, participants said what should be done. Those who had not abstained agreed that their recommendations were incompatible. They agreed that if they had the power to do so they would act accordingly no matter what the other said – recommendation would lead directly to action. The recommendations had the form of commands – 'do this' – and immediately elided into the language of ethical injunction – 'this should be done'. From the outset, agonistic dialogue is ethical through and through.

|'Dropping the bomb will end the war and save millions of lives.'

'Dropping the bomb will destroy hundreds of thousands of innocent lives.'|

The crew of Bock's Car, the plane carrying the bomb, found that an auxiliary fuel pump was not working. If there were no visibility over the target, they would not have enough fuel to bring the bomb back. They had been told only to drop it when they had visual sighting of the target.

Under the moment of justification, the conflict parties justified their recommendations. In the course of agonistic dialogue, many justifications are given. In the world of real decision-making, recommendations are justified to multiple audiences and for multiple purposes – to overcome external opposition, reinforce self-belief, mobilize internal support, persuade third parties. In the simulation, participants were asked to give only one justification to begin with – the main thing that they would appeal to if asked why they urge such action.

Participants agreed that in giving their main justification they were appealing directly to how things are in the world. Their appeal was spontaneous. They had not yet reached words like 'fact', 'true', 'know', 'reality', and the 'ought' of the moment of recommendation ('you should do this …') was already instantaneously fused with the 'is' of justification ('… because …'). 'Ought' and 'is' were combined in a single act of pointing. The conflict parties were in the unmediated presence of the purely ostensive: 'just look!'.

THE MOMENT OF ALIGNMENT

|('Dropping the bomb will end the war and save millions of lives.')

'The war would have ended anyway.'|

|('Dropping the bomb will destroy hundreds of thousands of innocent lives.')

'Conventional fire-bombing killed many more people.'|

At 0700 hours, the three planes were scattered in a squall and failed to make their planned rendezvous. When Leonard Cheshire, in one of the observer planes, saw the coast of Japan he said that he felt a pang of conscience because it reminded him of Cornwall in the UK.

Under the moment of alignment, the participants began to respond to each other's arguments. Under the initial moment of justification, the arguments missed each other. Participants were appealing to different things. Now they started the process of 'identifying and filling in the blanks' so that arguments would engage each other across the spectrum, as indicated in Chapter 4. Here the methodology of informal reasoning analysis is useful, but not essential, since it is more important that participants apply their own understanding.

The moment of alignment continually recurs in the development of agonistic dialogue to the point where participants discover that what is at issue includes the question of *whether* arguments have been met. At this point, the agonistic dialogue is carried to another level, as developed further below. This is where it moves beyond the territory usually marked out by the conventions of informal reasoning analysis as the distinction 'same/different' is also found to be involved.

THE MOMENT OF REFUTATION

|'It is not true that the war would have ended anyway without greater loss of life, Japanese as well as American. You refuse to face up to the facts at the time.'

'The destruction caused by conventional bombing is irrelevant. Two wrongs do not make a right. Besides, there were the radiation effects.'|

At 0800 hours, the weaponeer on Bock's Car found that the light went on at the top of the warning 'black box'. There was an electrical fault. The bomb had already been armed and the electronic controls were elaborate because the bomb had to be detonated in the air, directly over the target at 2,000 feet, for maximum effect.

Under the moment of refutation, the simulation participants said that they thereby distinguished between what was refuted (what the other mistakenly said) and what could be seen to refute it (how things are, what is so). What was refuted was seen as a whole, and more besides. It was seen against a background, and it was the background that was decisive. The background – what is so – was the same background appealed to under the moment of justification, and the same background within which, under the moment of recommendation, the action was or was not to be carried out. This, according to most of the participants, was what they were saying under the moment of refutation.

And now the whole language of 'fact', 'true', 'know', and their opposites, also sprang up – significantly late in the day – and was as immediately plunged into the vortex.

THE MOMENT OF EXPLANATION

|'You are arguing emotionally. This is a war. Millions have died. To refuse to act as responsibly as all the allied military and political leaders did at the time is to be more concerned with your own moral purity than with the effects of your actions.'

'You are like those who were brutalised by war. Your moral imagination is so weak that you are incapable of conceiving what it means to destroy a city. If you realised what you were doing, you would see that it is a monstrous war crime.'|

Leonard Cheshire, flying in an observer plane, said that it seemed unfair to be flying out of range of Japanese air defences or fighters. In Europe, where he had been a bomber pilot and won the Victoria Cross for bravery, the attrition rate was 20 per cent – you could expect to be shot down after five flights.

Under the moment of explanation, participants accounted for the fact that the other continued to argue the unarguable. Depending on the nature of the other's error, the other was thereby classified as uninformed, morally blind, logically confused – or any combination of these. If the other was sincere, then it was the sincerity described by Jonathan Swift as that state of perfected self-assurance that comes from being blissfully self-deceived. The passage from *ad rem* to *ad hominem* judgement happened spontaneously in a single movement. The other – as determined under the moment of refutation – already thereby stood within the realm of explanation.

This was the moment when psychological, political and socio-cultural explanation made its first phenomenological appearance. Significantly, its first and characteristic appearance is asymmetrical. This is easily tested and has been as regularly confirmed. In response to the question 'why do you say this?' participants invoked reasons under the moment of justification. In response to the question 'why does the other say this?' participants invoked explanations. The moment of explanation perpetually hovers over radical disagreement and threatens to bring the interchange to an end in mutual recrimination. What is the point of continuing to dispute with someone who is already conditioned to be blind to evidence and impervious to reason? We recognize the beginning of the slide that can eventually lead to mutual dehumanization.

THE MOMENT OF DESCRIPTION

|'I know that this is my perspective on things and you have yours, but ...'

'I hear what you say, and I acknowledge that if I was coming from where you are I might think differently, but ...'|

At 0900 hours, the planes arrived at their target. Bock's Car made two passes over the city but visibility was not good enough for a direct sighting.

Under the moment of description, the conflict parties, for various reasons, included themselves in third-party description of the radical disagreement: 'I know that this is my perspective on things and you have yours, but ...'. This was the reflexive moment when participants stepped back and reflected on the radical disagreement as a whole.

This is a key moment for conflict resolution specialists, who, as seen in Chapter 3, want to begin under the moment of description and to collapse the radical disagreement immediately into 'constructive dialogue', without pausing at the other staging posts along the way. *Assertions* about what is so, and *judgements* about the other, are to be immediately translated into *descriptions* of our own perceptions. These can then be equated with the perceptions of the other and space is opened up for mutual recognition of the validity of the different narratives for all conflict parties.

This is also the moment when social scientific explanation fully enters the scene. In its first entry, under the moment of explanation above, critical explanation only applied to the other. Now, under the moment of description, conceptual space has expanded so that explanation applies generally. I think that this late appearance of social scientific explanation in the phenomenology of radical disagreement is linked to the fact that what has gone before is not picked up on its radar screen.

But in the drastic economy of the phenomenology of radical disagreement, the moment of description does not play the role that either conflict resolution or social science has written for it. Repeated experience indicates, as in this case, that in ongoing agonistic dialogue, the moment of description has a very different – indeed, almost an opposite – function. 'I know that this is my perspective on things and you have yours, but ...' – and it is what follows the 'but' that signifies here. The symmetric and neutral language adopted by conflict parties under the moment of description is indeed indistinguishable from third-party description in general – such as the various forms of the 'common description' given in the prologue. But equally characteristic is the way this does not affect the nature of what follows 'but', when radical disagreement is resumed.

Empirical evidence suggests that the key function of the moment of description in continuing radical disagreement is to preserve *asymmetry*. Only meta-level symmetry of this kind is seen to guarantee the substantial asymmetry integral to the moments of justification and refutation. It does this by incorporating into its reflexivity whatever expressions of contingency and irony may arise, thus neutralizing them, and opening the way for a resumption of untrammelled ostensivity. The world the conflict parties refer to under the moment of description contains both their perspective and that of their opponent. So disputants establish, thereby, that in the continuing radical disagreement, they are not merely referring to their own references. They are referring to the world that also contains their references – but only as a part of it. With 'but', they once again look out on the world through clear glass – and act accordingly.

But this can be an uncertain and fluctuating process. Here is an example where the speaker struggles to accommodate this function:

> Is the US closer to truth and human dignity than the Taliban or Saddam Hussein? *Hell yes.* Understanding and dialogue with the cultures of the Middle East does not require us to abdicate our moral arguments for democracy, liberty and human rights, or our critique of nations that oppose those values in word and deed. I recognise the subjectivity of my own values. I happily acknowledge that many other value-systems can be just as 'true' as my own (I put 'true' in quotes because I'm not really comfortable calling any value system 'true' or 'false'). That said, my subjective values tell me in no uncertain terms that the values of the United States, flawed though they may be, are *better* than the values of reactionary Islamic extremists. Every public execution in Iran, every mass grave unearthed in Iraq, and every story of oppression in the Taliban's Afghanistan reinforces these values. I unapologetically believe that democracy is a better form of values than fascism.
>
> (Roth-Cline 2004)

THE MOMENT OF REVISION

|'It may be true that Russia's declaration of war on Japan on 8 August 1945 could have hastened a Japanese surrender, but ...'

'I accept that the figures for exactly how many died as a direct result of the dropping of the bomb on Nagasaki are contested, but ...'|

At 0900 hours, the planes were not over Nagasaki. The prime target of the 9 August 1945 attack was Kokura. Nagasaki had only been added to the list of targets in July 1945 when Kyoto was removed. It had already been attacked by conventional bombing, which was not usually the case with target cities in order to preserve them to maximize effect. And it was mountainous, which would again restrict impact. Only when there was no visibility over Kokura did the planes – the angels of death invisible to the citizens below going about their daily business at 0900 hours – fly on to the secondary target.

Under the moment of revision, participants adjusted their arguments under the impact of agonistic dialogue. In many cases, they produced arguments they had not thought about before.

The moment of revision is the second moment that conflict resolution aims for. In conflict resolution, the encouragement of a translation of aggressive statements about the world into reflexive descriptions of our own perceptions, under the moment of description (looked at above), prepares the way for mutual accommodation and transformation, under the moment of revision. In many cases this does, indeed, happen. But in the case of intractable conflicts and ongoing radical disagreement, it does not. In agonistic dialogue, the moment of revision is found to play a different role, and one that is akin to the moment of description.

At one end of the spectrum, as in this case, is reluctant admission of minor qualification accompanied by vigorous reassertion of the original case. Confidence, emotional intensity and intransigence may wax and wane, while core positions remain unchanged. Here the function of the moment of revision was, when under pressure, to readjust the periphery of the 'web of belief' that surrounds these positions. Discredited arguments were dropped and others were taken up. The purpose was not to reconsider and change the core, but to protect and sustain it.

At the other end of the spectrum – as it were leapfrogging the part of the spectrum that conflict resolution wants to occupy – lies radical conversion. On the road to Damascus, scales fall from our eyes. We see with blazing clarity that the other is right after all. And now we argue in reverse, but with intensified zeal. The blindness of our erstwhile companions is all the more plain to us because we, too, used to be like that.

THE MOMENT OF EXPLORATION

|'Deontology's refusal to recognise negative responsibility amounts to an abdication of ethical responsibility.'

'Consequentialism's failure to safeguard moral absolutes opens the floodgates to every kind of barbarism.'|

The three planes arrived over Nagasaki at 1100 hours. There was only enough fuel for one run over the target. Visibility was still bad.

Under the moment of exploration, conflict parties searched for the deep conceptual roots of the radical disagreement. In this case, participants were familiar with the distinction between consequentialist and deontological ethical approaches because of earlier discussion. The first speakers recognized that their position was consequentialist – the reason to drop the bomb was because the alternative would lead to many more Japanese and American deaths. The second speakers recognized that their position was deontological – the bomb must not be dropped because the deliberate killing of tens of thousands of innocent people is morally prohibited.

But under the moment of exploration in ongoing radical disagreement, uncovering the ethical and theoretical roots of the verbal contestation is not the end of the road, but only the beginning. What lies in turn behind the consequentialist and deontological positions – if anything? What is happening in this confrontation?

This is the gateway through which the investigation can move on into the pheno-menological territory that the enquiry most wants to reach and that lies beyond. This is the topic of the next section.

THE MOMENT OF ACTION

But always, lowering over agonistic dialogue, there is the moment of action. What is to be done to change the intolerable existing situation that conflict parties strive to eliminate? Or to preserve the justly achieved outcome that is defended to the death? Or to determine the as yet undecided result that combatants struggle to achieve or to prevent?

It is 1101 on 9 August 1945 and the planes are over Nagasaki. The moment of decision has arrived.

Under the moment of action, the time for deliberation is over. There is no room for third-party avoidance. One way or another, either through action or through inaction, the decision is made. Under the either–or pressure of decision in intense political conflict, indeterminate alternatives collapse into the crude yes-no of radical disagreement. Under the moment of action – often to our horror – the full enormity of what the other says is shown in what the other does. And we, too, dis-cover what we think by what we find that we do, or have done.

Should the bomb be dropped or not? In the simulation described here, at this point attention was unexpectedly switched to those who had abstained and had so far not fully participated. They would decide. In the real world, if those who could do something to change things do not, then what would have happened happens anyway. In this case, if the 'don't knows' did not intervene, the bomb would be dropped. The countdown began: 'ten, nine, eight, seven, …'. The tension became unbearable. On the count of 'four', two of the abstainers stopped the action. In the most intense and intractable political conflict. there is no room for abstention. In the ferocious intensity of the moment of action, the abstainers discovered what they really thought.

But that is not what happened historically on 9 August 1945.

In my book, *Choices* (Ramsbotham 1987), interviewees were all asked whether it had been right to drop the bombs on Hiroshima and Nagasaki. The polarization of the nuclear deterrence debate at the time was such that in nearly every case those who argued for continued deterrence said that the bombs should have been dropped, while those who argued against deterrence said that they should not.

Here is a radical disagreement between Leonard Cheshire, the witness of the events of 9 August 1945 who continually supported both nuclear deterrence and the dropping of the bombs (Cheshire 1985), and John Finnis, author of what is in my view the best book making the moral case against nuclear deterrence (Finnis *et al.*1987):

|'I hold that it was not wrong to bomb Hiroshima and Nagasaki. And the reason why I say this is that the only foreseeable alternative was the all-out invasion of Japan. Given the Japanese military mind at the time, that would

have involved a fight to the last man, total war across the whole of Japan, in which, not hundreds of thousands, but millions would have died.' (Leonard Cheshire)

'As to Hiroshima and Nagasaki, the dropping of the two atomic bombs on those two cities was indeed morally wrong. In fact, as one can plainly see from the records of those who made the decision, neither the motive nor the intention was to attack military targets. The intention was simply to cause maximum damage in largely civilian areas – which it did. Even if Leonard Cheshire is right, and this was the only way in which the war could have been ended short of a much more costly invasion of Japan, it was clearly morally wrong and should certainly not have been done.' (John Finnis)|

(Ramsbotham 1987: 197, 232)

Exploration of the moments of radical disagreeing sharply illuminates the enormity of what this radical disagreement shows. The defining link is between argument and action. Power dictates what happens. In this case, historically it was Leonard Cheshire who had been able to participate in bringing about the outcome he wanted.

At 1101 on 9 August 1945, bombardier Beahan shouted, 'I 've got it. I see the city. I'll take it now'. He released the bomb.

All the historical consequences immediately began to unfold. William Laurence of the *New York Times*, flying as an official observer, described the event (1946). He later won the Pulitzer Prize:

We watched a giant pillar of purple fire, 10,000 feet high, shoot up like a meteor coming from the earth instead of outer space. It was no longer smoke, or dust, or even a cloud of fire. It was a living thing, a new species of being, born before our incredulous eyes. Even as we watched, a ground mushroom came shooting out of the top to 45,000 feet, a mushroom top that was even more alive than the pillar, seething and boiling in a white fury of creamy foam, a thousand geysers rolled into one. It kept struggling in elemental fury, like a creature in the act of breaking the bonds that held it down. When we last saw it, it had changed into a flower-like form, its giant petals curving downwards, creamy-white outside, rose-coloured inside. The boiling pillar had become a giant mountain of jumbled rainbows. Much living substance had gone into those rainbows.

At noon on 15 August 1945, the Japanese Emperor broadcast to a Japanese nation who had never heard his voice before:

The enemy has begun to employ a new and most cruel bomb, the power of which to do damage is indeed incalculable, taking the toll of many innocent lives. Should We continue to fight, it would result not only in the ultimate collapse and obliteration of the Japanese nation, but also it would lead to the total extinction of human civilisation. Such being the case, how are We to save the millions of our subjects; or to atone Ourselves before the hallowed spirits of Our Imperial Ancestors? This is why We have ordered the acceptance of the provisions of the Joint Declaration of the Powers.

The rest was history. Power was allied to recommendation. The action was done.

But that was not the end of agonistic dialogue. Radical disagreement continues to this day about what was done and what should have been done on 9 August 1945. It still passionately informs current decision-making. Radical disagreement engulfs the 'lessons of history', sweeps up distinctions between past, present and future, and obliterates the efforts of those who want to close the chapter once and for all.

Exploring the resulting radical disagreeement

What is the radical disagreement about? How far does it reach? How deep does it go? With these questions, the heart of the radical disagreement is opened up, and, with it, the nature of the linguistic intractability that lies at the communicative centre of the conflict. It is no longer up to conflict parties individually or third-party analysts to answer these questions, because the radical disagreement is polylogical. That is also why this section of the book is the hardest to write. In the end, as a monological account, it can only point at examples of radical disagreement and hope that readers will see for themselves what these examples say.

What is the radical disagreement about?

This question proves much harder to answer than might be supposed because any answer given is found to be already part of what is at issue. What is the Israeli-Palestinian conflict about? What is its object?

'In the Israeli-Palestinian conflict two nations claim the same territory'.

This is a third-party description and is fine as far as it goes. But what are 'the two nations'? What is 'the same territory'? The description is innocuous. It misses the fact that in the radical disagreement, it is 'two nations' and 'the same territory' that is from the outset *part* of what is contested.

Which are the two nations? And already we are in the middle of the conflict. The name of Israel was introduced on 14 May 1948 when David Ben-Gurion performatively announced the creation of the new state. The naming of Palestinians and Palestine as their future state was accomplished through the birth of the PLO. The identity of 'two nations' has from the beginning been at the epicentre of what was fought over. Who are the people who in 1948 set up their state? What should they be called? Are they 'the Jews of Palestine'? Are they 'the Zionist colonisers'? Who are the non-Jewish inhabitants of Israel today – 20 per cent of the current population? What should they be called? Are they 'Arab Israelis'? Are they the 'indigenous Palestinians'? Who is to name them? The very naming of more than a million people is integral to the struggle.

Something similar applies to 'the same territory'. Readers are invited to reread the example of radical disagreement about Jerusalem on page 3. What was this radical disagreement about? Was it about Yerushalayim? Was it about Al-Quds? And let us not make the mistake – the almost irresistible mistake for third parties – of thinking that somehow *the city itself*, with its streets and houses and sounds and smells and inhabitants, is somehow distinct from subjective beliefs or narratives or perspectives or truths projected onto it by the conflict parties. As if it were the latter that constitutes the radical disagreement, whereas it is almost precisely the opposite that is the case. The war of weapons is a battle to conquer the city. The war of words is not a juxtaposition of subjectivities. It is a battle to *name* the city for *what it is*.

Or consider the radical disagreement between Jinnah and Nehru discussed earlier in Chapter 3:

|'There are two nations on this sub-continent. This is the underlying fact that must shape the future creation of Pakistan. Only the truly Islamic platform of the Muslim League is acceptable to the Muslim nation.'

'Geography and mountains and the sea fashioned India as she is, and no human agency can change that shape or come in the way of her final destiny. Once present passions subside, the false doctrine of two nations will be discredited and discarded by all.'|

Is this radical disagreement about 'two nations'? Once again the very concept 'two nations' is already equivocated and torn apart in the conflict. Jinnah refers to 'two nations', and the identification is made not as a subjective connotation that might be separated from a bare concept, but as part of what is concretely denoted. The identification is instantaneous. It is a pointing. The Muslim nation is named by Jinnah and there is a rapturous response – 'Pakistan'. The father of the nation had spoken.

'Two nations' – Nehru, in magisterial style, thereby gestures with anger at a pernicious false doctrine. He does not refer to a bare concept, but to a terrible and threatening delusion. He foresees the catastrophic ripping apart of the ancient unity of India to feed ephemeral political ambitions.

Already in 'two nations', the whole of the disagreement is contained. It is, as always, tempting to revert to harmless third-party description and say 'for Jinnah' two nations was a fact, whereas 'for Nehru' two nations was a false doctrine. But this trivializes the struggle, as if the radical disagreement were once again a mere coexistence of subjectivities, rather than a life-and-death struggle for the one object. Benedict Anderson famously describes nations as 'imagined communities' (1991). This is an informative third-party description. But how does it relate to the conflict? Was the contest between Jinnah and Nehru a conflict of imagined communities? Neither of them is saying anything like that. On the contrary, it was a fight to the death to determine, and dismiss, what was a *mere* imagined community – and to act accordingly. Prior even to any attempt to frame the conflict, the primordial struggle is to *name the object*. Whoever successfully names the object wins. The radical disagreement is about what it is about. And *that* is what gives insight into the nature of linguistic intractability.

This turns out to be the case across the board. Third-party description in general is true but banal when applied to radical disagreement. It breaks down. For example:

'One man's terrorist is another man's freedom fighter'

employs two possessives to present a juxtaposition of subjectivities. So what is the radical disagreement about? The object drops out of the description. But it is the object that is fought over.

Compare the innocuousness of the third-party description with the terrifying battle to name the object – in this case the terrorist – in the radical disagreement:

|'Israel's armed forces will root out and destroy the Hezbollah terrorists who deliberately target our civilians. The IDF [Israel Defence Forces], as always, will do all it can to minimise civilian casualties in Lebanon, although this is not easy when the terrorists go out of their way to hide among the wider population with the specific purpose of endangering them. They act entirely indiscriminately and have no concern for human life. We do not act indiscriminately but in a measured and proportionate manner. We did not seek this war. But we will win it.'

'The criminal Israeli army once again shows its contempt for the Lebanese civilians. They employ the modern weapons supplied to them by the United States and its terrorist lackeys without pity or any concern for the people whose lives and livelihoods they destroy. They deliberately target civilian infrastructure and always kill and wound many times more civilians than any Israelis harmed. They are war criminals. The resistance forces of the Party of God will drive them from our land with their tails between their legs. God is great!'|
(Lebanon 2006: composite, but verbatim, quotations)

What was the 'family quarrel' referred to in the prologue about? Was it about whether God is the creator of the world or a human creation? Let us not think that we can easily dispel this by some ingenious theory of descriptions or equivalent third-party analysis. In my experience, conflict parties who persist in the phenomenological exploration usually conclude that their radical disagreement is about |God|, where |God| is what is common between 'God' in 'God created the world' and 'God' in 'God is a human creation'. What is |God|? And that is where the greatest phenomenological discoveries are made.

A radical disagreement is a primordial struggle to name the object. A radical disagreement is about what it is about.

How far does the radical disagreement reach?

In radical disagreements, under repeated applications of the moment of alignment, conflict parties continually reach out for the decisive argument. In this way, more and more of what had been background is brought into the foreground – and is found to be already involved. A radical disagreement about the upbringing of children becomes a radical disagreement about God. A radical disagreement about dropping the bomb becomes a radical disagreement about the foundations of ethics. A radical disagreement about wages becomes a radical disagreement about capitalism. A radical disagreement about a piece of territory becomes a radical disagreement about history and religion. It is as if when someone has fallen through the ice, ladders are brought to rescue the person struggling in the water – and the ladders fall in too.

But what is the background? It is often said that in our social and intellectual relationships we cannot get outside our own culture or language or 'lifeworld':

> Communicative actors are always moving *within* the horizon of their life-world: they cannot step outside of it.
>
> (Habermas 1981 Vol II: 126)

We are told that there is no external 'skyhook' or 'view from nowhere' or escape from our *habitus* (Rorty, Nagel, Bourdieu), though some are still prepared to use the language of 'beyond the limits of thought' (Priest 2002).

But this is not what concerns the phenomenology of radical disagreement (unless this is itself the issue as, for example, in a radical disagreement about 'what cannot be said': Wittgenstein 1961: 6.54; Priest 2002: 191). The exploration of agonistic dialogue does not take up an extramundane position, nor can it because it is not a philosophy. Yet the phenomenological exploration that constitutes agonistic dialogue stretches, as it were, from the 'inside', as far as the appeals of those involved in it reach. In this sense, there is no limit. And whatever is referred to in this way is found to be already involved. Radical disagreement is the *prior involvement of background.*

Consider the radical disagreement between Thatcherite discourse and Marxist discourse introduced in Chapter 4.

Margaret Thatcher's interview is given on pages 99–100; She was famously forthright in her rejection of Marxism as a failed ideology. It was 'ideologically, politically and morally bankrupt'(Conservative Party Conference 1980). Conversely, she vigorously rejected any idea that there was such a thing as a Thatcherite ideology. She was not being 'populist'. She simply called a spade a spade. And the British people responded to her blunt language because they shared her values. Her appeal to the background was straightforward and complete – it was to how things are, the whole of discursive space. This was integral to her conviction and emotional determination.

But in the radical disagreement, Norman Fairclough, drawing on the panoply of Marxist critical weaponry of which he is an acknowledged master, finds no difficulty in exposing the Thatcher interview as a transparently thin linguistic 'veil' behind which continued political domination is being normalized. It is indeed an ideology, and the task of critical language study is to uncover it so that those who were previously unaware of it 'become conscious of the opaque causes and consequences of their own discourse'. Conversely, the background to which Fairclough appeals is not an ideology. It is discourse/society relations in general that he points to in accounting for the emergence, function and effectiveness of Thatcherite discourse in the first place:

> In our capitalist society, the dominant bloc exercises economic and political domination over the working class and other intermediate strata of the population ... Consequently, the relationship of power-holders in public life to the mass of the population is a controlling and authoritative one. In politics, as in other domains, those who aspire to power – the parties which seek governmental power – have sought to ameliorate to varying degrees the condition of the working class but not to challenge class domination. The authority element in political leadership, as in leadership in other domains, is thus determined by class relations. Why, then, have political leaders affected solidarity with 'the people'? ... This form of 'solidarity' functions as a strategy of containment: it represents a concession to the strength of the working class and its allies on the one hand, but constitutes a veil of equality beneath which the real inequalities of capitalist society can carry on, on the other ... This is the relationship which, I shall suggest, exists right across Thatcherite discourse.
>
> (Fairclough 1989: 194–5)

And now it can be seen why my own introductory third-party description of this radical disagreement as one 'between Thatcherite discourse and Marxist discourse' breaks down. The whole language of conflicting 'ideologies' or 'psychological projections' or 'social constructions' or 'discourse worlds' is inappropriate because these are plural terms. As such, they already contain ideas of coexistence and equivalence that, in their radical disagreement, the embattled parties deny. This is not a coexistence of rival discourses, but a fight to the death to impose the one discourse.

Religious leaders often do not want to acknowledge this. The Archbishop of Canterbury, for example, seeks to prevent conflict with other faiths – and scandal in his own church – by denying that there is radical disagreement:

> Faced with the disbeliefs of another discourse, each of the three participants in the Abrahamic conversation [Judaism, Christianity, Islam] should be prompted to ask whether the God of the other's disbelief is or is not the God they themselves believe in. If the answer were a simple yes, dialogue might be a great deal more difficult than it is; the reality of dialogue suggests that we do not in fact have to do with a simple 'atheism' in respect of the other's models of God.
>
> (Williams 2004)

This is somewhat like John Locke's idea that disagreement is usually verbal mis-understanding. The Archbishop may be right in many cases. But what when the Abrahamic conversation *does* take the form of radical disagreement? Unfortunately, it is not up to any single party to determine what 'the reality of dialogue' is in these cases. Here Taha Jabir al'Alwani, in his influential *The Ethics of Disagreement in Islam*, having argued that there can be no radical disagreement *within* Islam – 'dog-matism, discord and violent disagreement (ikhtilaaf) within the Muslim Ummah has no place in the authentic teachings of Islam' – makes it plain that this does not extend to radical disagreement *between* Islam and non-Islamic beliefs:

> No one should jump to the conclusion, however, that our keenness to pre-serve the brotherhood and solidarity of Muslims implies any negligence of the fundamental Islamic beliefs, which are not open to any speculation or com-promise. The determination to confront the enemies of the Ummah will prevent us from joining hands with those who do not have any affinity with Islam.
>
> (1997: 17)

So what when there is – as there undoubtedly is – serious doctrinal dispute bet-ween some Christians and some Muslims? Can this be adequately described as a *clash of belief systems*? I do not think so. Consider what such Christian believers say when they recite the creed, and what such Muslim believers say when they recite the Qur'an.

Those who recite the Nicene Creed are not thereby referring to a mere subjective belief in the divinity of Christ – still less to a mistaken belief as their opponents assert. 'Credo, I believe ...' – and with these great words the whole awe and maj-esty of the divine creation is invoked, and God's salvific grace in sending His only Son as our unique advocate and atoner for our sins. Through faith comes salvation. This is a solemn act of affirmation at the very core of Christian faith, an outpour-ing of gratitude and joy and love to the Second Person of the Triune Deity – our Saviour, Jesus Christ.

'O believers' – and there is no question in the repeated Qur'anic address to the faithful that this has anything to do with a possibly fallible (or as their opponents claim an actually deluded) human conviction. The believers are the Muslims who hear the Prophet's recital of the very words of the Almighty and obey His injunctions. The unbelievers are those who do not hear and do not obey. God is all-merciful and summons all humanity to His service. But the Qur'an is also a warning. Divine judgement is certain, unavoidable and very real, both for believ-ers and – to their great cost – for unbelievers. The unbelievers will learn that their fate is not a subjectivity. On the contrary. After the briefest of lives that will seem to them like a dream, they will wake to the shock of the eternal present and the never-ending reality of their punishment. 'Why did we not listen?' But now it is forever too late.

The very idea that this is merely a clash of belief systems, with its in-built assumption of coexistence and ontological equivalence, is anathema to the con-flict parties. How far do radical disagreements reach? They reach to the distant horizon – as far as the eye can see. Radical disagreement is the prior involvement of background invoked. It is not a gravitational war *between* worlds within a neutral third space. It is a war *for* and *within* the *one* world in which space itself is warped and familiar landmarks slide. A radical disagreement is a singularity in the universe of discourse.

How deep does the radical disagreement go?

In *The Theory of Communicative Action*, Jürgen Habermas distinguishes different ways of redeeming validity claims in order to settle disagreements and arrive at agreements. This is structured through the world-relations that communicative actors establish with their utterances or speech acts. According to Habermas, speakers raise claims that their utterances fit the world in three main ways – objectively, socially, and subjectively. In addition, there is the question of the 'well-formedness of the symbolic expressions employed'. These three world concepts (the one objective world, the shared social world, and the individual subjective worlds) 'constitute a reference system for that about which mutual understanding is possible'. The associated validity claims are that the given statement is *true* of the objective world, that the speech act is normatively *right* in the context of the social world, and that the speaker is *sincere* in references to the subjective world to which the speaker has privileged access (Habermas 1981/1991, Vol. I: 99–100).

What happens to these distinctions in the fiercely contested field of radical disagreement? In Chapter 6, I will say a bit more about Habermas' own account of radical disagreement. Here I will just use the idea of factual truth, normative rightness, subjective sincerity, and add logical consistency (roughly corresponding to 'well-formedness of symbolic expressions') and see what happens to them in the fiery furnace of radical disagreement.

It can be seen that these distinctions mirror those that were found to be invoked in phenomenological investigation into the moments of radical disagreeing looked at above. This is not surprising since distinctions of this kind emerge naturally from the validity claims made by conflict parties (communicative actors) in the course of agonistic dialogue – at the extreme boundary of the sphere of language oriented to reaching understanding analysed by Habermas. So I will look at what happens to the invoked distinctions between 'fact' and 'value'; 'reality' and 'perspective'; 'form' and 'content'; 'subject' and 'object'.

The distinction between fact and value

The distinction between fact (reference to the one objective world) and value (reference to norms in the shared social world) is regularly invoked. But the moments of radical disagreeing have shown that in the intense heat of radical disagreement they are fused together from the beginning. Under the moment of recommendation, value appears from the outset in the elision of the imperative (do this …) into the ethical (this should be done …), and this is, in turn, instantaneously welded into the factual under the moment of justification (… because this is how things are). This already-achieved complex exists prior to any explicit challenge and is carried as an amalgam into the ensuing radical disagreement. It is what is pointed at. So it is that, when the challenge comes – and is reciprocally rejected – it is the fact/value complex as a whole that is found to be already involved. To challenge (or defend) a fact is to challenge (or defend) what does not/does have that *value*. To challenge (or defend) a value is to challenge (or defend) what does not/does *have* that legitimacy. Contradictory appeals to the 'same' principle – for example the principle of justice – are found to involve the distinction between the principle itself (the very concept) and what does/does not come under it.

This is not just a grammatical point about how assertoric form and illocutionary force can be substituted for each other. It is linked to the central way in which *emotion* appears in the phenomenology of radical disagreement. Emotion is often interpreted purely subjectively or psychologically as, for example, an expressive penumbra that accompanies conflict and needs to be dispersed before conflict parties can get down to managing the substance of the contradiction that lies at its core. But the phenomenology of radical disagreement shows again and again that emotion is not separate from the fact/value fusion. It is the *fact* of the *outrage* that immediately elicits *indignation* and the steely *will* never to rest until the wrong is righted. The *indignation* felt by Palestinians is not separable from the *fact* of what happened in the *Naqba* and the fundamental *norms* of natural justice that were thereby violated and must now be restored. This fused complex is what may lie dormant, can be handed on down the generations, and at any moment can suddenly erupt with violent force. Emotion moves much quicker than reason. Emotion is woven through the fact/value complex at the core of radical disagreement. It is not a separable add-on that can be stripped away and treated psychologically. That is why in the praxis of radical disagreement (as considered in Chapter 7) tackling the *fact* of what is at issue and its *normative importance* is not distinct from handling the *emotion* that is already built in.

The distinction between reality and perspective

The distinction between reality and perspective is central in radical disagreement. It is invoked under the moment of refutation when what the other says is relegated from its spurious claim to refer to the external world (objective/social) and is thereby assigned to the subjective world of the other's 'mere' or 'mistaken' beliefs (the other may, of course, also make a validity claim *about* her/his subjective world). But in the radical disagreement, the other answers back. And now a battle royal is generated as what was referred to as the world in which the other's reference was a 'mere' or 'mistaken' subjective belief is in turn itself denied validity and attributed to the original speaker's 'mere' subjective world, together with the subjective desires and subjective emotions that mainly define it as such. What is happening now to the framework of world concepts invoked? This will be explored in Chapter 6 in relation to Habermas' putative model of radical disagreement, so I will not pursue this line of enquiry further here.

Instead, two key points can be made.

First, readers may recognize how light is now cast on the conflict resolution tradition that distinguishes the *contradiction* that lies at the heart of the conflict in question, from the *behaviour* that together with the contradiction makes up the instrumental aspect of the conflict, and the *attitude* that supplies the expressive aspect. The phenomenon of radical disagreement, interpreted as a conflict of subjective perspectives or beliefs, is here assigned *in toto* to the category *attitude*, and is thereby assimilated to emotions and desires. That is why the phenomenon of radical disagreement – which is constituted precisely by the struggle to determine what is *mere* attitude and to contrast this with what is the case independent of any attitude – is not recognized in the mainstream conflict resolution tradition.

Second, returning to the topic of the distinction between reality and perspective itself, it can also be seen how, in the radical disagreement, it is the very world concepts themselves invoked in the process of radical disagreeing – the one objective world, the intersubjectively shared social world, the subjective worlds of the communicative actors – that are thereby found to be already materially contested. The 'reference system for that about which mutual understanding is possible' is itself involved.

That is why in a context of radical disagreement I do not write 'reality' or *reality* or realities or Reality (or 'truth', *truth*, truths, Truth) or use any other 'scare' marks, but I am quite happy to refer to reality and truth. No notational twisting and turning will insulate itself from embroilment in whatever distinctions are invoked in the phenomenon being investigated – and are thereby found to be part of what is at issue. Radical disagreement is the prior involvement of such distinctions. The battle to determine what does and does not come *under* the categories 'external world' and (mere) 'subjective world' is found already to involve a battle to determine what those worlds *are*.

The distinction between form and content

Here conflict parties in radical disagreements accuse each other of logical errors. They invoke the central distinction between validity and truth in order to focus on the former. Whatever the truth of the propositions that make up an argument may be, the accusation is that it is the inference itself that is faulty.

Consider the (undeveloped) radical disagreement between Caspar Weinberger and Alec Fisher introduced in Chapter 4. Weinberger, with the full resources of the US Department of Defense, was making the strongest case possible in justification of US nuclear deterrent strategy in order to rally wavering allies during a critical phase of the cold war. Fisher, deploying the full resources of informal reasoning analysis, exposed a simple logical fallacy at the core of Weinberger's argument:

|'I am increasingly concerned with news accounts that portray this Administration as seeking to acquire a nuclear 'war-fighting' capability. This is completely inaccurate. If the Soviets know in advance that a nuclear attack on the United States could and would bring swift nuclear retaliation, they would never attack in the first place. That is exactly why we must have a capability

for a survivable and endurable response.'

> 'In this argument, Weinberger's main conclusion – "we must have a capabil-
> ity for a survivable and endurable response" – appears to flatly contradict his
> initial 'insistence' that "we are not seeking to acquire a nuclear war-fighting
> capability".'|

What is happening? In order to test this we would need to know how Weinberger
would respond. Although for obvious reasons we do not have Weinberger's
response, he was an interviewee in my book, *Choices*, and I have a good idea of
his thinking on this topic. Here is an extract from that book:

> The policy of the Western nations is to jointly preserve their freedoms and
> cultural values while preventing aggression and war – all war. The security
> provided by a strong defense provides the environment in which education,
> business, religion and freedom can flourish ... It would be a cruel 'economy'
> to jeopardise our national values by weakening our deterrence of the Soviet
> Union. In that our policy seeks to prevent war, and to ensure the continued
> existence of the Western political tradition which fosters and protects indi-
> viduals and human rights, democratic government and religious freedom and
> toleration, it is clearly and manifestly a most moral policy.
>
> (Ramsbotham 1987: 449)

Weinberger's central argument is that the aim of US nuclear deterrent policy is not
'war-fighting'. On the contrary, it 'seeks to prevent war'. This can only be done by
convincing Soviet leaders that they will never win a war, conventional or nuclear,
because of the manifest 'capability for a survivable and endurable response' of the
US. Without an evidently inviolable second-strike force, the Soviet Union would
not be deterred and war would not be prevented.

Fisher sees a 'capability for a survivable and endurable response' as *entailing* the
acquisition of a 'war-fighting capability' because it cannot be a bluff. US nuclear
forces prepare in all earnestness for nuclear war-fighting in case deterrence fails.

The key point illustrated in this example is that in radical disagreement *form* is
not separate from *content*. The logical fallacy that Fisher detects in Weinberger's
argument (form) is found to be already enmeshed in radical disagreement about
what Weinberger has said (content). That is to say, the question of the *validity* of
an argument is found not to be separate from the question of the *nature* and *truth*
of the propositions that make it up when arguments clash. A basic distinction
from informal reasoning analysis breaks down when applied in the drastically
constrained space of agonistic dialogue. Nor can this be 'cleared up' by further
logical analysis of the kind appealed to by Fisher, that is, the sets of distinctions
that constitute the theoretical framework for informal reasoning analysis. Fisher
has already invoked this in his original analysis of Weinberger's argument. See
Figure 4.1.

Phenomenological investigation repeatedly shows that, however many such appeals are made, in ongoing radical disagreement it is the framework for logical analysis appealed to that is involved, too. It is not just a question of *application* when the dispute is repeatedly found to involve the very distinction between *what* is applied and what it applies *to*.

This introduces an even more basic point. At the heart of radical disagreement itself in written notation is a contradiction, a logical scandal:

p   not-p

But in the normal 'third-party' convention this is written:

'p'   'not-p'

And now the notation of inverted commas – the usual notation for conversation in general – reduces the scandal to a banality. Form (*that* this is what people say – indicated by two sets of inverted commas) predominates entirely over content (*what* they say – what is contained within the two sets of inverted commas). This is the notation used generally in third-party description of radical disagreement, which is why it is so innocuous.

But the notation for radical disagreement used in this book – the bar line notation – is used precisely to mark the fact that in radical disagreement form does not predominate over content. On the contrary, what shows an exchange to be a radical disagreement rather than any other kind of verbal interchange is the *content*:

|'p'   ;   'not-p'|

It is what is contained within the two sets of inverted commas that makes the difference and defines this as radical disagreement. And now it is the fact that form cannot entirely contain content – that content, as it were, breaks out of the third-party descriptive straitjacket of form – that defines this as radical disagreement, and constitutes its linguistic intractability.

At this point. it is helpful to refer back to the four illustrations given in the Prologue (Figures P.1–P.4).

P.1 contains the radical disagreement recorded between the bar lines. But here the root of the inadequate third-party description is already firmly planted. The content of what is said is imprisoned in the form of the inverted comma notation, and the coexistence of the bodies of the two speakers on the seat in the illustration reinforces this in the visual field through suggesting that *what* is said is formally subordinated to the fact *that* it is said. This leads straight – and almost imperceptibly – to the third-party description indicated in P.2. The radical disagreement has already been attributed as a juxtaposition of equivalents to the two subjective worlds of the conflictants. From this flows the world of social-scientific and other monological third-party explanations. The demand for prior explanation short-circuits investigation, and the whole phenomenon of radical disagreement is already explained *away*. This is yet further reinforced by what the conflict parties themselves say under the moment of description – and the circle seems to be complete.

In contrast, P.3 and P.4 indicate what happens if the study of the phenomenon of radical disagreement (the phenomenology of radical disagreement) gets as far as uncovering the moments of radical disagreeing. It immediately becomes plain that, plausible – even inevitable – though it may at first appear, the third-party account assumed in P.2 is *explicitly rejected* by both conflict parties. That is what makes it a radical disagreement. And that is what lies at the heart of the linguistic intractability.

But there is a notable absentee from this set of pictures. Where is the picture that depicts the resulting radical disagreement itself? Where is the fifth picture? As Chapter 6 will underline, my own answer to this question, having spent a long time trying to find such a picture, is that it does not exist. There is no adequate third-party monological depiction. And now, in the light of the phenomenological exploration, it can be seen why this has already been said – in the original *example* of radical disagreement recorded in written notation between the bar lines in P.1 – if it is taken seriously in the first place.

A further point to be noted is that in radical disagreement the distinction between logical constants (not-) and propositional variables (p) is also compromised. What defines the radical disagreement as such is not the appearance of 'not-' on one side or the other (this can always be reversed), but the fact that there is *mutual contradiction* between the statements and the *reappearance of p* within both sets of inverted commas. For there to be radical disagreement, it has to be *the same* proposition that is here affirmed and there denied. That is why the involvement of the distinction between form and content plays such a critical role. Again and again under the moment of alignment, conflict parties find that the question whether they are each arguing about the same thing becomes what is at issue:

|'You have misunderstood me.'

'I have understood you perfectly – you are wrong.'|

And now the distinction 'same/different' is also found to be involved.

As a concluding note in this regard, perhaps it is apt that in mathematics the modulus sign |4| marks out what '+4' has in common with '−4'.

The distinction between subject and object

Finally, and from a somewhat different angle, what about the appearance of reflexive terms (I, you, here, now) in radical disagreement? Nothing could seem more distinct in Habermas' world-relations than, on the one hand, terms explicitly referring to the private worlds of communicative actors, and, on the other, terms explicitly referring to the external world (the one objective world and the shared social-normative world). But this distinction, too, turns out to be already involved – to break down – in the crucible of linguistic intractability.

How does the fact that this is *my* opinion (Oliver Ramsbotham's opinion), for example, appear phenomenologically in a radical disagreement in which I am a conflict party?

In this case, I do not think that it is the appearance of reflexive terms in general that shows this because reflexive terms can appear not only in what I say, but also in what my opponent says:

|'I am right; you are wrong.' ; 'I am right; you are wrong.'|

Which is which?

So could my appearance in the trammels of radical disagreement be conveyed phenomenologically by a feat of imaginative empathy? In one of Sartre's books (I cannot remember which), for example, there is an account of someone who looks through a keyhole in a hotel corridor at what is going on in one of the rooms. This is just as it should be. He is able to describe and make judgements about the world spread out before him. But all at once, there is a sound behind him. He springs back from the keyhole and looks down the corridor. Thank heavens! No one has seen him. He can relax again and is just about to return to his point of vision when he suddenly notices a door on the opposite side of the corridor – and is seized by an unaccountable dread. What has he instinctively apprehended? Why does he feel a shiver of self-conscious horror run down his spine? And then he sees a keyhole in this door. And through the keyhole – an eye.

This is a brilliant evocation of the experience of someone caught in a war of visual fields. Only a writer with Sartre's novelist's skill could portray the sense of uncanniness. But this still does not nail down what makes this *my* opinion rather than my opponent's.

So what *does* mark this out as my opinion?

I can only reach one conclusion. Within the nexus of a radical disagreement in which I am a conflict party, what makes this *my* opinion is – precisely and only – the fact that it is a *true* opinion. A *true* opinion is *my* opinion. And *that* is what is carried, as a single complex, into the radical disagreement – to be torn apart.

The wheel has come full circle. What looked like the most divergent of all distinctions invoked – not only the distinction between the private worlds of communicative actors in general and the external world, but *my* private world – turns out under the severe attrition of radical disagreement to transmute instantaneously into its opposite. And that is what *constitutes* linguistic intractability in this regard. I will return to the reflexive theme in the epilogue.

Conclusion

In the phenomenology of radical disagreement, the uncovering of the moments of radical disagreeing opens the way for an exploration by conflict parties of the resulting agonistic dialogue. This offers insights into the nature of linguistic intractability that are not available elsewhere. Radical disagreements are about what they are about – a life-and-death struggle to name the topic. Radical disagreements are the prior involvement of background appealed to – a fight to pin the label 'mere background' on what the other says. They reach as far as the eye can see. Radical disagreements are the involvement of distinctions invoked – the distinction between fact and value, the distinction between reality and perspective, the distinction between form and content, the distinction between subject and object.

In short, the phenomenology of radical disagreement shows that conflict parties are, *not nearer*, but *much further apart* than was supposed. Radical disagreements are not all-too familiar but, on the contrary, perhaps the least familiar features of intense political conflict.

How does this contribute to the project of systemic transformation in intractable conflicts at the point where attempts at settlement or resolution have (so far) failed? That is the topic for the rest of the book. But perhaps it can already be seen, first, that through agonistic dialogue, verbal exchange between conflict parties is continued in the only way that it can be during periods of intractability. Second, agonistic dialogue engages a greater number of those who make up the conflicting parties than would otherwise be the case – not just those predisposed to 'dialogue for mutual understanding'. Third, the evolving patterns of radical disagreement embedded in the complex conflict system are identified in a way they would not otherwise be – this provides essential information for conflict transformation. Fourth, the specific discoveries made in the phenomenology of radical disagreement illuminate the nature of the 'war of words' itself that constitutes linguistic intractability. Finally – although it is always possible that phenomenological exploration will make things worse rather than better – it is at least also possible that the phenomenology of radical disagreement, by showing conflict parties that they are much further apart than had been thought and making them strange to each other, might even itself begin to be transformative.

6 Epistemology
Understanding agonistic dialogue

Third parties, whether as analysts or as agents, find that their analyses and actions are already implicated in the conflict arenas that they seek to understand or transform. At a theoretical level, there is no adequate third-party account of agonistic dialogue. There is no theory or philosophy of radical disagreement. These largely negative results offer insight into the nature of linguistic intractability and have significant theoretical and practical implications.

This chapter turns from a consideration of conflict parties to a consideration of third parties. What happens to third-party accounts of radical disagreement in the context of the agonistic dialogues that they purport to analyse? In the world of action, it is a common experience that well meaning third-party interventions, even if initially welcomed by the combatants, all too often become embroiled in the ongoing intractable conflict. The epistemology of radical disagreement investigates the linguistic corollary. What happens when third-party *description* and *explanation* of the verbal exchanges between conflict parties generates third-party *prescription* for action in what nevertheless remain intractable conflicts?

In the first part of the chapter, I look at two of the best attempts to interpret embattled conflict narratives with a view to prescribing transformative action that I have come across – an attempt to read and respond to 'narratives of conflict' in the Israeli-Palestinian conflict, and a study of the way 'myths and truths started a war' in Kosovo.

In the second half of the chapter, I look in particular at Habermas' *The Theory of Communicative Action* and Gadamer's *Truth and Method*, the two most influential philosophies behind contemporary discursive and dialogic conflict resolution approaches respectively, as Chapter 3 showed.

Understanding narratives of conflict in the Israeli-Palestinian conflict: description, explanation, prescription

Pioneering work in this field has been done in many contexts, notably Northern Ireland, where, for example, the 1992–3 Opsahl Commission gathered a mass of testimony from all sides with a view to promoting mutual acceptance of the validity of discrepant traditions in the hope, thereby, of fostering 'parity of esteem'. Here the focus is on the Israeli-Palestinian conflict.

Third-party description, explanation, prescription

I use as an example the excellent analysis, description and prescription given in *Israeli and Palestinian Narratives of Conflict* (2006) edited by Robert Rotberg. The task in the epistemology of radical disagreement is to test the adequacy of putative third-party accounts by applying them to specific examples of radical disagreement. How should the phenomenon of radical agreement be understood?

Here are extracts from the editor's introduction (selected):

> 'The Israeli-Palestinian conflict for primacy, power, and control encompasses two bitterly contested, competing narratives. Both need to be understood, reckoned with, and analysed side by side in order to help abate violence and possibly propel both protagonists toward peace. This is an immensely tall order. But the first step is to know the narratives, the second to reconcile them to the extent that they can be reconciled or bridged, and the third to help each side to accept, and conceivably to respect, the validity of the competing narrative ...'

> Juxtaposing the 'two justifying/rationalizing narratives' helps us to 'understand the roots of the conflict and the differentially distorted prisms that fuel it'. At the core of such narratives lie 'symbolic constructions of shared identity' or 'collective memories', which do not usually so much 'reflect truth' as 'portray a truth that is functional for a group's ongoing existence'. Each is 'true' in terms of the requirements of collective memory'. Narratives are 'motivational tools'.

> What is required is a 'greater appreciation of the separate truths that drive Palestinians and Israelis', because this could 'plausibly contribute to conflict reduction'. The aim is 'to narrow, not eliminate, the chasm that separates one strongly affirmed reality from another. The lessons of this book are that the gulf between the narratives remains vast, that no simplified efforts at softening the edges of each narrative will work, and that the fundamental task of the present is to expose each side to the narratives of the other in order, gradually, to foster an understanding, if not an acceptance, of their deeply felt importance to each side.'
>
> (Rotberg (ed.) 2006: 1–17)

The radical disagreement between Israelis and Palestinians is described here in terms of 'competing narratives' or 'separate truths', and explained as 'symbolic constructions of shared identity' which serve as 'motivational tools' that are 'functional for a group's ongoing existence'. This leads to the transformational recommendation to 'expose each side to the narratives of the other in order, gradually, to foster an understanding, if not an acceptance, of their deeply felt importance to each side'. The methodology appealed to is that of promoting dialogue for mutual understanding.

In the body of the text, four main strategies emerge for doing this:

1 Ilan Pappe advocates 'bridging the narrative concept' along the lines already initiated by the new 'post-Zionist' revisionist Israeli historians, among whom he is a prominent figure, in order to narrow differences and if possible produce shared historiographical reconstructions.

2 Daniel Bar-Tal and Gavriel Salomon do not think that it is possible to overcome the way rival narratives oppose each other's fundamental truths, and, as psychologists, hope to promote reconciliation by 'building legitimacy through narrative' – fostering mutual acknowledgement of sincerity and therefore validity by recognizing 'that there are two (legitimate) narratives of the conflict'.

3 Mordechai Bar-On recommends acceptance of the fact that the Zionist and Palestinian narratives 'negate the very existence of the foe as a collectivity' and suggests that the focus should rather be on a critical re-examination of the historical record by each side separately. He sees this as a particular task for the Palestinians.

4 Finally, Dan Bar-On and Sami Adwan aim to promote 'better dialogue between two separate but interdependent narratives' that 'are intertwined like a double helix' through their work on the production of parallel texts on the Balfour Declaration, the 1948 war, and the 1987 Intifada, including the idea of getting Israeli and Palestinian schoolchildren to fill in intermediate commentaries.

An example of radical disagreeing for comparison

How does the editorial description and explanation of the radical disagreement, and the policy prescriptions and recommendations that flow from this, relate to *examples* of what is being described, explained and responded to? In this case, we do not have to look far. I will take one of the authors of the book as a spokesperson for the Palestinian narrative. This is Nadim Rouhana, a highly regarded Palestinian conflict transformation specialist and professor at a leading US conflict resolution centre (the George Mason University Institute for Conflict Management and Resolution). I think that what he says in his chapter would be accepted as objective and reasonable – indeed self-evident – by nearly all Palestinians. We would have to ask them.

How does Rouhana's 'narrative' relate to the editorial prescription and the four transformation approaches listed above? To make this clear I will use the same numbering sequence. And I will relate these extracts from Rouhana's text to the moments of radical disagreeing discussed in Chapter 5.

1 For Rouhana, 'bridging the narrative concept' cannot mean 'meeting the other half-way' when what is required is for Israelis to acknowledge the violence and injustice inherent in the Zionist project itself (as, in fact, Pappe does):

From the moment Zionism was conceived, force has been a central component of its relationship with Palestinians. The seeds of protracted conflict
are based in the relationship between colonizer and colonized, and thus are
inherent to the dynamics of the encounter between the Zionist movement and
Palestinians. It has always been naïve or self-serving to think that a Jewish
state could be established in a homeland inhabited by another people except
through the use of force.

(Rouhana 2006: 118)

Under the *moment of justification*, the reference in radical disagreeing is not to 'one
strongly affirmed reality' among others, but to what actually happened. Third-party
analysts should not try to deconstruct this prematurely if they want to reach the
radical disagreement itself.

2 In Rouhana's chapter, promoting reconciliation by 'building legitimacy through
narrative' does not mean recognizing 'that there are two (legitimate) narratives of
the conflict' because one of the narratives is fundamentally illegitimate:

The encounter has been one between an indigenous people in a homeland
defined by the political unit known as Palestine ever since the British mandate
was established, and another group of people, the Zionists, who came from
outside of Palestine, mainly from Europe, and developed a modern ideology
based on three key principles: The Jews are a nation and should establish their
own state ...; A Jewish state should be established in Palestine ...; Palestine
[should] become the exclusive homeland of the Jewish people and not the land
of both the Jewish people and the people of Palestine. Mainstream Zionists
... did not seek partnership with the people who lived in Palestine to build a
common homeland but rather [aimed] to transform the country into an exclu-
sively Jewish homeland.

(Ibid.: 116)

This is an example of invocation of the distinction between how things are, and
(false) ideology in radical disagreeing under the *moment of alignment* and the
moment of refutation.

On the issue of reconciliation, mentioned under 2 above, Rouhana emphasizes
that this means explicit Israeli recognition of the suppression of manifest facts
in their national narrative – the denial that the Palestinians even existed and the
refusal to acknowledge that they have been either expelled from their land or sub-
jugated as second-class citizens – and a resolve to remedy the ongoing injustice
in future by ensuring full equal rights for all those living in Palestine regardless
of race, religion or other differences. Reconciliation can only be based on truth
and justice:

Genuine reconciliation requires facing historic truths, taking responsibility
for past injustices, and framing future relations in terms of justice rather than

power. Reconciliation would also require a major political restructuring to enable full equality between individuals and national groups in Palestine, a change that would be incompatible with a Zionist framework or with Zionism.
(Ibid.: 127)

Radical disagreement is driven by recommendation for action, and, given power, by action itself. In this case, under the *moment of recommendation* and the *moment of action*, a loser in the resulting power play does not separate the question of the legitimacy of the oppressor's narrative from the question of the substantial recti-fication of the associated injustice.

3 For Rouhana, the idea that 'scholarly confrontations between conflicting nar-ratives can be fruitful only if each side concentrates on self-criticism, not on condemning the other' (Bar-On 2006: 153), and particularly the idea that this is a task mainly for the Palestinians because Israel already has its revisionist 'new historians' and 'post-Zionists', does not cut ice. The 'Palestinian narrative' is an attempt to rescue a record of suppressed reality, whereas even 'left-leaning' liberal Israelis who promote the idea that 'both sides have equally legitimate narratives' are thereby covertly supporting the hegemonic Zionist cause and reinforcing the *status quo*:

> Left-leaning Israelis and Zionist groups seek official and unofficial diplo-matic means to achieve the same result, while often paralleling the history of Zionism and the Palestinian national movement arguing that both sides have equally legitimate narratives as well as a history of violence, the need for recognition, and so on. This alternative approach seeks to achieve recognition of Zionism in return for a Palestinian state in the occupied territories.
> (Rouhana 2006: 128)

This is a clear example of how the very idea of equivalent 'narratives of conflict', central to the third-party understanding of the situation, is already lost in relation to the agonistic dialogue that constitutes linguistic intractability. This also illumi-nates the way that in intractable conflicts, the *moment of revision* plays a different role to that sketched out for it in conflict resolution and conflict transformation, reinforcing rather than weakening intransigence.

4 Finally, for Rouhana, it is not a question of 'promoting better dialogue between two separate but interdependent narratives' by producing parallel texts in both Hebrew and Arabic and inviting intermediate commentary so that 'hateful single narratives' are transformed into 'two mutually sensitive ones'. Instead, two other requirements are at issue.

First, the dominant narrative which supports and 'naturalises' the unjust power asymmetry stands in need of deconstruction in order to expose its subconscious, repressed roots in guilt and fear:

For obvious reasons, it is not easy [for Israelis] to face this fear, as it would mean challenging the national narrative and national and personal identity'.

(Ibid.: 127)

This can be seen to come under the *moment of explanation*.

Second, the marginalized narrative, which represents legitimate resistance to the injustice and a refusal to be suppressed or co-opted as 'one truth among many', needs to be reaffirmed:

For Palestinians, resisting the takeover of their homeland was a natural human reaction to injustice ... One of the most effective and least evident forms of resistance was the preservation of memories and the national narrative, at the core of which was a clinging to a right to the homeland – expressed now in the form of insisting on the principle of the right of return: Israel must be held responsible for the Palestinian exile, and the Jewish state in the Palestinian homeland must be denied legitimacy. This narrative is shared by all segments of Palestinian society, including Palestinians in Israel.

(Ibid.: 125)

For Rouhana, this is what the juxtaposition of two parallel texts in Hebrew and Arabic – or any other language – will demonstrate to any impartial reader. The appeal is ostensive – look and see.

An example of radical disagreement

But it is only when the other answers back in agonistic dialogue that the full dimensions of the radical disagreement itself are seen.

In *Israeli and Palestinian Narratives of Conflict*, the editor notes how some other authors 'take exception' to Rouhana's 'contribution'. What happens in these cases?

One of those to take exception is Mordechai Bar-On, an eminent self-styled 'veteran peace activist' and research scholar at the Yad Ben-Zvi Institute in Jerusalem. Bar-On has great experience of Israeli-Palestinian dialogue and a sophisticated capacity to 'read-off' for his own partisanship under what in Chapter 5 is called the *moment of description*:

Israeli historians should be able to explain the rational and moral indignation that motivated the Palestinians to provoke violence [in 1948], just as Palestinian historians should be able to explain why young Israelis could not but fight back at that stage.

(Bar-On 2006: 154)

Bar-On is happy to recognize that 'opposing narratives are conceived not only as untrue but also as insulting and morally corrupt' by the other, so that 'in the context of this volume, "truth" can be contested'. He goes further and recognizes the contingency of his own strong emotional response to Rouhana's utterances:

> I have no doubt that my arguments have little chance of influencing Rouhana, as his oral arguments (at our meetings at Harvard University) not only failed to convince me but also made me angry.
>
> (Ibid.: 148)

In Chapter 5, I noted that no matter how sensitive the invocation of equivalence under the moment of description may be, what signifies in ongoing radical disagreement is what follows the 'but …'. In this case the word is 'yet'. And in what follows 'yet', Bar-On does not use the language of mutual subjectivity appropriate to the moment of description, but the more direct language of objective 'faults' in the way the other tells the story, 'problems' with the other's thesis, and the dire consequences of the other's intransigence for prospects for peace – in short, the language appropriate to the moments of radical disagreeing.

Rouhana is the first speaker, Bar-On is the second:

> |'Israel will have to face at least part of the truth that the country that they settled belonged to another people, that their project was the direct cause of the displacement and dismantling of Palestinian society, and that it could not have been achieved without this displacement. Israel will also have to confront the realities of the occupation and the atrocities it is committing, and will have to accept that Palestinian citizens in Israel are indigenous to the land and entitled to seek the democratic transformation of the state so that they have equal access to power, resources and decision making, and are entitled to rectification of past and present injustices.'
>
> (Rouhana 2006: 133)

> 'There are many historiographical faults in the way Rouhana tells the story … The main problem with Rouhana's thesis … lies in his sweeping conclusion that "from the moment Zionism was conceived, force has been a central component of its relationship with the Palestinians" … Is it not possible for a Palestinian such as Rouhana to understand that, in 1948, the Jews of Palestine, to their chagrin, could not but use force to defend themselves and impose a solution that was legitimated by a majority of nations? … [T]here is no chance that I shall ever consider that my father and mother, who immigrated to Palestine as Zionists in 1924, were criminals. Nor do I consider my actions illegitimate when I gave the order "Fire!" and perhaps killed or wounded assailants in response to an ambush on the troop that I commanded on the way to Tel Aviv in December 1947 … There is hardly any question that, in December 1947, the fire that later spread throughout the country was ignited at that time by the Palestinians … The joy with which Arab intellectuals embraced the new [Israeli] narratives betrays a misguided assumption that, at long last, Israelis see the "truth" and are ready to adopt the Arab narratives of

the conflict ... The lesson Palestinians should learn from Israel's revisionist historiography is not how correct they are in their own narratives but rather how self-critical they, too, must become.'|

(Bar-On 2006: 147–8; 167–8)

Bar-On asks: 'Can even the most moderate and understanding Israeli agree to deny the legitimacy of the Israeli state? Can such an Israeli really be expected to embrace the original sin, or original crime, that Zionism inflicted upon the Palestinians?'

Rouhana asks whether even the most moderate and understanding Palestinian (including 'Palestinians in Israel') could agree to deny the legitimacy of Palestinian demands for equal rights in their own homeland, or be expected to accept responsibility for initiating violence in attempting legitimate resistance to disenfranchisement.

This example of radical disagreement is undeveloped. Very little direct agonistic dialogue is recorded. Yet already – in this brief exchange between two eminently moderate members of their respective communities, and colleagues in the production of the book – the entire lineaments of the linguistic intractability associated with the Israeli-Palestinian conflict can be glimpsed. To bring it into sharper focus, as outlined in Chapter 5 and developed in Chapter 7, what would be needed would be the promotion of the agonistic dialogue. The radical disagreement needs to be acknowledged, surface misunderstandings need to be cleared up, arguments need to be aligned (here they can be seen to miss each other), the moments of radical disagreeing need to be made explicit (as indicated above in relation to Rouhana's chapter), and the resulting fully engaged radical disagreement then needs to be properly explored.

The editor himself realizes something of this when he comments:

A next stage, too late for this book, would be for Jawad, Porat, Bar-On and others [he does not name Rouhana] to spend necessary hours together attempting to reconcile the discordant narratives, or at least delineating the precise contours of disagreement.

(Rotberg (ed.) 2006: 8)

This is, indeed, what needs to be done. It is what, surprisingly, is very rarely done so far as I can discover, even in critical political discourse analysis and coexistence studies. What would happen if it were done? Evidently it would be up to the conflict parties, undertaking phenomenological exploration of their agonistic dialogue, to find out. But Chapter 5 suggests that in general terms they might discover that they do not agree about the *object* in question in the first place – 'the indigenous Palestinian citizens of Israel', 'the Jews of Palestine', 'the displacement of Palestinian society', 'the solution legitimated by a majority of nations'. The radical disagreement is a primordial struggle to *name* the object. They might find that the background appealed to is in each case itself found to be already part of the conflict: 'the truth that the country that they settled belonged to another people', 'the many historiographical faults in the way Rouhana tells the story'. The radical disagreement reaches to the horizon. And they might find that emotions – Bar-On's anger, Rouhana's indignation – are not subjective adjuncts to the conflict, but are inseparable from what *causes* the anger and what *arouses* the indignation. In short, they might find that they are not nearer, but rather, much further apart than *Israeli and Palestinian Narratives of Conflict* suggests.

In this way, I think that great insight would be gained into the main linguistic reason why prescriptions for transformative action of the kind advocated in *Israeli and Palestinian Narratives of Conflict* – based as they are on prior third-party description and explanation – so often fail in the intensity of intractable conflict. In the drastic contraction of conceptual space constituted by linguistic intractability, there is not yet enough room for dialogue for mutual understanding.

In summary, what needs to be investigated in this respect is not narratives *of* conflict, but narratives *in* conflict.

Radical disagreement and the involvement of third-party impartiality

Before moving on to the next example of the prior involvement of third-party description, explanation and prescription in the conflict under investigation, it is worth extending the Israeli-Palestinian case to embrace the question of impartiality.

Dennis Ross was President Clinton's chief negotiator at the 2000 Camp David talks. In his 2004 book, *The Missing Peace: The Inside Story of the Fight for Middle East Peace*, he describes the radical disagreement between Israelis, Arabs and Palestinians as the subjective 'historical narratives of each side' which can only be understood once we learn 'why Israelis, Arabs and Palestinians see the world as they do' (Chapter 1). He regards himself as impartial between the conflict parties, with an interest only in securing a just peace.

Contrast what Ross says here *about* the radical disagreement between Israelis and Palestinians with what he says *in* the radical disagreement that he has himself been caught up in as a result, such as this response to the 2000 Camp David talks from Noam Chomsky:

> Bill Clinton and Israeli prime minister Barak did propose an improvement: consolidation to three cantons, under Israeli control, virtually separated from one another and from the fourth enclave, a small area of East Jerusalem, the center of Palestinian communications. The fifth canton was Gaza. It is understandable that maps are not to be found in the US mainstream. Nor is the prototype, the Bantustan 'homelands' of apartheid South Africa, ever mentioned.
>
> (Chomsky 11 May 2002 *The Guardian*)

Ross does offer maps in his 2004 book, contrasting a map of what 'official Palestinians' and critics like Chomsky 'inaccurately' cite as the 'final offer they turned down at Camp David', with a map outlining the 'actual proposal at Camp David'. In addition, he offers a third map reflecting 'Clinton ideas' in December 2000:

To this day, Arafat has never honestly admitted what was offered to the Palestinians ... [W]ith 97 percent of the territory in Palestinian hands, there would have been no cantons. Palestinian areas would not have been isolated and surrounded. There would have been territorial integrity and contiguity in both the West Bank and Gaza, and there would have been independent borders with Egypt and Jordan.

Had Nelson Mandela been the Palestinian leader and not Yasir Arafat, I would be writing now how, notwithstanding the limitations of the Oslo process, Israelis and Palestinians had succeeded in reaching an 'end of conflict' agreement ... Arafat either let the Intifada begin or, as some argue, actually gave orders for it ... Arafat was not up to peacemaking.

(Ross 2004: 767, 756–7)

The key point here is that Ross does not apply his subjectivist reading of the Israeli-Palestinian dispute to his own radical disagreement with Chomsky, Arafat and most Palestinians. Instead, he invokes the language of agonistic dialogue as examined in Chapter 5. That is what makes it a radical disagreement – and one that is integral to the ongoing conflict because many participants have quoted or criticized Ross in support of their claims. Ross's own appeal is not to 'subjective historical narratives', but to his objective knowledge of what really happened at Camp David. He was an insider. He refers to this as demonstrating the inaccuracy and dishonesty of the false assertions made by his opponents.

Jeremy Pressman is another third-party intervener – this time not a political activist, but an academic analyst. He also sees himself as an impartial well-wisher of the peace process. Having looked through the available documentation and supplemented this with extensive interviews with participants from all sides, he concludes, in diametric opposition to Ross, that

neither the Israeli nor the Palestinian version of the events at Camp David and subsequent talks is wholly accurate. The Palestinian version, however, is much closer to the evidentiary record of articles, interviews, and documents produced by participants in the negotiations, journalists, and other analysts.

(Pressman 2003: 5)

Pressman notes how closely aligned the view of 'some US officials' and 'major US newspapers' have been to the Israeli perspective, and consequently calls this the 'dominant version'. Others have said that the proposals put forward by the US at Camp David were coordinated in advance with the Israelis.

But the important point here is again the contrast between Pressman's language in his understanding of the radical disagreement between the Israelis and Palestinians, and his language in refuting false claims about the 2000–1 negotiations. He describes the former in familiar vein as divergent 'versions of events', 'visions in collision', 'narratives', 'stories', 'views', 'perspectives', and 'conflicting beliefs'. In his own argumentation, however, his appeal is directly and unequivocally to the historical evidence itself:

The Israeli conclusion ... is based on five contentions that do not hold up when assessed in light of the evidence from 2000–1.

(Ibid.: 23)

In the radical disagreements that third parties find themselves involved in, both with the original conflict parties, and with each other, whether as active interveners like Ross, or analysts like Pressman, the subjectivist third-party language of equivalence used to describe the original quarrel breaks down. Instead, the authentic language of agonistic dialogue emerges. This – when taken seriously and developed – gives third parties a chance to gain clear insight into the nature of linguistic intractability. They are not neutral or impartial because there is no room for that. They are trying to impose their own discourse on the continuing struggle. It is as well for them to realize this from the outset.

How myths and truths started a war in Kosovo

Julie Mertus' book, *Kosovo: How Myths and Truths Started a War,* is a rare study from a scholar who views what she calls the 'micro-analysis' of competing versions of the truth as a serious component in the dynamic of violent conflict, every bit as important as the more usual 'macro-analysis':

The kind of analysis that is most desperately missing is an analysis of history as told by the people of the Balkans themselves ...

(Mertus 1999: 5)

She took the trouble to gather material in Albanian and Serbo-Croat from local newspapers and personal interviews. She speaks the languages. In her book, she charts stages in the escalation of the conflict marked by inflammatory incidents, beginning with the 1981 student demonstrations, and ending with the alleged poisoning of Albanian schoolchildren in 1990. In each case, she summarizes the opposed views:

'the Truth for most Serbs was ...' ; 'the Truth for most Kosovo Albanians was ...'

And she offers verbatim interview statements from both sides. This is remarkable raw material for a study of the explosive significance of radical disagreement in intense political conflict. No one was better placed to explore specific examples of the radical disagreements themselves than Julie Mertus.

Yet Mertus herself does not undertake such a study. She sees no purpose in recording *exchanges* between the conflicting parties. She leaves the statements just as they are – juxtaposed, but not mutually criticized or commented upon.

Why does a scholar, who has undertaken the great labour of gathering such a significant corpus of ethnomethodological data – a very rare achievement – in the event not think it worthwhile to journey on to the exploration of the radical disagreements that she has so brilliantly exposed?

Once again, I think that the reason is related to Mertus' own understanding of the situation in the first place.

At the core of Mertus' reading, is the sharp contrast that she draws between 'facts' (factual truths), such that there had been years of 'gross human rights abuses against Albanians' by Serbian officials ('I was right about the abuse') and 'Truths' (non-factual truths) such as the conflicting accounts that she has documented:

> To understand how wars start we need to do more than examine factual truth, we need to unravel the 'more or less truths'.
>
> (Mertus 1999: 2)

In other words:

> for those who are interested in understanding and predicting behavior, what matters is not what is *factually true* but what people believe to be 'Truth'.
>
> (Ibid.: 9–10)

We are familiar with this idea and its consequences from Chapter 3 (although the notational slippage 'Truth' indicates the difficulty of maintaining the distinction).

Based on her sharp contrast between factual truth and non-factual Truth, Mertus sees the causes of the war operating at two levels.

At the top level, the leaders 'understood each other quite well' and knew that each wanted 'power and resources' in a 'zero-sum game'. There was conscious manipulation on both sides. In order to achieve their political purposes, leaders deliberately promoted fear and anxiety among their peoples by conducting a 'steady and intense propaganda campaign against the "other"'. At leadership level, therefore, the radical disagreement is entirely subsumed into the propaganda battle. There was no incentive to investigate further.

It was at the second level, among the 'general population', that sincerely believed conflicting Truths, perpetuated by institutionalized injustice and tied to competing but manipulated national identities, proved to be so potent. This is where mutual misunderstanding abounded because within local private communities on both sides

> feelings are played out in hidden transcripts of anger, aggression and disguised discourses of dignity, the modes whereby groups can act out the feelings they ordinarily must conceal, such as through gossip, rumour and creation of autonomous private spaces for assertion of dignity. Serbians and Kosovo Albanians are not privy to each others' hidden transcripts, nor could they understand each others' transcripts if they could gain access.
>
> (Ibid.: 10)

Within this context of mutual misapprehension, in which 'each society has its regime of truth', the opposite of a Truth is not necessarily a lie; rather, it is a competing Truth linked to an alternative self-image.

(Ibid.: 10)

For Mertus, these are not disputes about factual truth, only a coexistence of rival non-factual Truths. They are myths believed in as a result of material circumstance and induced fear. They are productions of power, and are linked to action (behaviour) through manipulated need (psychology). They themselves are all too easy to understand. It is what has generated them and the role that they have played in the conflict that need to be analysed. The radical disagreement has been reduced to a coexistence of manipulated subjectivities or beliefs. Once again there is no incentive to enquire further.

In Mertus' analysis, therefore, the radical disagreement itself drops out of consideration. It disappears between the limits of mutual convergence at leadership level, and mutual misunderstanding at general population level. That is why, I think, despite having wonderful material for a rich exploration of the radical disagreements at the core of the Kosovo conflict, Mertus has no inducement to investigate further.

When Mertus set out on her research, however, her original aim was not to study competing Kosovo Albanian and Serb Truths, but the factual truth about alleged Serb atrocities. She was then side-tracked into the former when the wide disparity between those accounts became apparent to her. But she did not forget her first intention.

On Serb atrocities she is clear that there had indeed been 'years of gross human rights abuses against Albanians by Serbian officials'. This was a factual truth:

I was right about the abuse.

(Ibid.: 9)

But this is nevertheless hotly disputed by many Serbs. So here is a radical disagreement between Mertus and those Serbs:

|'I was right about the abuse.'

'No you were not. You were hoodwinked by the Albanian provocateurs. The entire Western/NATO strategy was based on manipulated lies – just as in Afghanistan and Iraq.'|

In this (imagined) radical disagreement Mertus is not saying that the gross human rights abuses by Serbian officials were only 'Truth for Julie Mertus'. Nor that the opposite was, not an untruth, but 'Truth for those Serbs'. Nor that all that can be said is that 'each party has its own regime of truth'. No doubt each party does have its own regime of truth. But this does not touch what is at issue in the radical disagreement or the consequences in the world of action that flow from it – in this case, because Western leaders agreed with Mertus and had the power to act accordingly, the NATO assault, the ending of Serb rule in Kosovo, and the fall of Milosevich.

Consequent upon Mertus' descriptions and explanations are her prescriptions for preventative action in the communicative sphere. She is one of the few who recognize the limits to dialogue for mutual understanding in times of maximum intractability:

> Allowing competing Truths to float through the air in the same space, unjudged and unquestioned, can be a revolutionary act. The Truths may always exist. But the very telling can provoke self-reflection and dismantle the link between Truths and the degrading of an oppositional 'other'. The telling may narrow the gap between Truths, creating a common bridge toward something else. Yet sometimes the divisions between people are too great, the fear too intense, the desire of some to maintain or gain power too overwhelming. The mere telling is not enough to stem conflict. Thus we cannot stop after the story-telling. We must have the will to think of bold, even drastic interventions to change the status quo into a more peaceful something else.
>
> (Mertus 1999: 4)

But, because Mertus does not explore the phenomenon of radical disagreement and interprets what is said in terms of subjective Truths, there is no further linguistic recourse after the limits of 'story-telling' are reached. The rest is non-verbal intervention or linguistic therapy – or just 'something else'.

Philosophies of radical disagreement: Foucault, Barthes, Habermas, Gadamer

In the search for a philosophy of radical disagreement, I look first, briefly, at two philosophies underlying Mertus' interpretation – those of Michel Foucault and Roland Barthes. Then, at somewhat greater length, I turn to the two most influential philosophies in critical conflict transformation and hermeneutic dialogue respectively – those of Jürgen Habermas and Hans-Georg Gadamer. What do these philosophies say about the phenomenon of radical disagreement? Do they give an adequate account?

Michel Foucault

Mertus' concept of competing Truths is derived from Foucault:

> Knowledge of truth is not the product of reason operating independently of social and political relationships. Rather, truth can be understood as the product of complex power relations whereby Truth is produced through power and power is exercised in the production of Truth.
>
> (Mertus 1999: 2, with reference to Foucault 1980 131–2)

But does Foucault offer an account of competing truths or radical disagreement at all?

I do not find that in the structural nature of Foucault's early 'archaeological' approach there was any room for a concern with what he regarded as a throwback to phenomenological intentionality.

Nor in his 'genealogical' homage to Nietzsche did Foucault see any more significance in the phenomenon of human disagreement than did Nietzsche himself, and for loosely related reasons to those mentioned in Chapter 2. For Foucault, it would be superficial and entirely misleading to take truth claims seriously as phenomena worth studying in their own right, since truth is a child of multiple forms of constraint, and 'effects of truth' are produced by historical processes within discourses that are in themselves 'neither true nor false'.

Nor in Foucault's later re-interpretation of his work in terms of 'problematization' is disagreement any more prominent. Indeed, he specifically discounts the dialectical nature of negation and contradiction associated with verbal disagreement as both constraining and superficial. He saw his historical writings as attempts to liberate the future by showing the complex and contested ways in which the present has emerged from the past. He hoped that his patient and detailed tracing of the subtle modes by which intricate and swirling eddies of power and knowledge have been precipitated into current forms of reification, subjection and exclusion, would thereby help to open up new spaces of possibility for an emancipated subjectivity. Things that may otherwise appear ineluctable happen to have evolved like this, and can, therefore, evolve differently in future. The task is one of breaking down over-rigid categories, even those associated with resistance, such as the concept of ideology, with its inherent and problematic references to subject, infrastructure and the non-ideological. This includes the crude dialectic of disagreement, which, by negation, reproduces what it opposes in reciprocal oversimplification and violence. For Foucault, the solvent for the intolerable dominations associated with agonistic politics is micro-analysis and hyper-dispersal, not confrontation:

> The freeing of difference requires thought without contradiction, without dialectics, without negation; thought that accepts divergence; affirmative thought whose instrument is disjunction; thought of the multiple – of the nomadic and dispersed multiplicity that is not limited or confined by the constraints of similarity .... What is the answer to the question? The problem. How is the problem resolved? By displacing the question .... We must think problematically rather than question and answer dialectically.
>
> (Bouchard ed. 1977: 185–6, quoted Flynn 1994: 42)

Nothing could be further from the crude mutual refutation and the brutal either/or of radical disagreement. Foucault offers subtle and searching analyses of the nature and products of *agonism*, but is averse to including serious study of the *polemical* as part of this. He does not offer a philosophy of radical disagreement.

Roland Barthes

Turning to Barthes, I focus on his *Mythologies*, and in particular on the final essay in the collection, 'Myth Today'. Barthes' aim, writing as he was in the 1950s, was to unmask the 'naturalness' with which mythology was used by 'newspapers, art and common sense' to 'dress up a reality which, even though it is the one we live in, is undoubtedly determined by history' (1957/1993: 11). In this way, he sought to denounce 'the essential enemy' which was 'the bourgeois norm', because he thought that whereas left-wing myths were peripheral and merely tactical (the truly revolutionary speech of the authentic economic producer was the opposite of myth), right-wing myths ('myths of order') were fundamental to the continuing predominance of those who produced them:

> The oppressed *makes* the world, he has only an active, transitive (political) language; the oppressor conserves it, his language is plenary, intransitive, ges- tural, theatrical: it is Myth. The language of the former aims at transforming, of the latter at eternalising.
>
> (Barthes1957/1993: 149)

How does myth work according to Barthes? It is a second-order semiological system, in which the meaning (sign) of an original language-object is emptied of content to become pure form and the signifier of a second metalanguage. As signi- fier it is then filled with a new content by being absorbed into the concept that it is the purpose of the myth-maker to propagate (it becomes the signified in the new metalanguage). This appropriation creates the final signification (sign) of the meta- language, which is read as entirely natural and inevitable by the myth-consumer. The transfer of meaning thus operates instantaneously and below the threshold where the myth-consumer can recognize its contingency and duplicity. Only the myth-producer, in his cynicism, and the myth-decipherer/exposer (the mytholo- gist), in his sarcasm or anger, sees through the subterfuge. It is the naturalization of the concept that is the essential function of myth. If the political comprises 'the whole of human relations' in the reality of its social structure and power of making the world, then myth is 'depoliticised speech':

> In passing from history to nature, myth acts economically: it abolishes the complexity of human acts, it gives them the simplicity of essences, it does away with all dialectics, with any going back beyond what is immediately vis- ible, it organizes a world which is without contradictions because it is without depth, a world wide open and wallowing in the evident, it establishes a blissful clarity: things appear to mean something by themselves.
>
> (Barthes 1957/1993: 143)

How does this famous account relate to radical disagreement? What does it mean to suggest, with Julie Mertus, that under this conception conflicting myths can help to start a war?

I do not think that Barthes' idea of myth does, as it stands, relate to radical disagreement at all, which is why Barthes had no interest in it. Barthes' interpretation separates three linguistic levels: the level of the language-object, the level of the metalanguage where myth is constructed, and the level of the mythologist who deconstructs it. The mythologist, operating at level three, is thereby able to demystify and expose unchallenged the enemy subterfuge at level two, and in this way to release the level one non-mythical speech that it is his whole purpose to liberate.

This may work well within a context of Marxist theory. But it cannot easily be extended to describe what happens when myths are seen to be invoked equally on both sides in an intense political conflict such as Kosovo. In Mertus' adaptation, mythologists on each side compete to expose the myths of the other. Here, both invoke the three-level methodology, but in precise contradiction to the other's usage. What is at issue is found to be the levels themselves – or rather the distinction between these distinctions and what they distinguish, as identified in Chapter 4. What is at issue is what does and does not count as *mere* myth.

Jürgen Habermas: The Theory of Communicative Action

As seen in Chapter 3, Jürgen Habermas' discourse ethics is widely invoked in the conflict resolution field by those who are critical of 'dialogic' and 'problem-solving' approaches that ignore power asymmetries. So what does his seminal text, *The Theory of Communicative Action*, say about radical disagreement?

At first sight, disagreement is central to Habermas' thinking. The whole of this part of his social theory is grounded in a theory of argumentation, where disagreement appears both as a threat to linguistically coordinated social action that calls forth the role of argumentation, and as integral to the process of argumentation that is seen as the remedy:

> Thus the rationality proper to the communicative practice of everyday life points to the practice of argumentation as a court of appeal that makes it possible to continue communicative action with other means when disagreements can no longer be repaired with everyday routines and yet are not to be settled by the direct or strategic use of force. For this reason I believe that the concept of communicative rationality ... can be adequately explicated only in terms of a theory of argumentation.

> (Habermas 1981a: 17–18)

> The theory of argumentation thereby takes on a special significance; to it falls the task of reconstructing the formal-pragmatic presuppositions and conditions of an explicitly rational behavior.

> (Ibid.: 2)

To participate properly in argument is, therefore, to agree or disagree with reasons offered for or against validity claims, thereby defining the sphere of 'rational agreement' and 'rational disagreement'. Agreement and disagreement are inbuilt on an equal footing in this way into the very structure of the theory of argumentation together with the criticizability (challenge and redemption) of validity claims on which it rests:

> Agreement rests on common *convictions*. The speech act of one person suc-
> ceeds only if the other accepts the offer contained in it by taking (however
> implicitly) a 'yes' or 'no' position on a validity claim that is in principle
> criticisable. Both ego, who raises a validity claim with his utterance, and
> alter, who recognizes or rejects it, base their decisions on potential grounds
> or reasons. (original italics)
>
> (Ibid.: 128)

Indeed, disagreement has a special constitutive role:

> The binding effect of illocutionary forces comes about, ironically, through the
> fact that participants can say 'no' to speech-act offers. The critical character
> of this saying 'no' distinguishes taking a position in this way from a reaction
> based solely on caprice. A hearer can be 'bound' by speech-act offers because
> he is not permitted arbitrarily to refuse them but only to say 'no' to them, that
> is, to reject them for reasons.
>
> (Ibid.: 73–4)

The fact that Habermas describes this as 'ironic' may indicate an awareness of a moment of slippage when the conditional tense of *criticizability* (being able to say 'no') shifts into the indicative tense of *criticism* (actually saying 'no'). The former is integral to the emphasis that Habermas places on the fact that his theory is *intersubjective* in its focus on communicative action, in contrast to the *mono-logical* theories of, for example, Adorno. But the question is whether Habermas' theory is *polylogical*? Does it accommodate, not only the *potential* of criticizability that is inherently intersubjective, but also the *fact* of actual criticism and counter-criticism (radical disagreement) that is inherently polylogical? Do Habermasian communicative actors answer back?

Since this is Habermas' account, let us allow him to define the rules of debate, which he does quite stringently. He demands that the disagreement must take place without distortions of power and as if free from the political pressures of everyday life. The participants must aim to convince a 'universal audience', to 'thematize' a contested validity claim in a purely 'hypothetical attitude', and to let arguments speak for themselves (Habermas 1981a: 25). By shifting from political to hypo-thetical mode in this way, Habermas excludes the crucial link to partisan identities and imminent political action that defines radical disagreement. Nevertheless, we will follow Habermas in doing the same. What happens when people actually do answer back, choose the 'no' response, and reject the other's validity claim on purely rational grounds – as defined by Habermas?

Habermas' framework of analysis is based on a theory of communicative acts (CA1 CA2, etc.). In Habermas' words (1981b: 126–7), communicative actors

(A1 A2), moving in the medium of a natural language and drawing upon culturally transmitted interpretations, attempt to come to an understanding, as speakers and hearers from out of the context of their pre-interpreted lifeworld, about something in the one objective world, something in the common social world, and something in each of their own subjective worlds, with a view to negotiate common definitions of the situation and to coordinate action accordingly. The lifeworld is constitutive for mutual understanding as such, whereas the three formal world-concepts constitute a reference system for that about which mutual understanding is possible.

At the centre of this model lies the idea of a speaker who 'aims to come to an understanding *with* a hearer *about* something and thereby to make *himself* understandable'. So three world-relations are invoked by the raising of validity claims:

> In their interpretive accomplishments the members of a communication community demarcate the one objective world and their intersubjectively shared social world from the subjective worlds of individuals and (other) collectives.
>
> (Habermas 1981a: 70)

In particular, each participant in practical discourse 'understands a linguistic expression in the same way' as the other by 'knowing the conditions under which it can be accepted'.

Now what happens to this account in the special case of disagreement, when the other in the event rejects a validity claim? Habermas is clear. The fact of disagreement is already incorporated in the model. The rejection of a validity claim (a 'no' response) maps one-to-one onto his account of the redemption of a validity claim (a 'yes' response). Both count as 'success' for a speech act in formal-pragmatic terms:

> Someone who rejects a comprehensible speech act is taking issue with at least one of these validity claims. In rejecting a speech act as (normatively) wrong or untrue or insincere, he is expressing with his 'no' the fact that the utterance has not fulfilled its function of securing an interpersonal relationship, of representing states of affairs, or of manifesting experiences. It is not in agreement with *our* world of legitimately ordered interpersonal relations, or with *the* world of existing states of affairs, or with *the speaker's own* world of subjective experiences.
>
> (Ibid.: 308)

In short, according to Habermas, radical disagreement – |CA1; CA2| – can be substituted for communicative acts in general – CA1; CA2 – without thereby affecting the rest of the model, and in particular, the framework of world-relations that communicative actors establish with their utterances.

Is this true?

If someone responds to a validity claim with a 'yes' reaction, this not only helps to coordinate action in the public world, it also confirms the structure of world relations (the distinctions between the one public world, the shared social world, and the two or more subjective worlds of the speakers) and feeds the stock of language, culture and the lifeworld that make such communication possible:

> The lifeworld 'maintains itself' through 'the processes of reaching understanding.
>
> (Habermas 1981b: 124)

But, as seen above, in contrast to Gadamer, it is essential for Habermas that assent is not the only permissible response:

> To understand a symbolic expression means to know under what conditions its validity claim would have to be accepted; but it does *not* mean assenting to its validity claim without regard to context. (original italics)
>
> (Ibid.: 135–6)

If someone responds to a validity claim with an *abstention*, this may be seen as somewhat akin to the 'not proven' verdict in Scottish law because it is not the result of carelessness or indifference, but rather of proper scrutiny of the proffered reasons and arguments. Habermas toys with the idea of generalizing 'I do not know' into a principle of communicative reason itself. This takes the form of a capacity for self-criticism that can also apply 'the attitude of the other' (the other's subjectivity) to ourselves. We are familiar with this idea from Chapter 5, where we looked at it under the moment of description:

> By internalising the role of a participant in argumentation, ego becomes capable of self-criticism. It is the relation-to-self established by this model of self-criticism that we shall call 'reflective'. Knowing that one does not know has, since the time of Socrates, rightly been regarded as the basis of self-knowledge.
>
> (Ibid.: 74–5)

But, although a capacity for 'looking at things from the perspective of the other' is a hallmark of accomplished as against naive communicative actors, Habermas is aware of the danger of generalizing 'I do not know' to the point where the very possibility of framing redeemable validity claims in the first place evaporates:

> The concept of a subjective world permits us to contrast not only our own internal world, but also the subjective worlds of others, with the external world. Ego can consider how certain facts (what he regards as existing states of affairs in the objective world) or certain normative expectations (what he regards as legitimate elements of the common social world) look from the perspective of the other, that is, as elements of alter's subjective world. He can further consider that alter is for his part considering how what he regards as existing states of affairs and valid norms look from ego's perspective, that is, as a component of ego's subjective world. The subjective worlds of the

participants could serve as mirror surfaces in which the objective, the normative and the subjective-for-another are reflected any number of times.

(Ibid.: 69)

As it turns out, however, abstention does not threaten to do this because it is not
itself a validity claim. The framework of world-concepts invoked by the first
speaker remains intact. Absence of mutual agreement does not affect the mutual
understanding of what the situation would be for there to be such agreement:

> The function of the formal world-concepts, however, is to prevent the stock
> of what is common from dissolving in the stream of subjectivities repeatedly
> reflected in one another.

(Habermas 1981a: 69)

So now what happens when the response is a 'no' reaction? Can a hearer seriously
reject a speech-act offer while complying with the strict process, procedure and
product presuppositions of the 'ideal speech situation' noted above? Certainly,
according to Habermas. The hearer who says 'no' is rejecting the other's claim on
grounds of reason. In doing so, like the speaker, the original hearer is not trying
to exert influence beyond the force of the better argument. Rather, the hearer is
appealing as if to a universal audience, has thematized what is in dispute and is
prepared to enter hypothetical discussion while the pressure for immediate action is
held in abeyance, and not only aims 'to produce cogent arguments that are convincing in virtue of their intrinsic properties', but claims actually to have done so.

It is on these grounds that the hearer rejects the speaker's claim. The speaker's
utterance does not accord with the world of existing states of affairs (it is untrue)
or with the world of legitimately ordered interpersonal relations (it is normatively
wrong), or perhaps with the speaker's own subjective world (it is insincere). In
short, the hearer's act of rejection is a *counter-claim*.

And now what happens to the framework of world concepts thereby appealed
to? I will focus on the distinction between the external world (objective and social)
and the internal (subjective) worlds of speakers/hearers. Here Habermas sees an
integration of non-expressive and expressive components of speech acts. For
every proposition (p), there is an 'intention with the same meaning' (propositional
attitude):

> with the assertion '*p*', a speaker normally gives expression to the fact that he
> *believes p* ...

> In this way, a certain assimilation of convictions ... to the structure of emo-
> tional experiences take[s] place. It is only this assimilation that makes it
> possible to draw clear boundaries between the internal and external worlds,
> such that the beliefs of someone who asserts facts can be distinguished from
> the facts themselves ...

(Habermas 1981b: 67)

Beliefs are seen here to 'belong' mainly to the speaker's subjective world, but not in the same sense as the object of reference when a speaker makes an explicit public claim about his subjective experience in communicative argumentation. In the latter case, the belief referred to can be regarded as 'something analogous to the existence of states of affairs without assimilating one to the other', inasmuch as, like a state of affairs, it is what is at issue. As such, the speaker's claim about it can be accepted or rejected. It can, for example, be criticized on grounds of sincerity. In the former case, however, the speaker does not claim that he has certain subjective beliefs, but, in the process of making a validity claim about the external world, shows by his utterance that this is his belief ('gives expression to a belief or conviction'). For Habermas, this only becomes manifest when a speaker's belief (or opinion or interpretation) turns out to be mistaken because now the false belief is definitively assimilated to the speaker's experiential subjective world – chiefly defined in terms of desires and feelings:

> Desires and feelings have a paradigmatic status in this connection. Of course, cognitions [such as] beliefs ... also belong to the subjective world; but they stand in internal relation to the objective world. Beliefs ... come to consciousness *as* subjective only when there is in the objective world no corresponding state of affairs that exists ... It becomes a question of 'mere', that is, 'mistaken' belief as soon as the corresponding statement turns out to be untrue.
>
> (Habermas 1981a: 91–2)

Elsewhere, Habermas makes it clear that this is not the case in general, or the ground for making truth claims about the external world would be removed. We would be back to the closed system of subjective mirroring:

> If we ignore [the truth-claim that the actor connects with his opinion], we treat opinions as something subjective, that is, as something that, when brought forth by the actor as his opinion, [and] disclosed before a public, has to be ascribed to his subjective world. In this case we neutralize the claims to truth by treating opinions as expressive utterances; and these can be objectively judged only from the standpoint of their sincerity.
>
> (Ibid.: 117)

Within this model, therefore, a hearer rejecting a speaker's truth claim is rejecting a 'mistaken' belief on the grounds that 'there is in the objective world no corresponding state of affairs that exists'. What the hearer rejects is, in Habermas' terms, what thereby 'belongs' to the speaker's subjective world, together with the speaker's desires, feelings and so on – it is a 'mere' (mistaken) belief. That is to say, the hearer 'neutralizes' the speaker's claims to truth by treating them as expressive utterances. According to the model, this is what the rejection of a speech-act offer entails: it is what saying 'no' says.

But, also according to the model, this cannot be the end of the story. So far, we have only followed the logic inherent in the hearer's counter-claim. Habermas' analysis has been intersubjective, but not yet polylogical. In the communicative interchange that makes up the disagreement, the hearer's counter-claim is defined in terms of the speaker's original claim, and it is part of the definition of communicative action that neither has the last word:

> A definition of the situation by another party that prima facie diverges from ones own presents a problem of a peculiar sort; for in cooperative processes of interpretation no participant has a monopoly on correct interpretation.
>
> (Ibid.: 100)

That is to say, if the original speaker nevertheless persists in the assertion, as is the case in this model of disagreement, then the original speaker, as hearer, in turn thereby rejects the original hearer's counterclaim. The original hearer's counterclaim is thereby rejected as a mistaken belief that belongs to the original hearer's subjective world because no such corresponding state of affairs exists in the objective world.

The framework of world-relations appealed to can now be seen to be comprehensively involved (compromised) in the radical disagreement between communicative actors.

In fact, according to Habermas' account, this is what radical disagreement *is*. Habermas' account has arrived at the threshold of the territory of the phenomenology of radical disagreement. Yet, this is exactly the point at which he breaks off. Despite the formal equality that the 'yes' and 'no' reactions appear to have in constituting *criticizeability*, when it comes to actual *criticism*, Habermas privileges the 'yes' response:

> Reaching understanding is the inherent telos of human speech … [T]he use of language with an orientation to reaching understanding is the *original mode* of language use, upon which indirect understanding … and the instrumental use of language … are parasitic.
>
> (Ibid.: 288)

Verständigung (reaching understanding) is elided with the idea of *Einverständnis* (reaching agreement):

> Coming to an understanding (*Verständigung*) means that participants in communication reach an agreement (*Einigung*) concerning the validity of an utterance; agreement (*Einverständnis*) is the intersubjective recognition of the validity claim the speaker raises for it.

Habermas, for example, distinguishes 'collective like-mindedness' (*Gleichstimmenheit*) and 'de facto accord' (*Ubereinstimmung*) from genuine agreement (*Einverständnis*) and rationally motivated assent (*Zustimmung*) (1981a: 287) and so on, but nothing comparable is thought to be necessary in the case of the phenomenon of radical disagreement.

So it is that instead of exploring what actually happens to the framework of world relations when communicative actors disagree with each other, by asking the conflict parties, Habermas responds to the challenge of a 'definition of the situation by another party that prima facie diverges from one's own' by transposing his own third-party description:

> For both parties the interpretive task consists in incorporating the other's interpretation of the situation into one's own in such a way that in the revised version 'his' external world and 'my' external world can – against the background of 'our' lifeworld – be relativised in relation to 'the' world, and the divergent situation definitions can be brought to coincide sufficiently.
>
> (Habermas 1981a: 110)

The forest of inverted commas 'subjectifies' the third-party description without altering its nature. Habermas still does not follow through on what happens – in his new notation – when the radical disagreement is about 'the' world.

For the same reason, Habermas preserves his watertight distinction between the background conditioning lifeworld (together with culture and language) that is 'constitutive for mutual understanding as such' and provides the horizon that communicative actors 'cannot step outside', and the three formal world-concepts that 'constitute a reference system for that about which mutual understanding is possible' (1981b: 126). Here he does recognize that culture and language may themselves become problematic in 'rare moments', but sees this as merely in need of tinkering repairs from third-party specialists:

> It is only in those rare moments when culture and language fail as resources that they develop the peculiar resistance we experience in situations of disturbed mutual understanding. Then we need the repair work of translators, interpreters, therapists.
>
> (Habermas 1981b: 134)

Habermas does not explore what happens when, in radical disagreement, appeal is made precisely to the distant horizon – but this, too, is then found to be part of what is at issue. In short, radical disagreement itself is not acknowledged in Habermas' account. His is an *intersubjective*, but not a *polylogical* analysis. In the end, I do not think that Habermas offers a philosophy of radical disagreement at all.

Hans-Georg Gadamer: **Truth and Method**

As noted in Chapter 3, Gadamer's insights have been widely influential in conflict resolution. They are seen to offer a way of transcending cultural and political differences and managing conflict at the beginning of the twenty-first century. In her book on Gadamer, for example, Georgia Warnke says:

> To the extent that individuals and cultures integrate this understanding of others

and of the differences between them within their own self-understanding, to the extent, in other words, that they learn from others and take a wider, more differentiated view, they can acquire sensitivity, subtlety and a capacity for discrimination.

(Warnke 1987: 174)

So what does Gadamer's text say about the radical disagreements that are character-istic of the conflicts that Gadamerians are hoping thereby to overcome? Does *Truth and Method* offer an adequate or satisfactory account of radical disagreement?

Does Truth and Method *offer a philosophy of radical disagreement?*

The key move that has made Gadamerian hermeneutics influential in conflict res-olution is his appeal to conversation as equivalent to the interpretation of a text. The core of the hermeneutic process is viewed as a form of conversation or dialogue, and genuine conversation or dialogue is regarded as an exercise in hermeneutics.

In hermeneutics the application of the analogy enabled Gadamer to reinterpret tradition as a 'partner in conversation', thereby transcending the one-sided limits of the 'romantic' methodological hermeneutics of Schleiermacher and Dilthey, while incorporating insights from Husserl and Heidegger. But what has been the effect in the other direction, that is, in the application of Gadamerian ideas, drawn essentially from the hermeneutic tradition of textual interpretation, to conversa-tional dialogue between political opponents in intense conflict situations?

At first sight, the signs seem good. The entire hermeneutic world only springs into existence at the point where tradition becomes 'questionable' and where pre-conception meets 'resistance':

> Understanding becomes a special task only when this natural life in which each means and understands the same thing, is disturbed.

(Gadamer 1975: 158–9)

The hermeneutic enterprise begins when we are pulled up short by a text, or encounter a 'Thou' that stands over against us and asserts its own rights against our proto-assumptions and interests. This is the 'primary hermeneutical condition' (Gadamer 1975: 266):

> Let us consider what this idea of distinguishing involves. It is always recip-rocal. Whatever is being distinguished must be distinguished from something, which, in turn, must be distinguished from it. Thus all distinguishing also makes visible that from which something is distinguished. We have described this above as the operation of prejudices. We started by saying that a herme-neutical situation is determined by the prejudices that we bring with us. They constitute, then, the horizon of a particular present, for they represent that beyond which it is impossible to see.

(Ibid.: 272)

Fore-understandings and prejudices constitute our horizon, but we only become aware of this when we are confronted by what does not fit in or challenges them:

> A person who does not accept that he is dominated by prejudices will fail to see what is shown by their light.
>
> (Ibid.: 324)

What Gadamer calls 'true' or 'productive' prejudices are an integral part of the 'hermeneutic consciousness', and, as interpreters of human experience, we should actively seek out what is most likely to make us aware of them. These are the prejudices that 'make understanding possible'. Gadamer contrasts these with the 'unproductive prejudices' that 'hinder understanding and lead to misunderstanding' (Ibid., 263).

In view of all this, Gadamer might be expected to have made a strenuous effort to come to terms with the fact of mutual contradiction and disagreement as the most characteristic manifestation of 'resistance' in conversational mode and the decisive linguistic feature in the critical encounter with the 'Thou' that generates the whole hermeneutic experience.

Yet, this turns out not to be the case. Far from developing the theme of linguistic confrontation as an important part of the hermeneutic challenge, Gadamer says almost nothing more about it, and, where he does comment, he is invariably dismissive. He regards agonistic argument pro and contra as a purely formal and derivative aspect of the realm of dialectic whose serious purpose is, on the contrary, always a search for shared meaning and truth within the realm of lived experience. He associates disagreement with a generalization of those 'unproductive prejudices' that 'hinder understanding and lead to misunderstanding'.

This implies a severe downgrading of the status of the judgment or statement in Gadamerian hermeneutics:

> [The] concept of the statement, the dialectical accentuation of it to the point of contradiction, is … in extreme contrast to the nature of the hermeneutical experience and the linguistic nature of human experience of the world.
>
> (Gadamer 1975: 425)

Instead Gadamer's whole concern is with the opposite – the suspension of judgment and the transmutation of the statement into what he calls 'the question'. It is to an analysis of the logical structure of the question that he devotes his best energies and most of the subsequent space available, and it is only the 'true' question that ushers in productive dialogue and conversation and constitutes the dialectical link to the whole world of universal hermeneutics itself:

> All suspension of judgments and hence, a fortiori, of prejudices, has logically the structure of a question.
>
> (Ibid.: 266)

The art of questioning is called 'dialectic' because it is the 'art of conducting a real conversation' (Ibid., 330). It is identified with the 'art of thinking' itself.

That is why, when Gadamer is looking for a conversational equivalent in Part III for the hermeneutical insight in Part II that it is 'in situations in which understanding is disrupted or made difficult' that 'the conditions of all understanding emerge with the greatest clarity'(Ibid., 346), instead of finding it in radical disagreement, he turns instead to the safer analogy of translation between languages. It is 'the linguistic process by means of which a conversation in two different languages is made possible through translation' that Gadamer selects as being 'especially informative' here.

One language no more answers back another language than a text answers back an interpreter. Gadamer is aware of this. He acknowledges that 'the hermeneutic situation in regard to texts' is not 'exactly the same as that between two people in conversation' (Ibid., 349). The word 'exactly' suggests that he does not consider this to be a very significant difference. Unlike passages of conversation, texts are 'permanently fixed expressions of life', which means that

> one partner in the hermeneutical conversation, the text, is expressed only through the other partner, the interpreter.
>
> (Ibid.: 354)

In fact, Gadamer sees this difference as a gain for hermeneutic insight

> precisely because it entirely detaches the sense of what is said from the person saying it, the written word makes the reader, in his understanding of it, arbiter of its claim to truth.
>
> (Gadamer 1975: 356)

This is a decisive difference between textual hermeneutics and conversational dialogue, and it rules out the relevance of serious political disagreement at a stroke. Texts do not answer back as conversational partners do. So the hermeneutic-dialogic tradition must ignore the latter. The result is predictable. What Gadamer calls 'the really critical question of hermeneutics' – that of 'distinguishing the true prejudices by which we understand from the false ones by which we misunderstand' (1975: 266) – has to be left to the interpreter to answer as best s/he can acting as 'arbiter' in her/his own 'conversation' with the text.

Several other features of Gadamer's hermeneutics in *Truth and Method* rule it out as offering an adequate account of radical disagreement.

One example is that for Gadamer the 'true home of hermeneutics' is in the intermediate area 'between strangeness and familiarity' (Ibid., 262–3). In hermeneutics, these are not two different moments of apprehension. Instead, they are seen to constitute a single authentic hermeneutic experience (albeit constantly repeated and renewed), in which it is only through the awareness of conceptual limits that they are thereby transcended: 'in the process of understanding there takes place a real fusing of horizons, which means that as the historical horizon is projected, it is simultaneously removed' (1975: 273). In other words, the process of hermeneutic fusing of horizons is instantaneous and ongoing and is nothing other than the unfolding of understanding itself. Transferring this to the realm of conversation, there is no gap in Gadamerian dialogue between the 'strangeness' of 'talking at cross-purposes' (mutual misunderstanding) and 'agreeing about the object' (mutual agreement) (Gadamer 1975: 331). But these are precisely the limits to radical disagreement. So radical disagreement is not recognized in Gadamerian hermeneutics at all.

Gadamer offers the important insight, shared with the phenomenology of radical disagreement, that 'seeing each other's point' means acknowledging the other's point of view not merely as a point-of-view. This would be to ignore the other's 'claim to truth'. But Gadamer has no interest in what happens when there is a clash between claims to truth. His conclusion is that to see the other's point of view is to be moving towards agreement about the shared object of enquiry. In this sense, to understand is to agree about the object, and the alternative to agreement is once again, not radical disagreement, but misunderstanding. The hermeneuticist prevails over the analyst of conversation:

> We have already seen in the analysis of romantic hermeneutics that understanding is not based on 'getting inside' another person, on the immediate fusing of one person in another. To understand what a person says is, as we saw, to agree about the object, not to get inside another person and relive his experiences.
>
> (Gadamer 1975: 345)

But, as seen in Chapter 5, agonistic dialogue is *disagreement* about the object.

So it is that Gadamer's 'genuine' conversation is between interlocutors who are hermeneutically trained in the interpretation of texts (in this case each other's utterances). The emphasis in overcoming prejudice is placed throughout on the interpretative capacities of hearers. No account is taken of the possibility that a speaker may answer back independently of the interpreter and refuse to play the interpreter's hermeneutic game – for example by rejecting the interpretation, or even the whole hermeneutic enterprise, or by refusing to 'suspend the validity' of his own original 'prejudice' or belief.

This does not mean that Gadamer's hermeneutics does not offer valuable insights into the nature of radical disagreement. It does so at those points of slippage where it comes up against the shadow of radical disagreement without explicitly confronting it. These are the creative equivocations that accompany Gadamer's wrestlings with the concept of 'agreement about the object', the nature of 'naïve assimilation of horizons' or 'premature fusion of horizons' (how can we know when we are covering up the tension that would otherwise reveal our own horizon to us – would we not by definition be unaware that this was so?), and his magnificent concluding soliloquy in Part III of his book on the relationship between language and the world.

But *Truth and Method* is not, nor did it purport to be, a philosophy of radical disagreement.

Attempts to apply Gadamer's hermeneutics to the transformation of radical disagreement

Gadamer did not offer a theory of radical disagreement, but other philosophers have related his work more specifically to the task of transcending cultural and political differences and managing conflict at the beginning of the twenty-first century. In a collection of essays presented on the occasion of Gadamer's hundredth birthday in 2002 (Malpas *et al.* eds), for example, Ulrich Arnswald draws a parallel with the thinking of Ludwig Wittgenstein, while John McDowell and Charles Taylor invoke the philosophy of Donald Davidson in presenting Gadamerian approaches to the management of contemporary conflict. Arnswald is representative in arguing that:

> [Gadamer's] single most important insight may turn out to be a conceptual scheme that allows us to overcome cultural conflicts as well as clashes of different forms of life.
>
> (Arnswald 2002: 35)

McDowell equates Gadamer's hermeneutics with Davidson's work on radical translation and Gadmer's fusion of horizons with Davidson's 'principle of charity':

> What we are faced with before a fusion of horizons is the world, together with a candidate for being understood as another way of conceiving it, and we have a guarantee – if what confronts us is really another thinking subject – that it will be possible to understand the other's engagements with the world as expressive of another view of the world we had in view all along.
>
> (McDowell 2002: 180; see also 1994/6)

Davidson's rejection of the scheme/world dualism and refutation of the idea of total unintelligibility (untranslatability) between human cultures thereby opens the door to the possibility of radical disagreement (he removes one of the limits). Davidson also notes that 'giving up the dualism of scheme and world' does not mean giving up unmediated contact with the world of 'familiar objects whose antics make our sentences and opinions true or false' (1984: 198). This echoes Gadamer's rather more subjectivist wording: 'every worldview has the world in view as everything that is the case, not as everything that it takes to be the case' (1975: note 32, 192) – and is familiar from what is shown in the uncovering of the moments of radical disagreeing in Chapter 5.

At this highly abstract level, the phenomenon of radical disagreement can be said to exist between the limit of absolute misunderstanding ruled out by Davidson and the limit of a fusion of horizons delineated by Gadamer. But what happens phenomenologically if, when we 'face the world together with a candidate for being understood as another way of conceiving it', we find that this is a radical disagreement and that the other expressly rejects the idea that what s/he is saying is merely 'expressive of another view of the world we had in view all along'?

162 *Radical disagreement and the transformation of violent conflict*

To investigate this, it is illuminating to include Taylor's version of the Davidson/ Gadamer approach (Taylor 2002). Taylor does not claim to be dealing with radical disagreement, but with cross-cultural understanding. Nevertheless, his insight is instructive. He imagines a conversation between representatives from radically different cultures, who

> strive to come to an understanding, to overcome the obstacles to mutual com- . prehension, to find a language in which both can agree to talk undistortively of each.

So what happens when originally distinct horizons (the different 'way that each has of understanding the human condition in their non-identity') meet?

> For instance, we become aware that there are different ways of believing things, one of which is holding them as a 'personal opinion'. This was all that we allowed for before, but now we have space for other ways and can therefore accommodate the beliefs of a quite different culture. Our horizon is extended to take in this possibility, which was beyond its limit before.
> But this is better seen as a fusion rather than just an extension of horizons, because at the same time we are introducing a language to talk about their beliefs that represents an extension in relation to their language. Presumably, they had no idea of what we speak of a[s] 'personal opinions,' at least in such areas as religion, for instance. They would have had to see these as rejection, rebellion, and heresy. So the new language used here, which places 'opinions' alongside other modes of believing as possible alternative ways of holding things true, opens a broader horizon, extending beyond both the original ones and in a sense combining them.
>
> (Taylor 2002: 287)

Now let us apply this to an example. Taylor's central idea is that 'the horizon is extended so as to make room for the object that before did not fit within it'. How does this relate to radical disagreement between those who want to estab- lish western-style democracy in, say, Afghanistan or Iraq, and those who want to reject it?

> Democracy means sovereignty for man. And as a Muslim we believe sover- eignty for the Sharia.
> In the American form of democracy any issue is allowed to be put to a vote of the people, and the majority decision prevails upon all. Can we Muslims put an issue that has already been decided for us by Allah up for a vote and accept the will of the majority if they vote against the will of Allah? Of course we cannot, so therefore we can never accept democracy as defined, practised and promoted by America.
>
> (Abu Musab 2003)

In Taylor's version of Gadamer's fusion of horizons, let us begin by identifying ourselves with those who want to establish western democracy. We are confronted by an initially alien culture in which there is no place for the idea that 'personal opinion' should decide forms of government by majority vote. What we see as legitimate personal opinion, the other sees as rejection of the word of Allah, rebellion against His wishes, and heresy that must be stamped out before it spreads its corruption. So we expand our horizon to accommodate the realization that there are evidently other ways of believing things than our own. Beliefs are not just personal opinions after all. They are also the revealed word of Allah given to the people of the world as their religion, so that the true believers are those who obey His will as set out in His Holy Qur'an, the Sunnah of His prophet Muhammad and His laws (Sharia).

But in the political context of intractable conflict and radical disagreement – for example in Aghanistan – what does it mean to say that we are expanding our horizon to take in what was before outside it? If we are the only ones making the adjustment, what difference will this make to our actions? Will we submit to what the other wants and acquiesce in the establishment of Sharia? If not, is the other not likely to reject our self-proclaimed expanded understanding as yet another hypocritical ruse for getting our way? Is this, in fact, not what Islamists do say?

And what of the reciprocal move outlined by Taylor? For there to be a fusion of horizons must those wanting to impose Sharia learn to speak a 'new language' that 'places "opinions" alongside other modes of believing as possible alternative ways of holding things true'? Does this include non-Muslim opinions? What does 'alongside' mean in the context of the struggle between western democracy and Sharia? Is there room for this? Would not those who want to impose Sharia reject the whole idea that this 'opens a broader horizon, extending beyond both the original ones and in a sense combining them'? Would they not see this, too, as yet another way of insidiously indoctrinating Muslims and of undermining Islam from within? Is this not what many Muslims (and not only Muslims) do say about ecumenicism and the interfaith movement, for example?

Conclusion

I have yet to find an adequate third-party account of the phenomenon of radical disagreement. During the course of the search, I have reached the conclusion that there is no adequate theory or philosophy of radical disagreement. And that the reason for this is because monological models cannot chart what is polylogical. However subtle these models are, they cannot encompass a different order of complexity, that, as a result, appears only in the form of extreme simplicity.

But the fact that putative models of radical disagreement break down does not mean that they are uninformative. It is *why* they break down that signifies. The best models are those that, in their breakdown, shed most light. From Gadamer comes the idea of radical disagreement as a clash of horizons. From Habermas comes the idea of radical disagreement as a war between incompatible validity claims. From Foucault comes the idea of radical disagreement as a fight between historians to determine what are *mere* regimes of truth. From Barthes comes the idea of radical disagreement as a battle between (de)mythologists. From Davidson comes the idea of radical disagreement as the obstinate invocation of the scheme/world dualism by the conflict parties. From Derrida comes the idea of radical disagreement as the eruption of binaries that refuse to be pre-deconstructed. From Nietzsche comes the idea of radical disagreement as the sudden appearance of the counter-prophet and the exchange of hammer blow for hammer blow.

This chapter has shown why third party description and explanation breaks down in relation to specific examples of radical disagreement in intractable conflicts. And it has clarified how, as a result, dialogue for mutual understanding, based on such description and explanation, often proves premature in these cases. What are the practical implications of this? Are there alternative approaches that might gain more purchase? These questions are addressed in the next chapter.

7 Praxis
Managing agonistic dialogue

Lessons learnt from the exploration and understanding of agonistic dialogue assist the management of radical disagreement when conflict resolution fails. In these circumstances 'dialogue for mutual understanding' is premature. What is needed is the promotion of 'dialogue for strategic engagement', not less radical disagreement, but more. It is the strategic engagement of discourses (SED) – the logic of the war of words itself – that keeps open the possibility of future transformation when linguistic intractability closes down other forms of verbal communication. It clarifies what is at issue in the struggle between the challenging discourse, the hegemonic discourse, and the third-party (peacemaking) discourse, and what each of the competing discourses has to do in order to prevail. The distinction between extremism of ends and extremism of means is often a key to breaking the deadlock between undefeated conflict parties.

This chapter tests the implications of Chapters 5 and 6 for the management of linguistic intractability in the most difficult of all conflict arenas at the time of writing – the Israeli-Palestinian conflict.

Chapter 5 showed how in agonistic dialogue (dialogue among enemies) the radical disagreement is a struggle to define what it is about, reaching as far as the eye can see, and involving the very distinctions invoked in the process of disagreeing. This is not a coexistence of rival discourses, but a fight to the death to impose the one discourse.

Chapter 6 showed how, as a result of this, third parties, whether as analysts or as interveners, are not discursively impartial. There is no adequate third-party description or philosophy of radical disagreement. Third-party peacemakers find that they, too, are part of the struggle, seeking to transform the agonistic dialogue by substituting a third discourse of their own.

Serious political conflicts end in many ways: in victory for one of the conflict parties, in some form of agreed standoff or accommodation, in contextual change that transforms the parameters that defined them (who now remembers the never-resolved conflict between Guelphs and Ghibellines – supporters of the Pope and the Holy Roman Emperor – that convulsed Europe in the Middle Ages?). I return to these scenarios in Chapter 8. Here the concern is with what happens in the communicative sphere while intense unresolved political conflicts persist. How can continuing linguistic intractability between undefeated conflict parties be managed?

In these cases, conflict parties do not respond to conflict resolution efforts, such as those outlined in Chapter 3. Conflict parties refuse to distinguish positions from interests and needs, resist reframing competition into shared problem solving, will not convert adversarial debate into constructive controversy, do not change statements into questions or fuse horizons, fail to recognize the systemic nature of the conflict or that they only have a partial view of it, do not acknowledge the legitimacy of the other's narrative, do not recognise overlapping consensus, are not prepared to transform the language and practice of power into a non-politicized 'ideal speech situation', and in general, directly challenge the very bases on which third-party discourse analysis and third-party peace intervention are constructed.

What can be done in these cases?

In these circumstances, the practical implication of what has been shown in Chapters 5 and 6 is to abandon attempts at promoting *dialogue for mutual understanding* altogether. There is no point in persisting. There is no conceptual or emotional space for it yet. The effort is premature. Instead, the main effort shifts to the promotion of *dialogue for strategic engagement*, not less radical disagreement, but more. What is required is the *strategic engagement of discourses (SED)*. That is what is most lacking in the communicative sphere during times of greatest linguistic intractability.

How does this apply to the Israeli-Palestinian case?

As made clear in Chapter 4, a conflict system is made up of related and overlapping conflict complexes, such as the Middle East conflict complex, or the Afghanistan–Pakistan conflict complex. Each conflict complex encompasses nested conflict formations. The Israeli-Palestinian conflict formation, for example, is set within the wider Arab-Israeli conflict formation, which includes unresolved conflicts both between Israel and Syria, and Israel and Lebanon. The Arab-Israeli conflict formation is itself located within the still wider Middle East conflict arena that includes Iran and Turkey. This reaches out to affect global conflict dynamics that involve the aspirations of radical Islamic and Judeo-Christian fundamentalisms and the geo-political interests of the United States.

As analysis moves up and down between and among conflict formations, conflict parties become third parties and vice versa – although, as already shown, this distinction is itself found to be involved in the associated radical disagreements.

Axes of radical disagreement criss-cross the conflict arena and constitute the linguistic intractability that reinforces the complex as a whole. Important axes of radical disagreement cut cross the various conflict formations. In the case of the Israeli-Palestinian conflict formation, for example, internal discursive struggles within Israel and among Palestinians are often more bitter than those between the conflict parties themselves, and reach out to convulse the Jewish and Palestinian diasporas which are larger than the number of those living in the disputed territories. And the outcome of the conflict at the level of the Israeli-Palestinian conflict formation may mainly be a function of wider confrontations at a higher level, such as Egyptian and Saudi fears of Iran. Israelis see Hamas as an instrument of its exiled leadership in Syria, controlled and supplied from Iran whose regional ambitions – and the interests of its regime – include a need to demonize Israel. Nevertheless, without forgetting this, the emphasis in the rest of this chapter will be on the axes of radical disagreement that run *within* the Israeli-Palestinian conflict formation.

At the time of writing (April 2009), many say that the next few months will be the most critical in a generation as the determination of the new Obama US administration to end the conflict meets the equally determined resistance of the new Netanyahu Israeli government against ceding a viable Palestinian state to make this possible – nothing less than the 'last chance for a two-state Israel–Palestine agreement' (US/Middle East Project 2008).

By the time this book is published, we will see whose predictions are nearest the mark. But the main purpose of this chapter is not to make predictions, nor even to offer yet another third-party political analysis and list of recommendations. Predictions are, by definition, highly unreliable in complex conflict systems. The aim is to exemplify what the promotion of a strategic engagement of discourses (SED) implies in the Israeli-Palestinian conflict formation in its darkest hour, when all other communicative options seem to have run into the sand. The main evidence for the possibility of keeping strategic exploration open in this way, even during times of maximum intractability, is taken from an attempt to test this out in 2007 and 2008 as part of a European Union-funded project run by the Oxford Research Group together with Israeli and Palestinian partners.[1]

Preparations for this enterprise confirmed that few Israelis or Palestinians at the time were interested in dialogue for mutual understanding. Palestinians identified dialogue for mutual understanding with the normalization of oppression, and the interminable peace process with perpetual occupation. Israelis regarded dialogue for mutual understanding as pointless in view of past Palestinian unreliability, were not particularly interested in the Palestinian question now that security had been restored in the West Bank – continuing rockets from Gaza merely confirming the dangers of Israeli military withdrawal –, and were much more concerned by the nuclear threat from Iran. Arab peace overtures were interpreted as a trap to destroy a Jewish State of Israel. Persistent failure in the Oslo peace process since the assassination of Israeli Prime Minister Yitzhak Rabin in 1995 had led to mutual disillusionment.

Deep internal divisions on both sides, together with weak leaderships, had blocked progress on the 2003 Road Map and the November 2007 Annapolis initiative even among those who genuinely desired it. Israelis were deeply worried about national disunity as a result of immigration and demographic trends, socio-economic and cultural-geographic diversity, and above all, religious/secular divisions, which were exacerbated by the passing away of the first heroic generation of Israeli leaders. Palestinians were in despair about their internal religious/ secular and generational divides, geographical separation, and above all, the disastrous Hamas/Fatah struggle to fill the power vacuum after the death of Yasser Arafat. These divisions were seen to play into the hands of Palestinian enemies intent on 'divide and rule'.

These were the features that framed linguistic intractability and rendered *dialogue for mutual understanding* impossible. There was no discursive space for it. And this was the environment in which only *dialogue for strategic engagement* and the resulting *strategic engagement of discourses* (SED) could keep channels of communication open between the conflict parties, shed light on the internal economy of the radical disagreement that constituted linguistic intractability, and therefore illuminate what would need to be done in the linguistic sphere if violence was ever to be transmuted into non-violent struggle. It was also the only way in which third parties would be able to understand their own involvement and determine what was required if their own discourse was to prevail.

In these circumstances, the natural programme was to acknowledge the force of the existing conflict dynamic and to work with it, rather than against it. The programme was driven by the logic inherent in the very fact of linguistic intractability. As seen in Chapter 4, within a given conflict configuration, the strategic engagement of discourses operates at three interlocking levels.

*   Level 1: Intra-Party Strategic Engagement of Discourses (SED 1)
    The strategic engagement of discourses begins, not with dialogue between conflict parties, but with inclusive strategic thinking *within* each conflict party considered separately – as and when the desire to overcome the internal divisions seen to threaten the national project becomes strong enough to counteract the influence of would-be internal hegemons wanting to impose their own exclusive discourses. The motive for pursuing intra-party strategic discursive engagement of this kind is not to promote mutual understanding with the enemy. On the contrary, it is the fear that internal weakness will jeopardize the external national struggle.

*   Level 2: Inter-Party Strategic Engagement of Discourses (SED 2)
    Only in the light of sustained inclusive strategic thinking within each conflict party, and as a natural extension of the logic of strategic thinking itself, can the process evolve into the strategic engagement of discourses *between* conflict parties that is made possible as a result. In general, in asymmetric conflicts it is the challenging discourse (the discourse of the weaker party – the challenger) that has a greater incentive to promote strategic engagement, while the hegemonic discourse (the discourse of the more powerful party – the possessor) has a greater interest in ignoring or suppressing it. Either way, where there is strategic engagement, each party's main aim is, once again, not to understand the other, but to win.

*   Level 3: Third Party Strategic Engagement of Discourses (SED 3)
    Finally, and as a further natural extension of the logic of strategic engagement, comes the involvement of third parties – for example, third parties appealed to by the conflict parties in the course of their strategic linguistic struggle. Of particular interest here is the engagement of the discourses of those third parties, who see themselves as, or claim to be, disinterested peacemakers. These are now recognized as yet further discourses struggling to occupy the

whole of the discursive space and to dictate the course of unfolding events. To the extent that they acknowledge their lack of discursive impartiality, and the radical disagreements between themselves and the conflict parties (as also among and within themselves), would-be third-party peacemakers may be able to anticipate the consequences of their own involvement more clearly. And to the extent that they understand the detailed dynamics of the strategic engagement of discourses both within and between the conflict parties, they may be able to maximize their effectiveness.

This, in a nutshell, is the natural dynamic for managing agonistic dialogue and linguistic intractability when conflict settlement and conflict transformation avenues are blocked. It is a dynamic which is dictated by the very nature of the web of radical disagreements that constitutes linguistic intractability. It can certainly keep channels of communication open when other approaches fail. Whether it can eventually form a bridge for the reintroduction of these other approaches depends on all the other factors – including the non-linguistic ones – that drive the conflict.

In the case of the Israeli-Palestinian conflict, the Obama peace initiative, which was imminent at the time of writing (April 2009), may bear fruit. Most experts are sceptical or highly pessimistic, as are the conflict parties. On the other hand, in highly complex conflict systems experience suggests that it is when the outlook seems bleakest that possibilities for change can unexpectedly open up, and 'hard-liners' can sometimes deliver change more easily than 'moderates'. Either way, this chapter concerns the period before this became possible, which is the period of maximum intractability between the collapse of the Camp David/Taba talks in 2000–1 and the election of a right-wing Israeli government in April 2009. This period includes: the second Palestinian intifada and the suicide bombing campaign; the Sharon government's response to them; the building of the 'separation barrier' and support for continuing Israeli settler encroachment in the West Bank together with roadblocks, 'bypass roads' and military outposts; the Hamas takeover of Gaza in June 2007 and the rocket attacks on Israel; the Israeli retaliation in 2008–9.

The question to be addressed in this chapter is: in these circumstances of maximum polarization and linguistic intractability, how can the promotion of a strategic engagement of discourses – the exploration of agonistic dialogue itself – offer the best way of managing the radical disagreements that lie at its core?

In what follows, I will quote as much as possible and comment as sparingly as possible because in the internal economy of radical disagreement, it is what conflict parties and involved third parties say that speaks louder than any third-party commentator.

The strategic engagement of discourses level one: Palestinian–Palestinian – the challenging discourse

In asymmetric conflicts, the *challenging discourse* is the discourse of the materially weaker party. In this case, it is the Palestinian discourse, because in relation to the Israelis, the Palestinians are both qualitatively at a disadvantage (they do not have a state) and quantitatively much less powerful – in terms of control of territory, military capacity and economic resources. I turn in the next section to the fact that within the wider Arab and Islamic world, Jewish Israelis are a tiny minority and it is the Israeli discourse that is drowned out. This is in turn counter-balanced by the fact that, within the Judeo-Christian world, it is the Israeli discourse that once again predominates and in the United States has virtually become a joint Israeli-US discourse.

The prime initial consideration, then, is whether, despite their own severe internal radical disagreements, Palestinians have a strong incentive to engage in inclusive strategic thinking aimed at maximizing Palestinian national coherence and effectiveness in relation to the outside world. The answer in this case has been unequivocal. Palestinians from across the spectrum of difference (Hamas/Fatah, Islamist/secular, gender, profession, class, age, location including the countries of the diaspora) say that they have a very strong incentive to speak, if not with one voice, then at least in such a way that optimizes internal Palestinian cohesion and consequently projects it outwards with maximum force. This is the main driver of the first part of the SED process. It is not a wish by Palestinians to promote mutual understanding with the enemy, but rather a fierce determination to enhance their own strength.

The result of this logic was the setting up of an inclusive Palestine Strategy Group (PSG) in 2006–7. In his piece, *Palestinians Calculating Next Move: Coexistence With Occupation Not an Option*, Sam Bahour, a participant, wrote:

> Palestinians have been historically outmanoeuvred, politically neutralised, and made totally dependent on international handouts. Or have they? A newly released Palestinian strategy document which outlines strategic polit- ical options gives witness to a renewed breath of fresh air in the Palestinians' struggle for freedom and independence. After 60 years of dispossession and 40 years of brutal Israeli military occupation, many of the world's power brokers are convinced that the Palestinians are successfully being forced into submission and acceptance of the colossal injustices that have been carried out against them.
>
> What the international community fails to mention is that the dynamic on the ground is explosive. The Israeli military occupation is alive and well and causing structural, possibly irrevocable damage to Palestinian lands and persons. The Jewish-only Israeli settlement enterprise is off the leash and building more and more illegal settlements as if there were no tomorrow. The failing (or failed) health care system and education system in Palestine is producing a generation of Palestinians with much less to lose and little hope for the future.
>
> Over the past several months, I participated together with a group of 45 Palestinians from all walks of life, men and women, on the political right and left, secular and religious, politicians, academics, civil society, business actors, from occupied Palestine, inside Israel, and in the Diaspora. We were a group that is a microcosm that reflects the dynamics of Palestinian society.

We could not all meet in one room anywhere in the world because of the travel restrictions that Israel has created. Nevertheless we continue to plan and to act. Our mission is to open a discussion on where we go from here: What are the Palestinians' strategic options, if any?

After several workshops in Palestine and abroad and a continuous online debate, we have produced the first iteration of *Regaining The Initiative: Palestinian Strategic Options to End Israeli Occupation*, published in Arabic and English. The document is posted at www.palestinestrategygroup.ps and reflects an alternative to an official but impotent Palestinian discourse that will very shortly, in the judgement of most Palestinians, run head-on into a brick (cement) wall.

(Sam Bahour 30 August 2008)

Box 7.1 gives the Executive Summary of *Regaining the Initiative* 27 August 2008.

Box 7.1 Regaining the Initiative: executive summary 27 August 2008

Source: Palestine Strategy Group 2008: 2–6.

- The current negotiations in the 'Annapolis' peace initiative have reached a critical point. On the sixtieth anniversary of the *Naqba*, after twenty years of fruitless negotiation for a Palestinian state on the basis of the historic recognition by the PLO in 1988 of the existence of the State of Israel, it is time for Palestinians to reconsider this entire strategic path to their national objectives. Although already greatly inflated beyond the original 57% allotted in UN General Assembly Resolution 181 in 1947, Israel shows no sign of accepting even the 78% of historic Palestine that lies within the 1967 borders, but continues to encroach beyond them in order to create new 'facts on the ground' that will progressively render an independent Palestinian state on the remaining 22% inoperable. A weak Israeli government is confronted by strong internal resistance to any compromises whatsoever, while a divided Israeli public is not ready to take the necessary risks. Indeed, Israel refuses formally and consistently even to accept the fact that it is an occupying power with concomitant duties in international law. Instead, Israel calculates that a negotiated two state outcome on the 1988 basis is permanently available, and supposes that it can perpetually hold out for better alternatives to a negotiated agreement. The Israeli position rests on the assumption that procrastination will continue to tilt the strategic balance increasingly in Israel's favour. In short, Israel is not a serious negotiating partner.

- The central proposal in this Report is that Israel's strategic calculations are wrong. Israeli strategic planners overestimate their own strength and underestimate the strategic opportunities open to Palestinians. There are four main perceived alternatives to a negotiated agreement that are attractive to Israel and therefore prevent Israel from reaching a final settlement on the terms offered. It is a key strategic aim of Palestinians to make clear to Israel why these four alternatives are simply not available.

  First, the default option of prolonging negotiations indefinitely by pretending that 'progress has been made' and that suspensions are temporary, as during the past twenty years, with ongoing encroachments and military incursions, few burdens, and considerable financial and other benefits from continuing occupation.

Second, a pseudo provisional 'two state agreement' with a strengthened but severely constrained Palestinian Authority masquerading as a Palestinian government while Israel disaggregates and picks off the 'historic issues' and retains permanent control.

Third, a unilateral separation dictated by Israel as in the withdrawal from and siege of Gaza and the building of the illegal separation wall.

Fourth, a control of the occupied territories by Egypt and Jordan.

• But these four alternatives are unacceptable to Palestinians. They do not take Palestinian national aspirations seriously. Indeed, they aim to undermine Palestinians' national identity and rights altogether. So, if Israel refuses to negotiate seriously for a genuine two-state outcome, Palestinians can and will block all four of them by switching to an alternative strategy made up of a combination of four linked reorientations to be undertaken singly or together.

First, the definitive closing down of the 1988 negotiation option so long abused by Israel. This blocks the first two preferred Israeli alternatives to a genuine negotiated agreement.

Second, the reconstitution of the Palestinian Authority so that it will not serve future Israeli interests by legitimising indefinite occupation and protecting Israel from bearing its full burden of the costs of occupation (it may become a Palestinian Resistance Authority). This also blocks the first two preferred Israeli alternatives, and also helps to block the third.

Third, the elevation of 'smart' resistance over negotiation as the main means of implementation for Palestinians, together with a reassertion of national unity through reform of the PLO, the empowerment of Palestinians, and the orchestrated eliciting of regional and international third party support. The central aim will be to maximise the cost of continuing occupation for Israel, and to make the whole prospect of unilateral separation unworkable.

Fourth, the shift from a two state outcome to a (bi-national or unitary democratic) single state outcome as Palestinians' preferred strategic goal. This reopens a challenge to the existence of the State of Israel in its present form, but in an entirely new and more effective way than was the case before 1988.

Is this what Israel wants? Israel cannot prevent Palestinians from a strategic reorientation along these lines. Does Israel really want to force Palestinians to take these steps?

• The result of a reorientation of Palestinian strategy will clearly be much worse for Israel than the negotiation of a genuine two state outcome on the basis of the existing 1988 offer. Although many Palestinians may still prefer a genuine negotiated two state solution, a failure of the present Annapolis initiative will greatly strengthen those who argue against this. Most Palestinians are then likely to be convinced that a negotiated agreement is no longer possible. What is undoubtedly the case is that a reversal of the 1988 offer and the adoption of an alternative strategy is much preferable for Palestinians to any of the four preferred Israeli alternatives to a negotiated agreement. So, if current negotiations fail, Palestinians will be driven to replace the 1988 offer by a new strategy, not just rhetorically but in reality. The negotiated two state outcome will then be definitively cancelled. Palestinians will ensure that Israel is seen to be responsible for the closure of their 20 year offer. Israel will have lost a historic and non-recurrent opportunity to end the conflict and to secure its own future survival on the best terms available for Israel.

• In short Palestinians are able to block all four of Israel's best alternatives to a genuine negotiated outcome via a fundamental reorientation of strategy. Israel is not able to block this reorientation. The result of such a reorientation would be far worse for Israel than that of a genuine negotiated outcome. The result of such a reorientation would be far better for Palestinians than any of Israel's best alternatives to a genuine negotiated outcome. Therefore, when Palestinians calculate that a genuine negotiated outcome is no longer available, they undoubtedly will reorientate their strategy, not only rhetorically but in reality, and will finally close down their twenty year 1988 offer.

• Palestinians, therefore, have three main immediate parallel strategic tasks, which it is the central purpose of this Report to outline.

• The first strategic task is the detailed working out of a fundamental reorientation of Palestinian strategy along the lines outlined above, including the new preferred strategic path, and the full range of means of implementation. All of this is commented upon in the main body of the Report. This task must be undertaken in all seriousness and on the assumption that present negotiations will fail. Even if only used as a strategic threat in order to force Israel to negotiate seriously, the intention must still be to implement the new strategy should negotiations fail. An empty threat is strategically no threat. A mere bluff does not work. So it is now an urgent priority for Palestinians to agree and work out in detail their alternative to a negotiated agreement and to communicate this as soon as possible and as forcefully as possible to Israel. This must be the immediate focus of unified national strategic planning that includes all Palestinians, from different backgrounds, generations, genders, and political affiliations, both those living in the occupied territories and those living elsewhere.

• The second strategic task is to make sure that Israel understands the terms on which the 1988 offer is still held open by Palestinians and is clear about what Palestinians can and will do should these terms not be met. Has a national movement ever made a concession on a similar scale to that made by Palestinians in 1988? In November 1988 the Palestine Liberation Organisation, recognised by Palestinians as their sole representative, made the extraordinary sacrifice of accepting the existence of the State of Israel and determining to establish an independent Palestinian state on the remaining 22% of historic Palestine in accordance with UN Security Council Resolutions 242 and 338 (PNC Political Communique, Algiers, 15 November, 1988). In negotiations Israelis repeatedly say 'we do all the giving and the Palestinians do all the taking'. This is the opposite of the truth. Palestinians continue to demand no more than 22% of their historic land. It is Israel that has done all the taking through continuous government-backed settler encroachment on this remaining 22%. The second strategic task for Palestinians, therefore, is to spell out the minimum terms acceptable for negotiating a fully independent Palestinian state on 1967 borders, and to explain clearly why this is by far the best offer that Israel will ever get, including guarantees for Israel's future security from neighbouring Arab states. Palestinians will set out a clear timetable for judging whether this has been attained or is attainable. It is Palestinians who will judge 'success', and it is Palestinians who will decide how long to persist in negotiations and when the moment has come to change strategy entirely.

- The third strategic task is to ensure that it is the Palestinian discourse that frames international discussion of the Palestinian future. This is elucidated in the Report. The aim is to make clear to regional and international third parties that in all this it is not Palestinians who are lacking in commitment to a negotiated outcome, but Israel. Palestinians have persisted for twenty years with their historic offer of 1988. Israel has refused to honour it. That is why Israeli protestations are no longer credible to Palestinians. Israel has given Palestinians no option but to look elsewhere for fulfilment of their national aspirations. Israel bears full responsibility should negotiations fail.

- In conclusion, it needs to be understood clearly that we Palestinians will never allow Israel to continue its encroachments and domination under the pretence of insincere negotiations, nor to go on imagining falsely that there are better alternatives available to Israel. Israel will have to decide whether to accept the time-limited negotiation offer that is evidently in its own best interest, or not. And we Palestinians will then act accordingly at a time and in a way of our own choosing.

It is now up to us as Palestinians to regain the strategic initiative and to take control of our own national destiny. Israel, regional partners, and international actors, must understand definitively that Palestinians will not be divided in their strategic objectives, and that the Palestinian people, steadfast and determined, will never give up their national struggle.

The main body of *Regaining the Initiative* includes:

- prerequisites;
- strategic objectives;
- possible future scenarios with evaluations of their relative desirability or undesirability for Palestinians;
- evaluation of capacity to implement or block attractive or unattractive scenarios (feasibility);
- strategic options and the preferred strategic path (the preferred scenario, reserve scenarios, rejected scenarios);
- means of implementation;
- revision points and assessment of alternative strategies;
- review of alternatives to a negotiated outcome for Palestinians and Israelis;
- action plan.

Figure 7.1 shows a tabular outline of the evaluation of scenarios.

It is not so much the details of *Regaining the Initiative* that are significant for this chapter, but the process. Readers will come to their own conclusions about the force of the central argument given in outline here. But the report already clearly demonstrates two things. First, the great advantage of a sustained inclusive internal strategic engagement of discourses of this kind for the challenging party.in asymmetric conflicts. Second, its potential for opening space for inter-party exchanges even in the least propitious circumstances.

On the first count, the report was well received by many Palestinians who regarded it as the first serious attempt at coordinated and systematic public strategic thinking by Palestinians – hitherto jealously guarded as a preserve of the PLO leadership under Yasser Arafat:

> The overwhelming majority of the members of the project *Regaining the Initiative* are still in touch and extremely eager to further develop and continue the initial ideas they have agreed on and reached in their meetings and discussions. I have had the opportunity to speak with participants who are members of Fatah, Hamas, or women, student, academic, and human rights and democracy organizations. They all passionately agree about the desperate

Scenarios acceptable to Palestinians

Scenario	Palestinian capability to promote	Israeli capability to block	Third-party capability to influence
Two-state	low	high	medium (US high)
One-state	low (short term) increasing (long term)	high (short term) decreasing (long term)	low (short term) increasing (long term)
PA reform	high	low	low
UN trustee	low	medium	medium (US high)

Scenarios unacceptable to Palestinians

Scenario	Palestinian capability to promote	Palestinian capability to block	Israeli capability to promote
Status quo	high	medium	medium
Pseudo-Two-state	high	low	low
Unilateral separation	low (short term) high (long term)	high (short term) low (long term)	medium
Egypt/Jordan	high	low	medium

Figure 7.1 Evaluation of scenarios: preferences and capabilities

need to develop and sustain long term Palestinian strategic thinking. Indeed, this approach has already had a real major impact. A few months ago I received a phone call from a senior member of the Negotiation Support Unit (NUS) of the Palestine Authority informing me that the Unit has discussed thoroughly the Palestinian strategy document and adopted several parts of it.

(Bashir Bashir 2009)

Some were critical of the fact that the 'one state' alternatives were relegated to back-up status as if they were second-best for Palestinians, whereas for many Palestinians they are the only way to redress the historic dispossession of the *Naqba*. One commentator detected a damaging discrepancy in wording between the English version and the Arabic version on the strategic objectives (clearly the Arabic version is the authoritative one).

But this is all part of the ongoing inclusive internal strategic thinking. It is the SED process itself that shows up what still stands most in need of detailed thought and discussion by as many internal constituencies as possible and provides the main incentive to do so. It is, I would argue, what has been missing from the Palestinian national debate almost from the outset.

For example, in this case *Regaining the Initiative* showed up clearly how little thought had so far been put into public discussion about what the various 'one state alternatives' to a two state solution are. This is of vital strategic significance, because, as is widely recognized in negotiation studies, unless alternatives to a negotiated settlement are clearly thought through, weighed up and communicated, there is no sound foundation for effective internal strategic decision and strategic planning, or for its subsequent external projection. As Tony Klug puts it:

Depending on the proponent, 'one state' could be unitary, federal, confederal, bi-national, democratic, secular, cantonal (Switzerland), multi-confessional (Lebanon), Islamic (Hamas), Arab (PLO Charter) or Jewish (Greater Israel).

(Klug 2008: 3)

On the one hand, does the fact that nearly all Jewish Israelis vehemently reject a one-state outcome make it a strategic impossibility? On the other hand, would the indefinite perpetuation of the present situation not be equivalent to a one-state outcome since the only state (Israel) already has effective control of the whole territory (see below)? Would one state not be likely to end up, bloodily, in two states? And does the most likely route towards one state not in fact lie via two states – for example in the form of some future confederation? These are vital strategic considerations. Unless an inclusive internal strategic engagement of discourses is successfully promoted and sustained, they may never be properly thought through and planned for to the great impoverishment of the Palestinian national project.

This is an example of the creative possibilities opened up by the logic of internal strategic engagement of discourses. Participants in the *Regaining the Initiative* Palestine Strategy Group identified a number of other topics that called for further elucidation. For instance, the idea of dissolving the Palestinian Authority (on which thousands of families are dependent for wages) or transforming it into a Palestinian Resistance Authority. There was also the possibility of apparently doing the opposite – building an embryonic Palestinian state unilaterally with a view to a swift unilateral declaration of independence on 1967 borders with East Jerusalem as its capital, even though this has not yet been agreed with Israel, and then appealing to the international community for endorsement. This carries the risk that it might play into Israeli hands by appearing to condone a 'provisional' or 'quasi' state, but that is what the internal debate has continually to argue out.

Or there is the question of what would be required for Hamas to acquiesce in a two state settlement (including the possibility of formal de facto acknowledgement of the existence of Israel, of a long-term Hudna or truce, of a national referendum whose results Hamas would accept). This includes the question whether national reconciliation is, indeed, a prerequisite for effective Palestinian policy, or whether, say, the Palestinian National Authority in Ramallah would do better to carry on independently and wait for Gaza to follow later.

Or there is the requirement to clarify what exactly is meant by the 'smart resistance' called for in the Report, and what its implications are under various scenarios. This is a vital consideration in distinguishing extremism of ends from extremism of means identified as a key issue below, and requires maximum discussion from as inclusive a number of Palestinians as possible.

Above all what the promotion of a sustained and detailed strategic engagement of discourses of this kind does from the perspective of challengers (in this case Palestinians) at internal level is to enhance their capacity to match and outmanoeuvre their opponents (in this case Israelis) at their own game. It is thus a key component of *capacity-building* and *empowerment*.

Having now looked at an example of inclusive internal strategic debate, we are in a better position to address the next question. In relation to the main theme of this chapter – the management of agonistic dialogue between enemies in times of maximum conflict intractability – how does continuing inclusive *intra-party* strategic thinking of this sort (SED 1) contribute to the possibility of promoting an *inter-party* strategic engagement of discourses (SED 2)?

Another look at *Regaining the Initiative* clarifies why the possibility of an inter-party strategic engagement of discourses is always implicit in the very nature of strategic thinking. There are six main points to be made, each of which is illustrated by an extract from the text.

(A) *By its nature strategic thinking looks, not to the past, but to the future*

The Group met for extended three-day workshops in order to analyse and discuss strategic options for Palestinians in the months coming up to the sixtieth anniversary of the *Naqba*. These sixty years have been very long and bitter years for Palestinians. But the main focus of the Group is not on the past. It is on the future. What options lie ahead? What overall strategy best equips Palestinians to achieve success in our unwavering determination to achieve national independence? How can Palestinians refocus on the strategic objectives that all of us share? Can a common platform be articulated that will enable Palestinians to speak with one voice regionally and internationally? Can Palestinians regain the initiative in determining their own future?

(Palestine Strategy Group 2008: 9)

Intense and intractable political conflicts are fuelled by bitter past experience, traumas, hatreds and fears. Desire for revenge can overwhelm other considerations. Conflict parties can be trapped in recurring patterns of re-enactment. These do not go away and are certainly not forgotten. They fuel and shape the strategic thinking. But strategic thinking itself at least encourages reflection on what the future implications of this are. What strategic conclusions follow? It is up to conflict parties to define their strategic goals. But what are the implications for action, and how can these goals be best attained? The orientation is, by its nature, forward-looking.

(B) *Strategic thinking recognizes the prerequisite, not of cancelling internal radical disagreement, but of subordinating it to the priority of presenting a united front to the external world*

The second prerequisite is national unity. A house divided against itself cannot stand. Palestinian strategic action is impossible if the Palestinian nation is unable to speak with one voice or to act with one will. This does not mean agreeing about everything. Nor does it cancel internal Palestinian politics. But it does mean that, when it comes to formulating and enacting a national plan in relation to the outside world, Palestinians must subordinate internal politics to the superior demands of shared destiny and unity of purpose.

(Palestine Strategy Group 2008: 17)

As seen above, this is the main motive for counter-balancing the interest of the would-be internal hegemons, who want to monopolize strategic space and avoid inclusive internal dialogue. Overcoming this internal resistance is a central ingredient in the SED approach. Crucially, it also clearly lays out inner differences within broad political organizations like Fatah and Hamas, which are far from monolithic. This is of vital importance for would-be peacemakers, as emphasized later in the last section of this chapter:

For example, at the moment there is talk of a national referendum on the outcome of current negotiations with Israel. The problem is that, without extensive prior national strategic debate and consensus, the Palestinian voters are likely to be swayed more by political expediency than by strategic priorities. This is not a good basis for wise national decision-making. It weakens Palestinians and hands the major strategic card to their opponents. Nothing could indicate more clearly how important it is for political leaders to rise above partisan ambition when it comes to guiding public Palestinian debate about national strategic options. No doubt disagreement about strategy is sincere and not just a mask for partisan political interest. Even so the requirement is for political leaders from all parties to articulate a broadly agreed national strategy. Otherwise there is no prospect of rallying, coordinating, energising and empowering Palestinians. And, without the focused and determined effort of the Palestinian people, there can be no effective implementation of strategy.

(Palestine Strategy Group 2008: 44)

(C) *Strategic thinking links objectives to strategies through realistic assessments of relative power*

The analysis of relative power lies at the heart of strategic thinking. It is the main link between objectives and strategies. Power analysis revisits the scenarios in order to determine what is and what is not in the power of Palestinians, Israelis and third parties to achieve either on their own or via the actions of others. Power analysis assesses the capacity of agents to convert their aspirations into reality. This injects hard-headed realism into the procedure. It identifies the main obstacles that block preferred strategic pathways, and it suggests what can and should be done to reduce or remove them.

(Palestine Strategy Group 2008: 12–13)

This requirement of strategic thinking ensures that the discussion gets beyond empty sloganizing and uncriticized wishful thinking. It does not guarantee that 'pragmatic' outcomes will prevail. Conflict parties may still prefer to pursue options with little prospect of success, or may prefer damaging the other even when this entails a greater risk of damaging themselves.But at least this is done after a discussion and weighing up of the alternatives. As seen above, *Regaining the Initiative* considers various possible futures (scenarios) and weighs up preferences and dispreferences and the capacity to achieve the former and block the latter. From this, the preferred strategic path that gains most internal consensus is constructed. Strategic thinking translates wish lists into viable political options – at any rate in intention.

(D) *Strategic thinking understands that the chessboard must be looked at from the perspective of the opponent*

It is essential in strategic thinking to take constant account of how the chessboard looks from the perspective of the opponent. A player who does not do this ... will lose. The strategic purpose is to exert mounting pressure on the opponent to act as we want. This can only be done if we understand what the opponent desires and fears, and the sources and limits of the opponent's power. The same applies to inducing third parties to behave in the ways we want them to.

(Palestine Strategy Group 2008: 19)

Here is the seed from which a future inter-party strategic engagement of discourses (SED 2) can grow even in the most unpropitious circumstances when conflict resolution initiatives are still premature. Once again it does not have anything to do with 'helping each side to accept, and conceivably to respect, the validity of the competing narrative' or 'exposing each side to the narratives of the other in order, gradually, to foster an understanding, if not an acceptance, of their deeply felt importance to each side.' It flows from an entirely different strategic requirement – the requirement to win.

(E) *Strategic thinking chooses the most appropriate strategic and tactical means to attain its overall strategic ends – and keeps these under constant review*

> Power is the ability to get what you want done. If you get what you want done you have power. If you do not get what you want done you do not have power … In strategic planning agents must choose the most effective form of power (or combination of forms) in different circumstances, and must be prepared to be flexible in switching from one to the other where appropriate.
>
> (Palestine Strategy Group 2008: 18–19)

From the perspective of managing ongoing radical disagreement, this is perhaps the key aspect of the enterprise of promoting SED – working with it, rather than against it. As elaborated below, it introduces the distinction between *strategic ends* and *strategic means*, which is the key to opening up the possibility of separating radical disagreement from violence. There are different forms of power. Joseph Nye distinguishes hard power and soft power (2002). Kenneth Boulding distinguishes three 'faces' of power (1990):

1 *Threat power*: 'Do what I want or I will do what you do not want.'
2 *Exchange* or *bargaining power*: 'Do what I want and I will do what you want.'
3 *Integrative power*: 'Do what I want because you want it too.'

The Report advocates the use of all three forms of power as appropriate. The question then is: what are the most appropriate strategic means in relation to different strategic objectives and assessments of relative distributions of power?

Within this lies the question of 'smart resistance' also advocated in the Report. What forms of threat power are most effective and legitimate?

> The range of options open to Palestinians under the general heading 'resistance' is great, reaching from non-cooperation, through various forms of boycott and economic measures, and on to more active forms of resistance. This broad category of implementation can be deployed in support of all the strategic options so long as the tools are selected and applied with strategic precision. Here the distinction between civilian resistance and armed resistance is critical, and, within the latter, the distinction between armed attack on Israeli military assets and armed attack on Israeli civilians raises additional moral issues. Members of the Palestine Strategy Group were clear that in choosing means of implementation Palestinians must make sure that the

overwhelming justice of their cause is implemented by means that are also seen to be just.

(Palestine Strategy Group 2008: 44)

As further commented upon below, the distinction between strategic ends and strategic means is vital in distinguishing extremism of ends from extremism of means – one of the two keys to the way the strategic engagement of discourses can open the way to, or inform, a possible future peace process (the other is the framing of the political settlement).

(F) *Strategic thinking clearly understands that the communication of strategic messages to supporters, opponents, and third parties is an essential part of strategy*

> The second strategic task is to make sure that Israel understands the terms on which the 1988 offer is still held open by Palestinians and is clear about what Palestinians can and will do should these terms not be met ... The third strategic task is to ensure that it is the Palestinian discourse that frames international discussion of the Palestinian future.
>
> (Palestine Strategy Group 2008: 5)

This requirement of strategic thinking reinforces D above. It is not just that the chessboard must be looked at from the perspective of other players, but that signals must be given and received if strategic moves are to have the desired effect. So it was that it was decided, not without controversy, that the wording of *Regaining the Initiative* must itself be seen to be part of the strategic approach it set out, and as such was consciously addressed simultaneously to different readers (Palestinians, Israelis, others).

These six aspects of strategic thinking can be seen to offer scope for a possible strategic engagement of discourses (SED 2) between conflict parties. In this sense they might even be said to *mimic* conflict settlement and transformation approaches, which is why inclusive intra-party strategic thinking of this kind is capable of playing that role.

But this section should end with a reaffirmation of the fact that the prime discursive goal of inclusive internal strategic thinking (SED 1) is not to expedite conflict resolution, but to determine how best to ensure that the discourse in question, in this case the Palestinian discourse, prevails in the war of words. Quotations from *Regaining the Initiative* on this point have already been given in the prologue. They emphasized the importance of ensuring that it is the Palestinian discourse that frames all discussion about the Palestinian future, and the rejection of attempts by international power brokers prematurely to impose discourses of peacemaking and state-building. The 'requirement of a new discourse' is one of the three strategic prerequisites listed in *Regaining the Initiative*. Box 7.2 contains an extract from a later part of that section.

Box 7.2 The requirement of a new discourse

Source: Palestine Strategy Group 2008: 15.

Perhaps the most appropriate comparable discourse here is the discourse of decolonisation. This needs to be clearly understood by the international community. For example before 1947 Gandhi's primary discourse in India was not a peace-making discourse, because he was not making peace with Britain but struggling to end British occupation. And it was not a state building discourse because there was not yet an Indian state. His primary discourse was one of emancipation and national struggle. The same is true of the Palestinian discourse. Palestinians are of course ready to enter serious negotiations. They are more ready to do this than Israelis. But such peacemaking has to be defined within a context that genuinely aims to deliver Palestinian national aspirations. Anything less is simply not peacemaking but a confirmation of continuing occupation and repression.

There is no space to pursue this in detail further here, except to note the importance of combating a central idea in the peacemaking discourse that what is at issue is two equivalent 'Israeli' and 'Palestinian' 'narratives'. No doubt there are Israeli and Palestinian narratives. But what is centrally at issue is not a mere Palestinian narrative, but a series of incontrovertible facts – facts of expulsion, exclusion, dominance and occupation bitterly lived out by Palestinians day by day over the past 60 years and still being endured at the present time. This is not a narrative. It is a lived reality. Finding the best strategy for ending this lived reality is the main purpose of this Report. Transforming the discourse within which it is discussed is a major part of that effort.

Regaining the Initiative, therefore, is a clear example of the significance of what was shown in Chapter 5 to be the moments of recommendation, justification, refutation and explanation in the internal economy of radical disagreeing. At the root of linguistic intractability in this case is Palestinian determination to make the Palestinian discourse the primary language within which the Palestinian issue is discussed, not because it is a *narrative*, but because it is *true*. Dialogue for mutual understanding does not accommodate this – it tries from the outset to persuade conflict parties to drop the language of truth (this is so) and to adopt the language of self-reference (this is my perception). The strategic engagement of discourses, on the other hand, begins with it. Indeed, the very phrase 'Palestinian discourse' already contains the seeds of such misapprehension because it may thereby suggest that this is 'a mere Palestinian discourse'. And that, as became clear in Chapter 5 and is reaffirmed in this example, is to miss everything.

Meanwhile, here is the key question that the challenging Palestinian discourse – as shown through inclusive intra-party strategic engagement of discourses – poses for would-be peacemakers:

Why should Palestinians give up violent resistance and accept permanent dispossession?

Would this not be a betrayal of past sacrifices and an endorsement of perpetual occupation? Would it not be a capitulation in the face of manifest injustice? Would it not be a final defeat for the national project, an abandonment of the Palestinian homeland and the destruction of the Palestinian people?

The strategic engagement of discourses level one: Israeli– Israeli – the hegemonic discourse

In the context of the Israeli-Palestinian conflict formation, Israel is the hegemon, and the Israeli discourse is the hegemonic discourse in the sense that it is the discourse of the hegemon. Whether it is the hegemonic discourse in terms of the wider struggle is what is fought over in the war of words. At the moment within the Arab/ Muslim world clearly it is not. In the USA it still is.

The project that produced the Palestinian strategic response, *Regaining the Initiative*, also included a parallel process among Jewish Israelis. Once again, a representative group of a similar size, from across the spectrum of constituencies, convened for a series of meetings to explore and evaluate possible futures. The process is described here by an Israeli participator:

> The main criterion for selecting the participants was that together they represent the major currents of thought in Jewish-Israeli society … The group thus included several members of the Knesset with diverse political views, former heads of the security services (GSS, IDF), leading business people, key religious and spiritual leaders (ultra-orthodox, national-religious, [secular] Jewish renewal), prominent social activists, well-respected journalists, senior academics and various celebrities and publicly known figures.
>
> (Zalzberg 2009: assessment of the project)

Once again, quoting Zalzberg, 'to a large extent the group's thinking was led by the assumption that internal cohesion is the key to resolving the problems of Israel's Jewish population'.

But in this case, the outcome was different. To some extent, the difference was fortuitous and was the result of a different facilitation methodology. But I think that it was also a result of the fact that, in general, the discourse of the possessor does not concern itself with those who do not immediately threaten its possession. West Bank Palestinians no longer posed a major threat after the suppression of the al-Aqsa intifada, even though rockets were still fired from Gaza. Hegemons rely on military power for protection. In this case, participants showed little interest in discussing strategic alternatives vis-à-vis Palestinians, and were much more concerned with internal disputes about the character of the future Jewish State of Israel. The distinctions between Jewishness (cultural Jewish identity), Zionism (national Jewish identity), and Judaism (religious Jewish identity) were recurrently discussed. Jewish-Israeli society was seen to be fragmented:

> This is as a result both of social cleavages (religious-secular, socio-economic left-right, Ashkenaz-Sepharad, immigrants-natives) and of the pressures caused by the Israeli-Palestinian conflict … As a result the national conversation about the conflict has become a cacophony. To a large extent as time passes the discussion becomes increasingly polarised, filled with taboos and thus simplistic. This leaves Israeli Jews with no real capacity to agree on a

common strategy. Israel's significant power in the Middle East means that as long as it continues to muddle through without a conscious strategy the Israeli-Palestinian conflict is likely to continue to defy resolution efforts ... In short, a collective Jewish-Israeli focus on the plausible rather than the desired is needed. Experience of other conflict regions in the world has shown that such mapping provides the leadership and the public with a new vocabulary, which is needed for an effective national conversation ... After so many decades of violence, and with Israel facing a truly complex rapidly changing reality, a mapping of alternative scenarios should be used to broaden the discursive space, alleviate some taboos, and legitimise a conversation on certain futures that are so far unspoken. This is a requirement if Israeli Jews are to take a well-informed decision about their future – one that takes seriously into account the domestic, regional and international constraints, costs and benefits.

(Ibid.)

In the end, four 'future stories' were produced, based on four possible scenarios:

1 *A Jewish Home – from the Jordan to the Mediterranean*:
   A Jewish state in which Israel resumes full control in Judea and Samaria (the West Bank) and the demographic influence of National Religious and Ultra-Orthodox Jewish groups increases. Palestinians have full residential rights (personal and cultural), but not full political rights. Militant Palestinians are suppressed with severe violence.
2 *Two Homes for Two Peoples – Good Neighbours*:
   Two states for two people in which it is recognized that without a partition of the land between Palestinians and Jews, the outcome will be the creation of an untenable bi-national state between the Jordan and the Sea. A multinational force safeguards the security of Jewish populations on Palestinian territory, while in Israel efforts are made to close social gaps by including Israeli-Arabs and Ultra-Orthodox Jews in governmental institutions.
3 *One Home for Two Peoples – Isra-Palestine*:
   The bi-national State in which the dissolution of the Palestinian Authority forces Israel to resume full control of the West Bank and Gaza, and international pressure, including weakening American support, makes Israel comply. Both Israeli and Palestinian societies are torn amongst themselves between those who see the new reality as an opportunity and those who prefer a nation-state, either in a secular or in a religious version. Opposition on both sides is vehement. There is a mass emigration of Jews.
4 *A Shared Home – A Jewish Home as Part of A Regional Confederation*:
   The State of Israel enters the Confederacy together with Palestine (by agreement with the Palestinian Authority) and Jordan. Israel embodies the Jewish national identity and becomes the spiritual-educational centre for Jewish communities all over the world.

The process of production of these future stories was of great interest. Discussion was passionate, open and creative, as is characteristic of the vibrancy of Israeli society. The whole enterprise was an innovative attempt to widen Israeli debate, which it succeeded in doing. But the possibilities were not thought through strategically (that was not what participants wanted). And the decision was taken not to publish the results, so I will not comment – or quote – further here.

Instead, in the remainder of this section, I will partially shift focus away from the Israeli-Palestinian conflict formation and towards the Israeli response (or lack of response) to the main strategic initiative to come from the Arab side in the wider Arab-Israel conflict. This is the 2002 Arab Peace Initiative (API), or Saudi peace plan, endorsed by all 22 member states of the Arab League in Beirut in the aftermath of the 11 September 2001 attacks on New York and Washington, which partly conditioned it. This remarkable – and brief – document effectively reversed the three 'noes' famously enunciated at the Arab League meeting in Khartoum after the Six Days War in 1967: no peace, no negotiation, no recognition of Israel. Moreover, as careful readings show, the API buys into what had by then become the generally acknowledged framework for a final settlement as recently articulated in the December 2000 Clinton parameters (Alon 2007/8).

- The API for the first time explicitly refers to the June 4 1967 borders in relation to a final settlement, thus recognizing Israel's permanent claim to 78 per cent of the disputed territory;
- The API for the first time affirms that only East (Arab) Jerusalem will be the Palestinian capital, ceding the rest to Israel – it does not use the language of al-Quds or Holy Jerusalem, the place from which Mohammad made his 'night journey' to heaven, the site subsequently marked by the building of the seventh century Dome of the Rock, and the place to which the earliest Muslims turned in prayer before the *Qibla* was transferred to Mecca;
- The API for the first time says that a 'just solution' to the refugee problem will be 'agreed' with Israel, thus acknowledging Israel's right to negotiate an acceptable outcome and determine who will, and who will not, be allowed to settle in Israel.

All of this, it is argued by those who advocate a positive Israeli response, should be cause for Israeli rejoicing. Together with the 1988 PLO transformation of strategy described above, it represented an astonishing triumph for Israel. Now is the time to cash in on it and render the remarkable gains of the past 60 years permanent. UN resolutions will have been satisfied, there will be no further demographic threat from the three million Palestinians in the new Palestinian state, Israel's borders can be given cast-iron guarantees by a powerful UN-sanctioned peacekeeping force led by the US, any remaining Arab and Islamist irredentists will find their support drastically reduced and Iranian influence will be sharply curtailed. The economic rewards would also be great. And Israel could then set about inspiring its younger generation and restoring its reputation abroad as a progressive and principled exemplar of the Jewish vision.

The alternative to a positive Israeli response from this perspective is said to be a collapse of the two-state solution leading to a further radicalization of Palestinian and Arab youth, including the Arab citizens of Israel who make up 20 per cent of the Israeli population. The move is seen to be likely to be more in the direction of al-Qaeda jihadi nihilism than political Islamist movements like Hamas that are amenable to negotiation on concrete political agendas. Iranian influence would increase and strain would be put on relations with a new US administration wanting to mend fences with the 1.2 billion-strong Muslim world. Above all, the argument goes, blocking the creation of a genuine Palestinian state would be by far the greatest threat to the survival of Israel, not for military reasons, which would have become irrelevant, but for demographic reasons. Palestinians in Gaza, the West Bank, Jerusalem and Israel would come to constitute a majority of the population in mandate Palestine. The claims of these populations for full citizenship would become irresistible. It would effectively spell the end of the idea of a democratic Jewish state.

Such is the main case against current Israeli strategies at the level of the Israeli-Palestinian conflict formation. I will follow Tony Klug in calling it the *argument for an Israeli Peace Initiative*. It is the argument that led presidential candidate Obama, when he first heard of the Arab Peace Initiative on his visit to the region in July 2008, to say that it would be 'crazy' for Israel to refuse a deal that could 'give them peace with the Muslim world'. Drowned out by the move to the right in Israeli politics, and by the nature of Israeli coalition politics, which makes even public discussion of these issues electorally dangerous, it is a case that has so far hardly been seriously made – or rather heard – in Israel.

The text of the *Arab Peace Initiative* is contained in Box 7.3.

Box 7.3 Official translation of the *Arab Peace Initiative*

Source: www.al-bab.com/arab/docs/league/peace02.htm

The Council of Arab States at the Summit Level at its 14th Ordinary Session, Reaffirming the resolution taken in June 1996 at the Cairo Extra-Ordinary Arab Summit that a just and comprehensive peace in the Middle East is the strategic option of the Arab countries, to be achieved in accordance with international legality, and which would require a comparable commitment on the part of the Israeli government,

Having listened to the statement made by his royal highness Prince Abdullah bin Abdul Aziz, crown prince of the Kingdom of Saudi Arabia, in which his highness presented his initiative calling for full Israeli withdrawal from all the Arab territories occupied since June 1967, in implementation of Security Council Resolutions 242 and 338, reaffirmed by the Madrid Conference of 1991 and the land-for-peace principle, and Israel's acceptance of an independent Palestinian state with East Jerusalem as its capital, in return for the establishment of normal relations in the context of a comprehensive peace with Israel,

Emanating from the conviction of the Arab countries that a military solution to the conflict will not achieve peace or provide security for the parties, the council:

1. Requests Israel to reconsider its policies and declare that a just peace is its strategic option as well.

2. Further calls upon Israel to affirm:
   I – Full Israeli withdrawal from all the territories occupied since 1967, including the Syrian Golan Heights, to the June 4, 1967 lines as well as the remaining occupied Lebanese territories in the south of Lebanon.
   II – Achievement of a just solution to the Palestinian refugee problem to be agreed upon in accordance with U.N. General Assembly Resolution 194.
   III – The acceptance of the establishment of a sovereign independent Palestinian state on the Palestinian territories occupied since June 4, 1967 in the West Bank and Gaza Strip, with East Jerusalem as its capital.

3. Consequently, the Arab countries affirm the following:
   I – Consider the Arab-Israeli conflict ended, and enter into a peace agreement with Israel, and provide security for all the states of the region.
   II – Establish normal relations with Israel in the context of this comprehensive peace.

4. Assures the rejection of all forms of Palestinian patriation which conflict with the special circumstances of the Arab host countries.

5. Calls upon the government of Israel and all Israelis to accept this initiative in order to safeguard the prospects for peace and stop the further shedding of blood, enabling the Arab countries and Israel to live in peace and good neighbourliness and provide future generations with security, stability and prosperity.

6. Invites the international community and all countries and organisations to support this initiative.

7. Requests the chairman of the summit to form a special committee composed of some of its concerned member states and the secretary general of the League of Arab States to pursue the necessary contacts to gain support for this initiative at all levels, particularly from the United Nations, the Security Council, the United States of America, the Russian Federation, the Muslim states and the European Union.

But instead of a vigorous internal strategic engagement of discourses and inclusive national debate around the argument for an Israeli Peace Initiative, from 2002 to 2008 the API was 'greeted with a yawn by the Israeli government' and aroused surprisingly little public interest in Israel. This was no doubt partly due to its timing, coinciding as it did with the beginning of the al-Aqsa intifada (including a suicide attack killing 29 Israelis on 27 March 2002), the early months of the Sharon government which rejected the premise on which the API was constructed, and the Bush administration's reorientation of US policy as a 'war on terror' after the 11 September 2001 attacks. The incremental nature of the 2003 Road Map and Israel's strategy of 'unilateral separation' entirely sidelined the API. Nor was it mentioned in the Joint Understanding that initiated the Annapolis summit on 27 November 2007, even though this revived 'end-state' negotiations.

From 2007, a belated attempt was made by a number of Israelis, with outside support particularly from Europe and the United States and to a limited extent coordinated with the Arab League, to revive interest in the API in Israel with a view to eliciting an official response from the Israeli government.[2] In November 2008, for example, more than 500 former Israeli generals, diplomats and intelligence, military and security officers signed a full-page advertisement in Israeli newspapers urging the country 'not to ignore a historic opportunity which a moderate Arab world presents us with' (*Financial Times*, 27 November 2008). At about the same time President Peres, in a letter to the Oxford Research Group, wrote:

> The Arab Peace Initiative of 2002 broke the united front of the Khartoum policy of the Arab League. This represents a revolution in the Arab approach, which should not go unanswered by Israel.

But the right wing response was swift. Yuval Steinitz of the Knesset's Foreign Affairs and Defense Committee, for example, reiterated why the Saudi plan was a non-starter:

> It doesn't recognize Israel's right to defensible borders and demands that Palestinian refugees settle in the Jewish state as well as the Palestinian state, which is totally unacceptable and contradicts the essence of the two state solution.
>
> (*Haaretz* 19 October 2008)

Israeli Ambassador to London, Ron Prosor, elaborated this theme in a letter to the *Guardian*. See Box 7.4.

Box 7.4 Letter from the Israeli Ambassador to the UK

Source: Ron Prosor, Israeli Ambassador to London, the *Guardian* December 2008.

A Revived Peace Initiative Will Stumble Unless Arab States Recognise Israel and Make Rhetoric Reality

The Palestinian Authority recently took the unprecedented step of advertising the Arab Peace Initiative in Hebrew in the Israeli press. Adverts also appeared throughout the international media, including this newspaper. Many Israelis welcomed it as a step in the right direction.

Yet before the world shouts 'eureka', it is important to realise that the Arab initiative cannot be seen as a 'take it or leave it' offer. It cannot serve as a diktat, or replace the need for bilateral negotiations, on both the Palestinian and Syrian tracks. The plan is an interesting starting point for negotiations, but the international community should be under no illusions. Elements of the text are a cause for grave concern as regards the survivability of the state of Israel.

The demand that Palestinians should be able to relocate to areas inside the borders of the state of Israel jeopardises Israel's very existence. Most Israelis understand and support the creation of a future Palestinian state. It is difficult, however, to understand why Palestinians, having created a state of their own, would subsequently insist on sending their own people to the Jewish state. Instead of demographically undermining the state of Israel, surely Palestinians would be better able to help build their own nation within their own state.

Israel's concern over the future of Jerusalem should also not be underestimated. From time immemorial, Jerusalem has been the eternal capital of the Jewish people, and will always remain so.

Meanwhile, the final borders between Israel and the Palestinian state can only be determined bilaterally. The 1967 borders might provide a reference point for negotiations, but the demographic realities and security concerns of Israel's population must be taken into account.

Nevertheless, the revival of interest in the plan, first proposed by the Saudi king in 2002, met with interest in Israel. In contrast, the reception elsewhere in the Middle East ranged from the sceptical to the hostile. Several Arab papers refused to publish an advert with an Israeli flag. For many, the very notion of Israeli statehood, as represented by our national flag, is still taboo.

[Paragraphs on Iranian hostility to Israel, and how oil-rich Gulf countries encourage unrealistic Palestinian irredentist dreams but fail to provide the funds needed to build a viable Palestinian infrastructure and do not 'steer their less fortunate counterparts towards the path of moderation and progress']

For too long the Middle East has been crippled as Arab populations have been force-fed the lie that Israel's destruction is both desirable and imminent. Today, as Iran continues to inject these poisonous concepts into the body of the region, the Middle East must abandon the mindset of the 1967 Khartoum conference and its infamous three noes.

For the twenty-first century, three realities must instead be acknowledged: Israel exists, Israel belongs, and recognising Israel would be to the benefit of every Arab society. Everyone in the region with the ability to promote this understanding must be urged to do so.

Ambassador Prosor says that 'most Israelis understand and support the creation of a future Palestinian state'. Why is it, then, that, when it comes to it, most Israelis have not been prepared to take the necessary steps in this direction? Some Israelis resist on principle because they identify Eretz Israel (the land of Israel) with Judea and Samaria (the West Bank). But Ambassador Prosor says that they are a minority, as regularly confirmed in opinion polls. So where has the inhibition lain, at any rate up to the time of writing?

The only way to answer this question is once again to ask Israelis. And that is precisely the aim of the SED process. The answer given is that there is a structural strategic reason for this, which needs to be clearly understood by anyone wanting to participate effectively in the debate. Although there is a persistent majority in favour of a two state solution in principle, there is an equally persistent majority that, when it comes to it, does not think that the Palestinians are 'ready for self-rule'. A key moment in the eyes of most Israelis was what they see as the refusal by Yasser Arafat to settle at Camp David in 2000, followed by the catastrophic outbreak of the 'second intifada' which left Israel with no option but to crush it. The Hamas take-over of Gaza – seen to be orchestrated by Iran – and subsequent rocket attacks confirmed this. Only when 'the circumstances are right' can Israel safely relinquish its iron grip on Gaza (controlled by siege) and the West Bank.

This is a function of deep history, the overwhelming fear of a second holocaust, fuelled by past wars, rocket and suicide attacks, the existential nuclear threat from Iran, and what ambassador Prosor calls the poisonous 'lie that Israel's destruction is both desirable and imminent'. A blatantly racist passage like this from the Hamas Charter (1988), which could have been lifted straight from *Mein Kampf* and is echoed by the current rhetoric of Iranian President Mahmoud Ahmadinejad, certainly confirms this, and effectively silences those in Israel who argue for dialogue and accommodation with Hamas:

> [Pro-Zionist forces] were behind the French Revolution, the Communist revolution, and most of the revolutions throughout the world ... Concerning local and international wars ... they were behind the First World War in which they destroyed the Islamic Caliphate, picked the material profit, monopolized the raw wealth, and got the Balfour Declaration. They created the League of Nations through which they could rule the world. They were behind the Second World War, in which they grew fabulously wealthy through the arms trade. They prepared for the establishment of their state; they ordered that the United Nations be formed, along with the Security Council, so that they could rule the world through them. There was no war that broke out anywhere without their hands behind it ... Today it is Palestine and tomorrow it may be other countries, because the Zionist scheme has no bounds; after Palestine they want to expand from the Nile River to the Euphrates. When they have occupied the area completely, they look toward another. Such is their plan in the *Protocols of the Elders of Zion*. The present is the best proof of what is said.
>
> (*Hamas Charter* 1988: Articles 22 and 32)

Through bitter experience Israelis have learned that they can rely on no one but themselves. Their security depends on their enemies' fear of the deterrent power of the Israel Defense Forces – Jabotinsky's 'iron wall'. From this perspective, a prime purpose of the December 2008–January 2009 Gaza action was to restore deterrent credibility after the perceived failure of the 2006 campaign against Hezbollah in South Lebanon.

In sum, the strategic root of the Israeli reluctance to respond positively to the API – to regard it as a deceptive and dangerous ploy – lies in *perceived balance of strategic risk*. However great the long-term inducement of a final settlement might be, as the possessor it will be Israel that has first to relinquish its grip on the West Bank in order to reach out for what remains a distant prize offered by those who remain Israel's enemies. So even if the long-term balance of risk of retaining control may be greater, since the short-term risk of letting go is seen to be palpable, immediate, and dangerous, it will never get to the point where decision-makers will irrevocably commit themselves to it.

So it is that all Israeli governments since 1967 have been determined not to lose the 'strategic depth' necessary to make Israel defensible. Even Yitzhak Rabin was clear that he had no intention of permitting a truly independent Palestinian state in this vital area. The rate of increase of Israeli settlements around Jerusalem and on the West Bank itself increased between 1993 and the time of his death in 1995. Ariel Sharon's 1982 blueprint map for the permanent carving-up and subjugation of the West Bank has not been put away. President Bush endorsed a section of it in his April 2004 confirmation that the large settlement blocs on the West Bank should be assigned to Israel.

Looking eastward from the sea, the West Bank is a small piece of territory, beyond which lies the large Palestinian population in Jordan, and beyond that Iraq, and beyond that proto-nuclear Iran, and beyond that the 'Stans' (Kazakhstan etc). If the West Bank is vacated, what forces will pour into the void? When Gaza was vacated, the result was the Hamas take-over and rocket attacks. Israeli intelligence understands exactly how Iran controls its protégés and how military supplies reach Gaza from East Africa. Only preemptive attacks such as the Israeli raid on Sudan in early 2009 can in the end halt supply. Is there any prospect that an immature Palestinian state will be able to control the situation, even if it wanted to? Once ceded, there will be no possibility of reasserting control. The Israeli military-security community is adamant that no possibility of hostile armed forces operating on West Bank territory or airspace is tolerable. This is a one-way ticket. Why should Israel buy it when it gets nothing in return but unreliable and probably disingenuous promises from those who in the past have done all they can to destroy it? That is how the argument goes.

Such is the strategic logic that binds Israelis to current policies – the Catch-22 situation where military control of the West Bank by the IDF renders the building of a Palestinian state to the point that it might be strong enough to take over and control forces hostile to Israel impossible. Some Israelis welcome this. The majority, who sincerely say that they favour an eventual two-state outcome, find that they cannot escape it.

At the time of writing, therefore, the broad challenge that the prevailing Israeli strategic discourse poses for would-be internal and external peacemakers at the level of the Israeli-Palestinian conflict formation to match that given above in relation to Palestinians above is:

Why should Israelis give up violent defence/repression and share power?

Is this not the only thing that has worked in the past? Is it not what has forced Israel's enemies to sue for peace? What can Israelis possibly get in return other than a dramatically increased security risk? Why should Israel abandon everything that has been gained at such cost? Would this not immediately open the floodgates to Israel's worst nightmares?

The strategic engagement of discourses level two: Israeli–Palestinian – the hexagon of radical disagreement

Turning from the promotion of inclusive internal strategic engagement of discourses on both sides separately (SED 1) to the possibilities thus opened up for their extension into a strategic engagement of discourses between the conflict parties (SED 2), the significance of the wider conflict formations is not forgotten – for example the regional power struggles between Israel, Egypt, Saudi Arabia and Iran. It may well be that this is the decisive arena within which the fate of the Palestinians will be decided. But that is beyond the scope of this chapter. The focus here is only on possibilities for strategic discursive exchange at the level of the Israeli–Palestinian conflict formation during a time of maximum conflict intractability.

It has already been seen that the strategic engagement of discourses at intra-party level (SED 1) can lead naturally to some form of inter-party strategic engagement (SED 2), because: strategic thinking looks to the future not the past; strategic thinking prioritizes internal national unity; strategic thinking assesses capability and relative power as well as preference; strategic thinking entails looking at the chessboard from the perspective of the opponent; strategic thinking continually reviews the most appropriate means to attain its strategic ends; and strategic thinking requires the continuous delivery of strategic messages to supporters, opponents, and third parties.

Moreover, it can be seen how, as a result, the existence of internally inclusive strategy groups on both sides at least keeps open the possibility of continuing channels of communication across the spectrum of internal constituencies, even at times of maximum political attrition when other communicative avenues shut down. This is best illustrated by means of the simplest model of inclusive composite two-party strategic discursive engagement – the *hexagon of radical disagreement*. See Figure 7.2.

In this model, there are two conflict parties (A and B), each of which is internally composite (both contain extremists and moderates). This generates six *axes of radical disagreement*. Evidently this is a highly simplified model. There may be

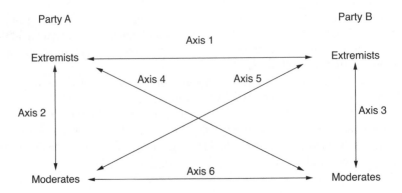

Figure 7.2 The hexagon of radical disagreement

more than two conflict parties. There are many cross-cutting internal divisions. The terms 'extremist' and 'moderate' will vary across different issues and are themselves contested. Third parties have not been included. And so on. Nevertheless, the model is useful for illustrating the main dynamics involved.

Axis 1

Radical disagreement is popularly identified with Axis 1 – the disagreement between extremists (as normally defined). But this is, if anything, the least significant axis. As demonstrated in Chapter 6, it is radical disagreement between moderates (as normally defined) that is by far the most important element. Extremists often feed off each other and are mutually dependent. Leaders who want to resist compromise rely on enemy intransigence and may deliberately provoke it. Extremists play on the well-known psychological and strategic-political dynamics of mutual polarization and escalation:

|'What is called a "peaceful solution" to resolve the Palestinian problem is contrary to the beliefs of the Islamic Resistance Movement, because giving up any part of Palestine means giving up part of religion ... There is no solution to the Palestinian problem except by Jihad.' (Hamas Charter 1988: Article 13)

'No government has the authority ... to abandon parts of the Land of Israel (Eretz Israel) to foreigners, and anything done to this end is null and void, in the name of the God of Israel.' (*Union of Rabbis for the People of Israel and the Land of Israel*, quoted Dershowitz 2005: 46)|

Axes 2 and 3

These constitute level 1 of the SED process. They form the basis for the possibility of strategic engagement between a majority on either side. It is via axes 2 and 3 that the other axes remain operational. It is often here that the most bitter strategic discursive engagements take place – for example, between the American Israel Public Affairs Committee (AIPAC) lobby and the J Street lobby among Jewish Americans.

Axes 4 and 5

These are the exchanges (often indirect) that are only made possible so long as Axes 2 and 3 remain inclusive and Axis 6 remains active. Extremists do not want to participate directly in, or to encourage, these axes of communication (Iranian President Ahmedinejad preferred dealing with US President Bush than with US President Obama). Extremists are more at home in the stark stand-off of Axis 1. These are axes of radical disagreement that SED makes possible and – if the aim is to dilute extremism – promotes.

Axis 6

This is the most crucial – and underrated – axis of radical disagreement. It is easy to assume that, being moderates, there is bound to be agreement across this axis about most of the main issues. But that is not the case in intractable conflicts. On the contrary, this is where the central lines of radical disagreement lie and where agonistic dialogue that explores this is most urgently needed. Chapter 6 showed how it is radical disagreement between moderates like Nadim Rouhana and Mordechai Bar-On that encapsulates the linguistic intractability at the heart of the Palestinian-Israeli conflict. And how, even in a book dedicated to accommodating narratives of conflict to which they were both contributors, this was exactly the strategic exchange that even there did not take place. Exploring and understanding Axis 6 is fundamental to the possibility of managing radical disagreement in intractable political conflicts.

In short, structurally it can be seen that, so long as prior inclusive strategy groups (Axes 2 and 3) are created and maintained on each side, then, even if direct exchanges only take place across axis 6, this is enough to keep channels of communication open generally across all six axes. This allows a possible space for that most crucial (but rare) eventuality – *a strategic engagement of discourses between majorities, issue by issue, on either side*.

This is one of the main mechanisms through which, when dialogue for mutual understanding gains no purchase, dialogue for strategic engagement can nevertheless sustain some sort of contact between the conflict parties.

But there is no reason why this should be conducive to positive management and peacemaking. There is no reason why a majority on either side should be amenable to compromise on any specific issue. This information is vital for peacemakers, but dialogue for strategic engagement does not assume that more contact means more understanding. It may result in the opposite. The SED process does not in itself determine what strategic decisions will be made by conflict parties, nor what will emerge from the promotion of strategic discursive engagement between them. Unlike dialogue for mutual understanding, dialogue for strategic engagement is not necessarily orientated towards peacemaking.

Nevertheless, I would strongly argue that, when there *are* opportunities for movement in the direction of a possible future settlement, it is the promotion of strategic engagement of discourses at level 2 that optimizes chances that these will be noticed and can be acted upon. Strategic discursive engagement raises sails to catch any stray winds that may be blowing. The sails may not catch enough wind to propel the ship forward in a particular preferred direction. But one thing is certain – if the sails are not raised, there will be no motion, however many winds are blowing.

I have already given two reasons why SED 2 can be sustained during periods of intractability – the intrinsic nature of strategic thinking itself, and the capacity of inclusive intra-party strategy groups to keep communication channels open across the spectrum.

There is also a third related reason. This is derived from the difference in strategic thinking between *strategic ends* and *strategic means* as exemplified in *Regaining the Initiative* above, which highlights the crucial distinction between *extremism of ends* and *extremism of means*. The key point is that in managing intractable conflict, there is always scope for detaching violence from ongoing radical disagreement, because it is always possible to pursue uncompromising strategic ends by non-violent means. Mahatma Gandhi, Martin Luther King and Ibrahim Rugova were *extremists of ends* who unwaveringly pursued their strategic objectives – the end of British rule in India, the overthrow of racial discrimination in the US, Kosovan independence – with a view to ultimate victory. They engaged in vigorous radical disagreement and agonistic dialogue with their opponents. As part of their goal to destroy the unjust system, their discursive aim was to eliminate the unjust discourse. Indeed, in order to achieve this, they wanted to *raise* the level of intractable conflict, not to reduce it. Here is King in his famous Lincoln Memorial Address in Washington on August 23 1963:

> We have also come to this hallowed spot to remind America of the fierce urgency of *now*. This is no time to engage in the luxury of cooling off or to take the tranquillising drug of gradualism. *Now* is the time to make real the promises of democracy. The whirlwind of revolt will continue to shake the foundations of our nation until the bright day of justice emerges.
>
> (King 1992/1963: 533–4)

But Gandhi, King and Rugova were *moderates of means*, pursuing their strategic objectives non-violently. All three believed that non-violence was strategically more effective than violence.

We can remind ourselves of the radical disagreement looked at in Chapter 6:

> |'Can even the most moderate and understanding Israeli agree to deny the legitimacy of the Israeli state? Can such an Israeli really be expected to embrace the original sin, or original crime, that Zionism inflicted upon the Palestinians?'

> 'Can even the most moderate and understanding Palestinian agree to deny the legitimacy of Palestinian demands for equal rights in their own homeland? Or be expected to accept responsibility for initiating violence in attempting legitimate resistance to disenfranchisement?'|

This tells us that a majority of those who would normally be called moderates on either side – most Israelis and Palestinians – are, in the context of this radical disagreement, *extremists of ends* on issues such as the rights of Palestinians to rectification of past injustice, or on questions such as recognition, not just of the State of Israel, but, as the current Israeli Prime Minister insists, of Israel as 'the state of the Jewish people'. No Israeli government can acknowledge responsibility for the former and survive. No Palestinian government can recognize the latter and survive. In other words, no matter what settlement may be achieved, the deep core of the conflict, together with its associated radical disagreements, will go on.

The main lesson for peacemakers is to focus on managing the continuing radical disagreement between extremists of ends (who may be a majority on key issues) so that this does not fuel support for extremists of means (who thus remain a minority).

But before moving on to this question, I offer a reminder of what it is at ground level that such engagement seeks to transform. This is the tragic core of the agonistic dialogue that the third party is attempting to address (Brown 2007).

Kenize Mourad travelled through Israel, Gaza and the West Bank in 2002 at the height of the al-Aqsa intifada and at exactly the time the Arab Peace Initiative was being launched. Here is her conclusion, having spent months interviewing 'ordinary Palestinians and Israelis' so that they could 'tell their stories'. It is not surprising that the API did not make an impact in these circumstances:

> During my time there, I was filled with the sense that every encounter was weighted down by a terrible misunderstanding. Manipulated by extremists at either end, most of the people whom I interviewed were convinced that the other side wanted to annihilate them.
>
> (Mourad 2004: 2)

This is an example of a radical disagreement recorded by Mourad involving the mother of the first female Palestinian suicide bomber and the Israeli sister of a bomb victim: the two younger women were both 27:

> |'[My daughter] had joined the Red Cross as a nurse and there she saw the worst. She witnessed atrocious things in Nablus, Jenin, Ramallah – women and children killed when they broke the curfew to go and buy food, wounded people dying without her being able to help. Three times when she had tried to go to people, she had been shot with rubber bullets. She had seen women give birth in front of checkpoints and lose their baby and sick people dying because they could not get to hospital. She told me how she had pleaded in vain with soldiers to let ambulances through … Every night she would come home exhausted and stressed and tell us everything she had seen. She was more and more outraged by what the Israelis were doing to civilians and by the world's indifference. But she never talked to me about the suicide bombings.'

> 'Arafat is no different from Hitler – you can't negotiate with him. Why doesn't the world understand that? How can the world not see that we have nothing but this country? Where can we go? It is the only place we Jews have. The Palestinians want to force us to leave … How can you compare Sharon and Arafat? … Perhaps you think I hate Arabs? Not at all. There are two Arab women in the firm where I work. I don't have any problem with them, even since my sister died. I have nothing against Palestinians or Israeli Arabs. I will never hate them. It's Arafat that I hate. He exploits his people and doesn't give them any means of educating themselves. All he can do is teach them how to kill … You think the Israelis are just as much to blame. You don't understand. You put us on the same level, but it's false. We are not the same. Our soldiers are not there to kill. It's a war and they are defending themselves; sometimes there's an accident, that's all. The Palestinians want a bloodbath. They don't care if they die or if they see

their children dying. You can't compare us and you don't have the right to do that.'|

(Mourad 2004: 76; 80)

Why should Palestinians give up violent resistance and accept dispossession? Why should Israelis give up violent defence/repression and share power? Any answers given by internal and external peacemakers to these questions will have to satisfy this Palestinian mother and this Israeli sister.

The strategic engagement of discourses level three: third-party peacemaking

Third parties are engaged in great numbers at every point in the Israeli-Palestinian conflict and play many different roles. Sometimes they are involved or intervene on their own initiative. Sometimes they are appealed to by conflict parties. Sometimes they are brought in by other third parties. Their discourses compete with each other and with those of the conflict parties to occupy the whole of discursive space. They participate as combatants in the war of words. In this sense, they become conflict parties.

As mentioned in Chapter 4, the introduction of third parties opens the complex network of relations that make up the wider conflict formations within which the Israeli-Palestinian conflict is embedded. The formal definition of a 'third party' depends on the conflict formation under consideration.

In this case, the Quartet formed by the US, Russia, the EU and the UN represents the international community. All are deeply implicated historically in the Israeli-Palestinian conflict. Russia in its former embodiment in the Soviet Union was among the earliest to encourage the creation of the State of Israel and played a highly intrusive role thereafter. Russian immigrants to Israel have had a profound demographic and political impact. The US was at first more ambivalent, at one point in 1948 advising against the setting up of an Israeli State and forcing Israel to withdraw from lands taken in 1956, but is now the main guarantor of Israeli survival. The EU contains Germany, France (provider of Israel's first nuclear reactor in 1957) and the UK, prime actors in the events in question. The UN set up the commission that advised that Palestine be partitioned and the General Assembly voted in support.

Peacemaking analysis repeatedly shows that, given the strategic impasse, it is only a third party that can break the deadlock. At the time of writing (April 2009), all eyes are turned towards the new US administration of President Obama. George Mitchell has been appointed Middle East envoy and the President plans to visit the region next month. This is the period of maximum activity for those who want to influence the US administration. So here, as an example of would-be third-party discursive peacemaking, I take the Executive Summary of *A Last Chance for A Two-State Israel–Palestine Agreement*, presented immediately after the November 2008 Presidential election by the US/Middle East Project. This was a bi-partisan 'statement on US Middle East peacemaking' by ten former senior government officials, including former Democrat National Security Adviser, Zbigniew Brzezinski, and former Republican National Security Adviser, Brent Scowcroft (see Box 7.5). Although by the time the book is published this report will be out of date, it is a useful text for illustrating the main points made here.

Box 7.5 A Last Chance for a Two-State Israel–Palestine Agreement: executive summary

Source: US/Middle East Project 2008: extracts.

We urge the next U.S. administration to engage in prompt, sustained and determined efforts to resolve the Arab-Israeli conflict....

Unless the president tackles this problem early it is unlikely to be done at all. Political capital will erode; domestic obstacles will grow; other issues will dominate; and the warring parties will play for time and run the clock.

Failure to act would be extremely costly. It would not only undermine current efforts to weaken extremist groups, bolster our moderate allies and rally regional support to stabilize Iraq and contain Iran, but would also risk permanent loss of the two-state solution as settlements expand and become entrenched and extremists on both sides consolidate their hold. In short, the next six to twelve months may well represent the last chance for a fair, viable and lasting solution.

To maximise the prospects for success, we urge the following key steps, drawing on lessons from past successes and failures.

1   Present a clear U.S. vision to end the Israeli-Palestinian conflict

The dispute between the two sides is too deep, and the discrepancies of power between them too vast, for them to solve their conflict without the U.S. acting as a determined and evenhanded advocate and facilitator.

The most important step President Obama should take early in his presidency is to flesh out the outlines of a fair, viable and sustainable agreement, based on principles that both Israel and the Palestinians have previously accepted by signing on to UN Security Council Resolutions 242 and 338, the Oslo Accords, the 2003 Road Map, and the 2007 Annapolis understandings. The charge that advancing such principles would constitute improper "outside impositions" is therefore groundless.

The U.S. parameters should reflect the following fundamental compromises:

• Two states, based on the lines of June 4, 1967, with minor, reciprocal, and agreed-upon modifications as expressed in a 1:1 land swap, to take into account areas heavily populated by Israelis in the west Bank;

• A solution to the refugee problem consistent with the two-state solution, that does not entail a general right of return, addresses the Palestinian refugees' sense of injustice, and provides them with meaningful financial compensation as well as resettlement assistance;

• Jerusalem as home to both capitals, with Jewish neighbourhoods falling under Israeli sovereignty and Arab neighbourhoods under Palestinian sovereignty, with special arrangements for the Old City providing each side control of its respective holy places and unimpeded access by each community to them;

• A non-militarized Palestinian state, together with security mechanisms that address Israeli concerns while respecting Palestinian sovereignty, and a U.S.-led multinational force to ensure a peaceful transitional security period. This coalition peacekeeping structure, under UN mandate, would feature American leadership of a NATO force supplemented by Jordanians, Egyptians and Israelis. We can envision a five-year, renewable mandate with the objective of achieving full Palestinian domination of security affairs on the Palestine side of the line within 15 years.

[The Executive Summary ends with advice to 'encourage Israeli-Syrian negotiations', to 'adopt a more pragmatic approach toward Hamas and a Palestinian Unity Government'.]

Readers will have their own views on the particular recommendations made in the Executive Summary of the US/Middle East Project Report. By the time they read this, they will know to what extent the new US administration has acted along the lines recommended here and how successful the new Israeli government has been in postponing any irrevocable move towards a genuinely independent Palestinian state. Perhaps the US administration will try to orchestrate international pressure on Israel, if not use the leverage of its economic and military support. Perhaps the Israeli government will mobilize the pro-Israel lobby in the US press and Congress, or try to deflect attention to Iran and court Saudi fears, or play up the Syrian track as a delaying tactic, or enmesh negotiations in detail and play for time, or work to prevent the consolidation of a united Arab front, or attempt to focus on economic alleviation for Palestinians but not significant political concessions. Or perhaps, conversely, Israel may be induced to make concessions towards a Palestinian state in exchange for a free hand against Iran, and Arab states (Egypt, Saudi Arabia) will connive at such arrangements. Predictions are perilous in complex conflict systems.

But for would-be third-party peacemakers, this example of attempted third-party peacemaking can already demonstrate some of the main lessons to be drawn from a strategic engagement of discourses in intractable conflicts. Lessons can be drawn from all three levels – third-party, inter-party, and intra-party.

Level three

At third-party level, the authors of the Report describe the recommended US intervention as *neutral* (the US is an 'even-handed advocate and facilitator'), *impartial* (the word 'fair' is repeated) and *disinterested* (it is not a case of imposing a US solution). The third level of the strategic engagement of discourses, however, shows why interveners would be wise to accept that in the cauldron of intractable political conflict, it is not up to them to define this. Everything is politicized. The intervention will be widely seen as not even-handed or fair, and to be driven mainly by US regional and global interests – as is, indeed, already explicit in the text. As clarified in Chapter 6, third-party peacemakers want to occupy the whole of discursive space.

Also at *level three* come the complex of relations among other third parties, which includes the containing conflict formations (Arab-Israel, wider Middle East) that are not the focus of this chapter, but may now play the decisive role. Has shared fear of the Iranian threat shifted priorities both for Arab regimes in Cairo and Riyadh, and for the Israeli government – opening the way for concessions on the question of Israeli settlements and moves towards a Palestinian state in exchange? Here the would-be peacemaker can use the knowledge gained from analysis of intra-third party strategic engagement of discourses in general to orchestrate pressure accordingly.

Level two

The strategic engagement of discourses between conflict parties within the conflict configuration in question clarifies the daunting nature of the challenge facing third-party peacemakers in relation to the two chief components of any future settlement. The first is the formulation of a mutually acceptable political framework that reflects relative balance of power and can accommodate unresolved political struggle and continuing radical disagreement. The second is the persuasion of the conflict parties that their undefeated political and moral-religious aspirations are from now on best pursued non-violently.

On the question of political framework, the US/Middle East Report assumes that a 'two-state Israeli–Palestine agreement' is the only viable political framework. But what does this mean? As seen in Chapter 5, it is the *naming* of what is in contention that lies at the heart of linguistic intractability. If and when the new Israeli Prime Minister eventually refers to a 'Palestinian state', what is he naming? Does this bear any resemblance to what Palestinians refer to? And, crucially, how does what Israelis see as the *alternative(s)* to a two-state solution relate to the *alternative(s)* as envisaged by Palestinians – along the lines invoked in *Regaining the Initiative*, for example? Only a strategic engagement of discourses can clarify this so that third-party peacemakers can act accordingly.

On the question of a possible renunciation of violence, the strategic engagement of discourses specifies what is required of the two linked tasks.

Within the disputed framework, Palestinians must be persuaded that giving up violent resistance and accepting a settlement, far from amounting to capitulation and dispossession, represents the most potent way to continue the struggle and reach the strategic goal of a final rectification of injustice. A key argument for the challenging discourse here – as in Northern Ireland – is that a definitive giving up of violent resistance will put *more* pressure on Israel to shift in the desired direction, not *less*. As also that it may be *through* a two-state solution that a 'one-state outcome' – perhaps in the form of some future confederation between the two states – will be most easily attained, however remote the idea may seem at the moment. The horizon may be 50 years or more. But the rights of those unjustly expelled have not been abandoned. The Palestinian fear, as made clear in *Regaining the Initiative*, is that to make this move will be to fall into the Israeli trap of a 'quasi-state' and result in the Palestinian cause being ignored, not only by Israelis, but also by the Arab world and the international community. Third-party peacemakers have to focus all their persuasive powers on meeting this fear and persuading Palestinians that, on the contrary, this is the only way to secure full and sustained international support for a genuine, sovereign and independent Palestinian state – a transformation that will then make all other things possible.

The possessor, in this case the Israelis, must be persuaded that ending violent repression and sharing power is the most effective way to maximize gains over the longer term. Is the possessor 'doing all the giving'? Yes, in the sense that it is already in possession of what is disputed. If the possessor has a monopoly of power, it can keep everything with impunity. The enemy has been definitively defeated. But in ongoing intractable conflict this is, by definition, not the case. The question then is: what cards does the possessor have to play, and when, in order to stabilize its gains at the maximum level possible? Israel made peace with Egypt in 1979. When, if ever, will the strategic calculation be seen to favour peace with Palestinians? It is always timing that is of the essence in wise and flexible strategic thinking. Third party peacemakers need to convince key Israeli advisers and decision-makers that the moment is now – the driving consideration once again is not giving up and compromise, but maximizing long-term gains and winning. The Israeli fear is that to relinquish control is to open the floodgates through which their sworn enemies will swiftly pour. The third-party peacemaker has to be prepared to do everything that is necessary to allay this fear.

The US/Middle East Report makes several concrete proposals of a familiar kind: on the determination of future borders (including Israeli settlers), the right of return of Palestinian refugees, the status of Jerusalem, security arrangements, economic resource control and management. This is a well-worn litany repeated with variations through the 2000 Clinton parameters, the 2001 Taba discussions, the 2002 Arab Peace Initiative, the informal 2003 Geneva accords, and so on. 'Everybody knows what a final settlement will look like' is the common refrain. But the strategic engagement of discourses shows that everyone does not know what a final settlement will look like. That is the problem. For example, a land-swap to accommodate Israeli West Bank settlements inside Israeli borders entails equivalent incorporation of largely Arab-populated territory currently in Israel into a new Palestinian state. What are the views of the Arab Israelis/Palestinian citizens of Israel affected? Indeed, should Arab Israelis/Palestinians in Israel not form a distinct inclusive strategy group as part of the SED process – as has to some extent already happened (the Haifa Declaration)?

In short, the main lesson for third-party peacemakers from the strategic engagement of discourses is that in making peace between undefeated conflict parties, the language to use is not the language of compromise or giving up. It is the language of strategic victory. The proposed settlement means that the conflict party in question will *win*. Above all, those who need to be convinced on either side and to be transformed into peacemakers are not the habitual doves, but precisely the extremists of ends who, the strategic engagement of discourses shows, are a *majority* on both sides on the existential issues. The settlement is not itself the terminus and end of conflict. The conflict – and the radical disagreements that go with it – continues. The precious gift that third-party peacemakers have to offer is *hope*. This is taken further in Chapter 8.

Level one

And now the great benefit of all the hard work that has gone into the level one inclusive intra-party strategic engagement of discourses becomes available.

Supplied with this information, third-party peacemakers can learn in detail, issue by issue, how each element in the list of specific recommendations plays among the various internal constituencies. *The focal point here would be to channel third-party efforts through small groups of influential military, security and political advisers and opinion-formers on each side.* This would be developed further in a more detailed study. It includes vital insight into the make-up of cross-cutting sub-groups – who the pragmatists and ideologues are within Hamas on different issues, or which ultra-orthodox Jewish groups oppose Zionism and in what ways. Under-tested areas of strategy can also be analysed – for example, how true is it that economic factors are decisive and that challengers will accept political and ideological compromise in return for the future prospect of material well-being? Is the current Netanyahu strategy of economic peace likely to work? Why not ask?

If the new US strategy to be announced in a few weeks from the time of writing follows anything like the line suggested in this Report, it will be closely akin to what I earlier called the 'argument for an Israeli Peace Initiative'. Although Palestinians would have many difficulties with it, at the moment it is most profoundly at odds with prevailing Israeli strategy. In that case, third-party peacemakers will find themselves on course for a head-on collision with one of the conflict parties. They will need all the skill they can muster to win the resulting discursive battles, at the different levels of the interlocking conflict formations, along the lines indicated above.

Conclusion: let words die, not people

In intractable conflicts in which dialogue for mutual understanding proves premature, it is dialogue for strategic engagement that offers the best hope for conflict management in the discursive sphere. This may not deliver a settlement. It is not pre-negotiation. Nor is it even pre-pre-negotiation. But at least all the sails are kept up and spread to catch any hopeful gusts of wind that may unexpectedly arise. Otherwise, without sails permanently hoisted, it will be much more likely to be a continuing story of mistiming and missed opportunities.

The idea is not to muzzle or silence radical disagreement, but, on the contrary, to amplify and develop it. It is to promote the war of words so that the full lineaments of linguistic intractability can be seen and understood. In this way, the struggle between the challenging discourse, the hegemonic discourse and the third-party (peacemaking) discourse becomes manifest. This clarifies what is at issue and what each of the competing discourses has to do in order to prevail.

The promotion of an inclusive internal strategic engagement of discourses is undoubtedly good for the challenging discourse. It is more likely to lead to wise, flexible and realistic strategies for attaining transformative goals including back-up strategies in case first preferences fail. It helps to clarify what messages need to be sent to opponents and third parties and when. It maximizes active and orchestrated participation and support to mobilize the full energies of the people behind the national project. It sustains determination and hope.

I would strongly argue that promotion of an inclusive internal strategic engagement of discourses is also in the interest of the hegemonic discourse by helping to ensure that no strategy goes untested or uncriticized. The process does not dictate which particular outcome will prevail. But it helps to ensure that the pilots are not flying blind and that the rapidly opening and closing opportunities for a safe landing are noticed in time. 'Default' strategy and instinctive reliance on brute power is highly vulnerable to wishful thinking and strategic sclerosis.

In both cases it is ongoing strategic engagement of discourses that best clarifies the shifting cost-benefit analysis that can provide the best incentive for a peace process (Strategic Foresight Group 2009). A sustained strategic engagement of discourses of this kind was missing in the 1990s in support an apparent break-through. And it was missing after 2000 to help fill the dangerous vacuum after the collapse of the Camp David talks. It will be needed in the current peace efforts, both if they succeed (the immediate post-settlement period is often the most dangerous) and if they fail.

Unlike dialogue for mutual understanding, dialogue for strategic engagement has no natural bias towards peacemaking. It is up to the conflict parties and third parties to conduct their own strategic thinking and reach their own conclusions. But I have suggested four ways in which a strategic engagement of discourses can at least provide communication channels and vital information for peacemakers, when all other avenues have shut down:

1 the inherent nature of strategic thinking itself, as exemplified in the six points noted earlier in this chapter;
2 the possibility of interchange permanently held open by the promotion of inclusive intra-party strategic groups, as exemplified in the hexagon of radical disagreement;
3 the light continually cast by the SED process on the constantly changing relation between extremism of ends and extremism of means, and the consequent early warning of danger and openings for peace;
4 the detailed information constantly made available for internal and external peacemakers, with consequent invaluable guidance on whom to put pressure on and how, at the three SED levels commented upon above.

Even when this is not the case, and no realistic possibilities for a sustainable settlement have yet emerged, at least the quality of systemic strategic thinking fully cognisant of the complex conflict environment may be improved. Perhaps promotion of the battle of discourses may rule out some of the worst decisions for action in advance. Perhaps in this way, and to this extent, it may even be that, more often than would otherwise be the case, words will die rather than people.

Notes

1 The Directors of the ORG EU project were Gabrielle Rifkind (Director of the ORG Middle East programme) and Ahmed Badawi; the Palestinian track was advised and guided by Husam Zomlot and facilitated by Ahmed Badawi; the Israeli track was led

by Avner Haramati, Mario Schejtman and Ofer Zalzberg, with workshop methodology devised and conducted by Adam Kahane assisted by Shay Ben Yosef and Tova Averbuch. Oliver Ramsbotham is Chair of ORG and has been a major contributor to the project, as has Middle East expert Tony Klug.

2 The Oxford Research Group played a modest but quite influential part in this, convening a three-day meeting in November 2008 between leading Arabs, Israelis and internationals to determine ways in which the API could be moved higher up the agenda – particularly in Israel.

8 Re-entry

Feeding back into conflict settlement and conflict transformation

When the management of radical disagreement via a strategic engagement of discourses is successful, conflict parties otherwise not amenable to transformative dialogic approaches are brought to a point where they may have an incentive to participate. Dialogue for mutual understanding again becomes possible, space for conflict settlement is opened up, and continuous monitoring and exploration of radical disagreement can play a key role in early warning for prevention and postwar reconstruction. In these circumstances, the strategic engagement of discourses is a pump-primer for conflict resolution.

But difficult questions remain. In what circumstances is dialogue for strategic engagement not possible? Can it make things worse? How does it impact on relative discrepancies of power in asymmetric conflicts? What when conflict parties conclude that violence works? Who are the enemies of peace and how should they be dealt with? Answers to these questions lead to a reconsideration of the roles of moderates, peacemakers and spoilers in intense political conflicts when radical disagreement is ongoing.

In Chapter 4, objections to the enterprise of taking radical disagreement seriously in conflict resolution, discourse analysis and conflict analysis were bracketed. This opened the way for the phenomenology, epistemology and praxis of radical disagreement – exploring, understanding and managing the agonistic dialogue between enemies that constitutes linguistic intractability. The claim in Chapter 7 was that, in intractable conflicts, it is only by actively promoting a strategic engagement of discourses – by taking the war of words itself seriously – that the full force of the discursive battle is grasped, intra- and inter-conflict party verbal exchanges are kept open, and conflict parties – including third-party peacemakers – learn best what is required if they are to prevail.

Chapters 8, 9 and 10 now unbracket the objections from conflict resolution, discourse analysis and conflict analysis outlined in Part I in order to see how much of the investigation undertaken in Part II survives.

This chapter unbrackets *conflict resolution*. Conflict resolution is taken as a generic term that encompasses *conflict settlement* at one level and *conflict transformation* at another. See Figure 8.1.

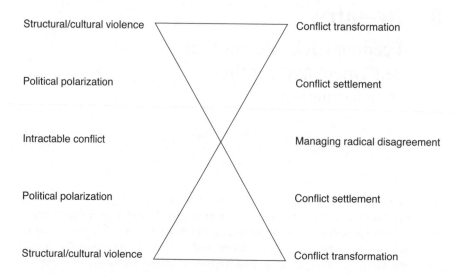

Moving from the top to the bottom, the hourglass model illustrates in highly schematic form the escalation and de-escalation of intense political conflict. The two triangles represent decreasing political space during the escalation phase (the top triangle), and increasing political space during the de-escalation phase (the bottom triangle). The aim of conflict resolution is to maximize political space. It aims to prevent escalation by addressing underlying structural and cultural violence, and by settling disputes once conflict parties have formed and polarized (top triangle). If this fails, it tries to contain and end direct violence as soon as possible, to achieve some form of political settlement, and then to (re)build sustainable peace by transforming the structural and cultural exclusions, exploitations and inequities that might otherwise ignite another cycle of conflict (bottom triangle). It can be seen that the management of radical disagreement offers a means of maintaining channels of communication and keeping open possibilities for future settlement and transformation at the point of zero political space – when conflict settlement and conflict transformation themselves can no longer or cannot yet gain purchase.

Figure 8.1 The hourglass model of conflict escalation and de-escalation

The chapter begins by revisiting the conflict resolution enterprise of dialogue for mutual understanding in general, and then moves on to conflict settlement and conflict transformation. Conflict transformation includes attempts to prevent violent conflict pre-war, and attempts to build sustainable peace post-war.

Radical disagreement and dialogue for mutual understanding

Before looking at the promotion of a strategic engagement of discourses in relation to conflict settlement and conflict transformation, it is worth revisiting the rich tradition of constructive dialogue and problem solving looked at in Chapter 3. What contribution, if any, can the exploration of agnostic dialogue (Chapter 5) and dialogue for strategic engagement (Chapter 7) make to dialogue for mutual understanding in general?

The Gadamerian approach to dialogue – recognizing and thereby overcoming prejudice through a fusion of horizons that creates a 'third culture' – is close to David Bohm's idea that in genuine dialogue, participants attempt to overcome these 'blocks' by suspending judgement:

> What is called for is to suspend those assumptions, so that you neither carry them out nor suppress them. You don't believe them, nor do you disbelieve them: you don't judge them as good or bad …
>
> (Bohm 1996: 22)

Perhaps here, the exploration of agnostic dialogue and dialogue for strategic engagement can help bridge those situations where conflict parties do not recognize their prejudice and are not ready to suspend judgement.

I think that something like this applies generally across the field of dialogue for social change. For example, the authors of *Mapping Dialogue* (2006) see the 'underlying structure' of dialogue for mutual understanding as a process of divergence followed by convergence:

> The *divergent* phase of a process is a time of opening up possibility. It is about generating alternatives, gathering diverse points of view, allowing disagreement in, and suspending judgment. We are often afraid of really opening up, to allow for full divergence to occur, because we are uncomfortable, or even fearful of the messiness of too many new and divergent ideas and perspectives. Yet the greater the divergence at the beginning of the process, the greater the possibility of surprising and innovative outcomes.
>
> (Pioneers of Change Associates 2006: 13)

But what when the disagreements that are 'allowed in' during the divergent phase are radical, that is to say, when they cannot be described merely as 'divergent views', but involve fiercely contested political incompatibilities? Once again, I think that in these circumstances, dialogue for strategic engagement offers additional resources to keep parties engaged who would otherwise drop away. One example is Harold Saunder's Sustained Dialogue approach, which focuses on underlying relationships linked to identity, interests, power, perceptions of the other, and patterns of interaction. This approach has proved effective in conflict arenas such as Tajikistan (Saunders 1999). In this approach, there are five stages of sustained dialogue. Dealing with disagreement comes at the beginning of stage two, when stories are told, grievances are expressed, and an attempt is made to 'clear the air'. At the end of stage two, the conversation changes:

> 'Me' becomes 'We'. 'What' becomes 'Why'. Participants shift from speaking 'to' each other to speaking 'with' each other.
>
> (Ibid.: 60)

In this case, I think that dialogue for strategic engagement may help to handle those situations in which conflict parties are unable, or unwilling, to move from 'me' to 'we' at such an early stage in the programme, or from 'what' to 'why', or from speaking 'at', to speaking 'with' each other.

An example from the Israeli-Palestinian conflict is the long-standing *Israeli-Palestinian School of Peace* project, which goes back to 1972, when Arab and Jewish Israelis created a joint village – Neve Shalom/Wahat El Salam (Oasis of Peace) – to embody peace and reconciliation in their daily lives. At first, the emphasis in the School of Peace was on individual relationships. Then, it came to be accepted that collective identities could not be ignored and needed to be explicitly worked through. Arabs and Jews meet uni-nationally as well as bi-nationally, and one of the tasks of the uni-national groups is to negotiate wide internal differences. There is also a focus on political inequalities, with Arab-Israeli participants often expressing resentment about disempowerment and needing to overcome initial feelings of inferiority, and Jewish-Israeli participants needing to acknowledge the equality of their fellow-citizens and shed instinctive feelings of superiority. These groups are regarded as microcosms of Israeli society, and the process aims to redress mutual ignorance and bring Arab and Jewish Israelis together to shape a common Israeli future. But what is to be done when Arab Israelis challenge the very basis of a democratic Jewish state, or when Jewish Israelis question whether such citizens should be part of it? Perhaps dialogue for strategic engagement may help to sustain communication even across such chasms (Halabi and Sonneschein 2004).

An example from Northern Ireland is provided by the Corrymeela Community, whose founder, Ray Davey, describes the remarkable transformative potential that dialogue for mutual understanding can have between individuals from divided societies:

> When Sean and Damian, from a Catholic inner-city school in Derry, agreed to come on the weekend, they feared that they would be in the minority, and no-one would be prepared to listen to their experiences and views. So they arrived wearing sweatshirts ablaze with the colours and the flag they supported, and brandishing slogans proclaiming their cause. Then, expecting to be put down by their opponents, they adopted a macho image, projecting their outlook in the most aggressive tones. Their first surprise was to discover that they were not in the minority. Their second was when they learnt that many of the other Catholics present did not share their political outlook. Their biggest surprise was to discover that most of the others were prepared to accept without reaction their dress, listen calmly to what they said, and ask them why they felt that way rather than arguing back.
>
> As the weekend went on their voices went down by decibels, their aggressive behaviour subsided, and they acknowledged that they were not sure themselves about all of the most extreme positions they had proclaimed on the Friday night. Most importantly on Sunday at the final worship they said that the group gave them hope that it was possible to pursue change through negotiation rather than force as the only way that people will consider. As a

result they planned to meet together with others of the group in their home town and keep in touch and hopefully to come back to Corrymeela.

(Davey 1993: 135)

When this works, there is no more to be said. But perhaps the exploration agnostic dialogue and dialogue for strategic engagement could usefully supplement the process in cases where the other does answer back, or political differences are too stark to be bridged in this way, or 'contact', far from helping to ameliorate the situation, only serves to make things worse.

Finally, an example from South Africa is offered by Adam Kahane's Montfleur process (Kahane 2007). In 1991, after Nelson Mandela's release from prison and at a time of great uncertainly in South Africa, Kahane convened a group of 22 leading figures from across the political and social spectrum in South Africa to explore and discuss possible future scenarios for the country. Participants came from the white business and academic community, and included leaders from the main challenging parties (including the ANC, PAC, South African Communist Party). Over a period of months, the group identified and explored four scenarios in relation to the question: *How will the transition go, and will the country succeed in 'taking off'?* In the first scenario (the ostrich), the white government tries to avoid a negotiated settlement. In the second scenario (the lame duck), the transition takes too long in an unsuccessful attempt to satisfy everyone. In the third scenario (Icarus), a black government takes power and bankrupts the economy by over-spending. In the fourth scenario (the flight of the flamingos), the transition is successful and all South Africans rise slowly together. The group ended by unanimously choosing the fourth scenario as the best blueprint. This was a very successful and influential exercise. Clearly, in this case, there was no need for a supplementary methodology because the process worked perfectly. But perhaps dialogue for strategic engagement might be useful where the former hegemon is in a stronger position than was the tottering apartheid regime, and where all participants do not agree on a joint scenario (in this case, even the names of the three rejected scenarios were pejorative).

At this point, it is worth revisiting Heidi and Guy Burgess' 'Constructive Confrontation' approach to transforming intractable conflicts, looked at in Chapter 4:

Constructive confrontation is a way to approach resolution-resistant conflicts that utilizes the best aspects of consensus-based conflict resolution processes, but does not require consensus to be effective. It can be used by disputants themselves, or by third parties who want to help individual or multiple parties confront these conflicts in the most effective way. Rather than replacing negotiation or consensus-based techniques, we see constructive confrontation as a complementary process that can be used when traditional consensus-building has failed or appears unlikely to yield a consensual agreement.

(Burgess and Burgess 1997: 9)

Burgess and Burgess have developed Constructive Confrontation primarily to deal with unavoidably intractable public policy conflicts. The ultimate goal is still to transform conflictual into cooperative relationships by stressing the primacy of 'community values over selfish values' (1996: 320). But the emphasis is on process and incremental improvements rather than comprehensive resolution, within a frame that shifts emphasis away from short-term disputes to a 'long-term view of the underlying conflict'. Conflict parties are encouraged to develop approaches that serve their own interests, but in the light of an awareness of other parties involved and of principles of justice and fairness. The diagnosis distinguishes 'core issues' from 'overlay problems' such as misunderstandings, fact-finding problems, escalation dynamics, and procedural controversies. Power relations are addressed by empowerment of conflict parties through the encouragement of intra-coalition consensus building and external assistance in advocacy by 'constructive confrontation advisers'.

There is much in common with dialogue for strategic engagement here, as acknowledged in Chapter 4. But I think that the focus on radical disagreement, agonistic dialogue and linguistic intractability makes dialogue for strategic engagement more directly adapted to the kinds of intractable conflict mainly considered in this book, rather than the public policy arena from which constructive confrontation has come. So perhaps dialogue for strategic engagement, and the strategic engagement of discourses that it promotes, may have something to add in cases where the question of 'incremental' vs 'final state' processes is part of what is at issue – for example Israelis as possessors favour the first, Palestinians as challengers the second. Or the distinction between 'core issues' and 'overlay problems' is itself embroiled – for example, core issues include questions such as whether there has been misunderstanding or what counts as fact-finding. Or appeals to justice and fairness are themselves contested – it is the very distinction between these distinctions and what they do/do not distinguish that lies at the heart of the dispute.

Radical disagreement and conflict settlement

At the core of the extensive literature on conflict settlement is the question of how to facilitate agreement between undefeated conflict parties. This book deals with intractable conflicts where, by definition, settlement has not yet proved possible. In terms of Friedrich Glasl's 'U-procedure' the focus in this book has been on the *gap* between his four 'diagnostic stages' that 'take us step by step from a description of factual, observable behaviour to the deeper, underlying assumptions and principles which govern behaviour' on the one hand, and his 'new maxims' that transform the conflict in stages five to seven on the other (Glasl 2008: 48). Chapter 7 suggested ways in which, even in these circumstances, a three-level strategic engagement of discourses might help prepare the ground for an eventual resumption of efforts at direct settlement. But now it is worth considering briefly what happens when the search for a settlement does succeed. Is this suddenly the end of radical disagreement? In the light of what has been seen earlier in Part II, my response is that in the case of undefeated, and as yet unreconciled antagonists, I do not think so.

As seen in Chapter 7, the heart of the settlement in these cases is usually a framework that reflects relative strength at the time (military and non-military), together with an arrangement whereby challengers have been induced to give up violent resistance, and possessors have been induced to give up violent repression and share power. But the undefeated parties have not yet surrendered their long-term aspirations or dreams. What Glasl calls the 'cognitive turning point', 'the 'emotional turning point' and the 'intentional turning point' are not yet complete (2008: 47). They have been persuaded that their continuing incompatible strategic goals are now best served by different strategic means. In short, the core of the settlement is what I call 'Clausewitz in reverse' – not the end of the conflict, but its transmutation into a different – and it is hoped permanently non-violent – form.[1]

The misconception that settlement means an end to conflict is encapsulated in the popular misnomers that the aim of conflict resolution is 'conflict prevention' or 'post-conflict reconstruction', whereas the proper aim is to transform actually or potentially violent conflict into non-violent forms of ongoing political struggle. Conflict lies at the heart of all serious politics. And radical disagreement, as its chief linguistic manifestation, remains integral to it.

The Middle East conflict is often compared to conflicts in South Africa and Northern Ireland. In this respect, what can the latter teach the former?

In South Africa, Nelson Mandela did not give up his long-term strategic goal in the confrontation with apartheid. In this sense, like Gandhi and Martin Luther King, he was an extremist of ends. Although he still had testing conflicts to manage within the black majority, it became plain relatively soon after his release from prison in 1991 that the white minority dominance that he had devoted his life to bringing down was effectively finished, despite what seemed at the time a dangerous rearguard resistance. He showed great skill and vision in reassuring the former hegemons that they would not be victimized in the transfer of power, but the outcome was decisive. The discourse of apartheid was defeated. Mandela's discourse triumphed. Mandela's achievement at this stage was to be magnanimous and wise in victory.

In Northern Ireland, in contrast, the settlement was made between undefeated parties. In this sense, it is nearer to the Israeli-Palestinian case. A changing complex conflict environment constantly closes and opens opportunities for settlement. Changing relations between the Irish and British governments within the EU played a major role, as did economic transformation in the Irish Republic. The mediation role of centrist politicians like John Hume of the SDLP was important. But, whatever the systemic nuances, at the strategic core of the Good Friday Agreement of April 1998 was the willingness of the challengers (republicans) to give up violent resistance and of the possessors (loyalists) to share power. As with the Palestinians, the fear of the challenger was that to give up armed resistance was to give up the challenge. As with the Israelis, the fear of the possessor was that to share power was to give up possession. What each feared was defeat. And the art of the peacemaker was to persuade both that, on the contrary, their continuing incompatible strategic goals (a united Ireland, a permanent union with the UK) were more likely to succeed through an agreed non-violent but power-sharing framework.

So it was that both republicans and loyalists hailed the Good Friday Agreement of April 1998 (and in the case of the DUP, the St Andrews Agreement of October 2006) as a victory. This is, indeed, the 'discursively paradoxical reality' so carefully and revealingly charted by political discourse analysis (Hayward and O'Donnell eds forthcoming 2010):

> [I]t can be claimed that the ambiguity of the language of the Agreement has allowed the creation of a discursively paradoxical reality which is manifested through different nuances of discourse, which lie, in turn, at the heart of the success of the peace process as we know it today.
>
> (Filardo forthcoming 2010)

The key point here is that in the years leading up to the Good Friday Agreement, settlement only became possible when the Sinn Fein/IRA leadership decided that, in altered circumstances, the unchanged strategic goal of a united Ireland would now be more likely to succeed by non-violent means – the political route would in future be more effective than a continuation of the armed struggle. Gerry Adams, the Sinn Fein leader, like former IRA prisoners and nearly all staunch republicans, continued and continues to interpret the conflict in exactly the way he did before the peace deal and, as a result, openly expects to achieve a united Ireland in the near future. Some have said that this is disappointing – that he should now be using the language of political moderation and reconciliation. But it is *because* he has been unwavering in his radical political disagreement with the unionists (he has remained an extremist of ends) that he has not been politically 'outbid' and therefore outflanked by more than a handful of IRA die-hards (extremists of means). He has succeeded in carrying the bulk of the republican movement with him in the decision that continuing and unchanged republican political goals are now best attained non-violently. A brief glance at the Sinn Fein website makes this clear.

Political discourse analysis also shows the same to be true of loyalist counterparts. They, too, have not changed their ultimate strategic goal of maintaining the union indefinitely. This may explain why, contrary to some people's expectations, whatever role may have been played by centrist politicians in helping to bring about the initial agreement, once it had been secured, centrist parties (Alliance, SDLP) suffered heavy electoral losses.

This is the main lesson for the Israeli-Palestinian conflict from the Northern Ireland case. The settlement does not end the conflict, nor does it end the radical disagreement that is part of it. It transmutes it into non-violent mode to be fought out – in the Northern Ireland case – constitutionally. Conflict parties still retain their dreams. Republicans dream of a United Ireland. Loyalists dream of a perpetual Union. They have not given them up.

This lesson has not been lost on other challenging groups. In May 2009, Murad Karayilan, acting leader of the Kurdistan Workers' Party (PKK), offered an end to the 25-year war of independence with Turkey in which 30,000 had lost their lives:

Kurds do not want to continue the war. We believe we can solve the Kurdish question without spilling more blood. We are ready for a peaceful and democratic solution in Turkey – to be solved within Turkey's borders.

(*The Times* 26 May 2009)

Was this a capitulation on behalf of the 12 million Turkish Kurds? Not in the eyes of the Kurdish leader:

Britain accepted the will of the Scots by giving them a parliament of their own, and that's what the Turks have to do with us.

His eyes were on the distant horizon. Scots today have the chance of full independence after 300 years of union. Their future is in their own hands. Kurds can plan accordingly. Alsace-Lorraine was fought over between France and Germany for a century. The 'two-state' option of partition (Lorraine to France, Alsace to Germany) never transpired. In the end, France won. But now there is open access and freedom of movement.

Settlement between undefeated conflict parties does not terminate the conflict or the radical disagreements associated with it, but transmutes them. Only by continuing to take the ongoing radical disagreements seriously can the settlement be consolidated and made secure. As noted in Chapter 7, ongoing strategic engagement of discourses is needed both to underpin apparent success and to provide fall-back positions in case of apparent failure. That is the chief way in which the management of radical disagreement remains relevant even when the door is at last opened once again for conflict settlement, and – beyond that – eventual conflict transformation.

Radical disagreement and conflict transformation

The primary task of conflict transformation – to overcome structural and cultural violence and to lift conflict parties out of the mire of antagonism into wider relations and visions that can accommodate paradox, inclusiveness and diversity – is a long way from the embattled terrain of intractable conflict where dialogue for strategic engagement is rooted. But the previous section has already suggested why taking the phenomenon of radical disagreement seriously, and continuing to manage it accordingly, is also of significance for early warning, both in the prevention of violent conflict (the top triangle in the hourglass model) and in post-war peacebuilding (the bottom triangle).

Preventing violent conflict

The enterprise of early warning and prevention of violent conflict has been a major international enterprise, particularly since the end of the cold war (see Ramsbotham, Woodhouse and Miall 2005: 106–31). The well-known *Carnegie Commission Report* of 1997, for example, distinguished 'structural prevention' that addresses underlying causes from 'operational prevention' that addresses particular confrontations once they have formed (Carnegie Commission 1997). This follows from earlier studies of conflict escalation that point to a pattern where failure to satisfy basic human economic, political, security and identity needs provides fertile soil for violent conflict, but whether this in the event leads to the formation of political groupings, polarization and the emergence of armed resistance depends on strategic choices made by possessor and challenger leaders and their mutual impact (Azar 1990).

Ted Gurr's analysis of 'minorities at risk' concludes that on average it takes 15 to 20 years from the first manifestation of an organized political challenge to the outbreak of armed conflict – for example in Sri Lanka or Kosovo or the formation of the Taleban (Gurr 2000). This is the window of opportunity during which taking the phenomenon of radical disagreement seriously gives ample notice and clarifies what needs to be done to keep unfulfilled political aspirations separate from militarization and the control of those who espouse extremism of means, and to minimize the chances of uncontrolled escalation. It gives detailed early warning of three fatal rubicons that are very hard to reverse once they have been crossed:

1 the transition from internal discontent to a direct challenge to the state (its nature in ideological conflicts, its integrity in secessionist conflicts, control of its resources in economic conflicts);
2 the moment when police and judiciary are no longer seen by significant communities as administering impartial law;
3 the formation of armed militia and the counter-violence of forcible repression.

At these points, intransigent leaders on both sides are much more likely to rise to the surface, exert control over their constituencies, and increase the momentum towards war. It is too late to put the genie back into the bottle. Systemic reinforcers of intractability and intransigence lock in.

Post-war reconstruction and peacebuilding

At the other end of the spectrum is post-war reconstruction – another extensive topic that cannot be properly covered here (see Ramsbotham, Woodhouse and Miall 2005: 185–245). But once again the phenomenology of radical disagreement – the exploration of the agonistic dialogue associated with linguistic intractability – offers indicators of progress or lack of progress that cannot be secured in any other way.

Since, as seen, the cessation of direct violence between undefeated conflict parties is a transmutation of conflict, not an end to it, it is not surprising that the failure rate of interim settlements is high (Hampson 1996; Doyle and Sambanis 2006). Radical disagreement persists into the post-settlement environment and has to be managed in circumstances that are often increasingly volatile. The conflicting interpretations of the settlement, deliberately left ambiguous, often become more difficult to accommodate as the terms and consequences of the settlement become clearer.

And there are other, much studied, factors that dictate that conditions will deteriorate further before they finally improve. Increased levels of conflict are seen by most analysts to be likely in weakened or divided post-war states seriously depleted by long periods of fighting. Mutual loss and victimization is compounded by disillusionment at lack of quick economic returns, the cumulative disappointment of thwarted political interests, unemployment among returning refugees and former combatants, the frustrations of those who had profited from the fighting, or ideologically irreconcilable 'spoilers' inside and outside the country implacably opposed to the settlement. In the post-cold war world the prevailing convention for how to end major violent conflicts has been to rely on *democratization, market economies*, and *regulatory justice systems* as long-term underpinnings for sustainable peace. During the transition phase all three increase instability and conflict – elections create power struggles, markets generate economic competition, judicial reform stokes up the fight for legal redress.

This is the arena in which constant awareness of the level and nature of radical disagreement gives early warning of danger while there is time to counter it, warns against complacency, and teaches that the challenges of post-war reconstruction are not to be underestimated.

Difficult questions

Chapter 7 and Chapter 8 up to this point have been written from a broadly conflict resolution perspective. Dialogue for strategic engagement in intractable conflicts has been treated as a placeholder for a possible future revival of settlement and transformation approaches. And, when settlement and transformation become possible, the strategic engagement of discourses has been seen to retain its relevance as a source of early warning and information. The exploration, understanding and management of radical disagreement has been treated as an extension of or pump-primer for conflict resolution.

But at this juncture I have to part company with that assumption. I have to face a number of difficult questions that challenge the idea that taking radical disagreement seriously and exploring agonistic dialogue can always – or even often – play that role.

When is dialogue for strategic engagement not possible or appropriate?

Are there circumstances in which even a strategic engagement of discourses is not possible or appropriate? How typical is the Israeli-Palestinian case?

What when brutal authoritarian regimes crush opposition and succeed in silencing discursive challenge – as in Myanmar (Burma), or North Korea, or the Chinese suppression of Tibet? What when a hegemon is ruthless in monopolizing internal control – like the late Velupillai Prabhakaran and the LTTE in Sri Lanka? What when extremism of means is integral to strategic ends – as in the case of al-Qaeda? What when the conflict is not about political or ideological differences, but about economic gain – not 'grievance' but 'greed' – as in the drug wars in Mexico? What when the war zone has disintegrated into a chaotic confusion of clan- or family-based factions where fighting has become a means of sustenance and a way of life – as in Somalia?

When does dialogue for strategic engagement make things worse?

What of the possibility – or is it probability – that promoting a strategic engagement of discourses may deepen rather than alleviate conflict intractability? Is it not likely that the focus on incompatibilities, divisions and strategies for victory will, as noted in Chapter 3, just stoke up antagonism and make conflict parties realize all the more clearly why they hate and fear each other? Does this not link to the culture critique, which says that the whole idea of radical disagreement and a strategic engagement of discourses is western and inappropriate in cultures based on different practices, conventions and ways of life? Does it not just make things worse to introduce or encourage such oppositional approaches?

Is dialogue for strategic engagement not superficial, if not counter-productive, in relation to the systemic structures of domination, oppression and exclusion?

What of the deep systemic drivers of conflict, such as the profound structural inequalities and manipulations of power that characterize late capitalism and are studied through critical political economy analysis? What when it is the international system itself that generates exploitation and oppression? All of this is prior to the emergence of conflict parties and dictates why protest and challenge is stifled before it appears.

This is part of a wider critique of the whole peace industry. The critical theoretic question 'whose peace?' is conjoined to the question 'whose justice?' (Pugh *et al.* eds 2009). And the answer regularly given is 'not a form of peace and justice that is in the interest of the weak and vulnerable'. 'Victor's peace' may have evolved into various hybrid forms of the 'liberal peace' that now shape prevailing international norms and institutions (Richmond 2005). But this is still seen to retain its original character, stamped in the image and interest of the dominant epistemic community of Western nations that created it, and subsequently exported it to the rest of the world. Conflict on the unruly periphery of global capitalism is seen to be contained and policed by the hegemonic powers in their own interest, and is treated pathologically within a therapeutics of aid, development and peacekeeping whose aim is to perpetuate, not reform the system (Duffield 2001).

What is the relevance of taking radical disagreement seriously in these circumstances? The oppressed and excluded are denied a voice, so the idea of a strategic engagement of discourses has no relevance. This is what I called the 'silence of the oppressed' at the beginning of Chapter 4, and recognized in the preface as the long – the very long – pre-history of radical disagreement.

Does violence work?

This question relates to the core assumption in conflict resolution that direct violence does not work and is always wrong.

Certainly in intractable conflicts, embattled parties often believe that violence works and act accordingly. As a challenger in Kosovo, the KLA (UCK) rejected the pacifism of Ibrahim Rugova, deliberately provoked Serb retaliation, and was instrumental in triggering NATO intervention. As a possessor in Russia, President Putin cancelled earlier attempts at accommodation with secessionist Chechens and a few years later declared victory over the rebels. In both cases, the argument is that (only) violence works.

Is violence right?

What about the further question, whether violence can be, not just effective, but right?

Frantz Fanon famously invoked the need for violence in the bloody process of decolonization:

> 'The last shall be first and the first last.' Decolonization is the putting into practice of this sentence ... The violence of the colonial regime and the counter-violence of the native balance each other and respond to each other in an extraordinary reciprocal homogeneity.
>
> (Fanon 1961: 28)

Sartre agreed and was dismissive of post-colonial advocates of non-violence in his preface to Fanon's book:

> A fine sight they are too, the believers in non-violence, saying that they are neither executioners nor victim. Try to understand this at any rate: if violence began this very evening and if exploitation and oppression had never existed on earth, perhaps the slogans of non-violence might end the quarrel. But if the whole regime, even your non-violent ideas, are conditioned by a thousand-year-old oppression, your passivity serves only to place you in the ranks of the oppressors.
>
> (Sartre in Fanon 1961: 21)

This is echoed among the 'lost generation' of Palestinian youth in Gaza and the West Bank, the 'children of the second intifada':

> We never see anything good in our lives. Ever since we were little, we see guns and tanks, the sound of the apaches and the F-16s, and the little kids wanting

little guns to fight against Israel. A negotiated agreement is not possible. None of us believes a Palestinian state will be established like that. All of us expect a more violent struggle over the next years. The first intifada failed. The Oslo peace process was useless and benefited Israel. No one can resist with stones or build a nation without violence.

(*International Herald Tribune* March 2007: adapted)

Conclusion: who are the enemies of peace?

Previous chapters have shown how, in intractable conflicts, peacemakers are also combatants in the discursive sphere. The discourse of peace seeks to occupy the whole of discursive space. It aims to transform (eliminate) its rivals. Who are the enemies of the discourse of peace?

The enemies of the discourse of peace are not *discourses of conflict*, for reasons made clear at the outset in this book. The discourse of peace may actively promote discourses of conflict in cases where it is necessary to alleviate power asymmetry or confront injustice. And, as seen earlier, in intractable conflicts a majority of the conflictants may be extremists of ends on the key issues – these are not spoilers.

Nor are the enemies of the discourse of peace *discourses of force* as such. Although militarism has historically been widely identified as an enemy of peace, there is unresolved internal controversy about the use of police force in restraint of criminality, and about the use of military force in national defence, in peacekeeping, in protecting the vulnerable, in maintaining or restoring international peace and security, and so on. This extends to controversy over whether the use of force on a vast scale may in some cases, as in World War II, be the only way to overthrow a ruthless and intractable enemy of peace. For many pacifists, on the other hand, the use of military force *is* violence.

The most succinct definition of the enemy of the discourse of peace is to say that it is the *discourse of violence*. There are many discourses of violence that embrace the *discourse of violent repression* as well as the *discourse of violent resistance* at 'conflict settlement' level, and extend to the *discourse of structural violence* and the *discourse of cultural violence* at 'conflict transformation' level.

In line with this idea, those working in the conflict resolution field might respond to the difficult questions accordingly. In situations where there is not yet enough space even for a strategic engagement of discourses, the response might be not to give in, but to persist in efforts to open the inclusive agonistic dialogue up. There may be cases where the promotion of dialogue for strategic engagement will make things worse, or even where it would be better for the stronger party to win quickly, but this is already well known – there are no exceptionless rules: it is always a matter of chance and judgement.

On the key question of global institutions and practices of exclusion and dominance, these might be confronted by identifying them with the associated discourses of structural and cultural violence and combating them accordingly, although it would be well understood that this reintroduces the whole of politics via the struggle to define what counts as global injustice. Where the silence of the oppressed still prevails, the aim would be, not to *speak for* the oppressed, as can happen in the more didactic tradition of prior critical third-party analysis, but to create a space where the oppressed are able to speak *for themselves*, however ignorant, mistaken or politically incorrect this may seem to be from a sophisticated critical perspective. For Oliver Richmond:

> This points to a need for international actors and institutions, such as the UN, EU, World Bank, USAID, state donors and major NGOs to think and operate in terms of local ownership of the peace projects that they engage in, which must be focused on developing the agency of those actors on their own terms.
>
> (Richmond 2008: 147)

And now the questions whether direct violence works and whether in some cases it may be right become even more central. It might well be that a different answer is given in the two cases. But advocates of conflict resolution do not want to accept that violence works and argue that it just breeds further violence. In Sri Lanka, for example, the challenger, the LTTE, chose violence rather than acceptance of the 2002 peace agreement and lost. Although the Sri Lankan government also chose violence and won with external help, the argument is that none of this would have been necessary if non-repressive policies had been adopted forty years before, and that the violent crushing of the revolt is now only likely to perpetuate it in future. The debate goes on.

Is violence sometimes *right*? Here, I think, the discourse of peace is likely to make a final stand and simply say 'no'. What answer, then, is given to the 'lost generation' of Palestinian youth in its claim that violent resistance is the only recourse left in the face of violent national dispossession and continuing violent Israeli occupation and repression? Perhaps the only response is to redouble efforts to transform the hegemonic discourse of violent repression so that the challenging discourse of violent resistance is not necessary – as well as to transform the deeper discourses of structural and cultural violence. This may be extraordinarily difficult to do since violent repression and violent resistance are symbiotic. But, as Chapter 7 showed, it is the strategic engagement of discourses in the communicative sphere that best informs the discourse of peace in such an ambitious and hazardous mission.

I end this chapter with one or two further illustrations of the discursive struggle of the discourse of peace against its enemies. In what follows it is not forgotten that, in the history of terror, state terrorism (including 'counter-terrorism') is responsible for much greater numbers of atrocities than insurgent terrorism. Nor are political or religious movements in general being conflated with the advocacy or practice of direct violence against civilians associated with some of them. Here is an example of a discursive challenge to the violence of the discourse of Muslim jihadism from a 38-year-old Muslim woman in the UK, Gina Khan:

It's all happening on your doorstep and Britain is still blind to the real threat that is embedded here now. All these mosques are importing jihad. The radical teaching is filtering through, and these mosques are not regulated. They are supporting everything that is wrong about Islam. Most of the British Muslims from my community are ignorant, uneducated, illiterate people from rural areas. It is very easy for them to be brainwashed. These are people who have been taught from the beginning that our religion is everything. It is the right way. You are going to hell simply because you were not born a Muslim. Everyone is being taught that Islam is going to take over, there are going to be mosques everywhere. This is something jihadists have been planning for centuries. They were just looking for our weaknesses, which they have found. They've turned the bombers' graves into shrines, when they're just killers. They say we're being victimised. We're not. The truth is coming out at last, but it's 20 years too late. Muslim society is based on male domination and the oppression of women. The mosques are run by men. The Sharia councils are run by men. The 'voice' of the Muslim Community is always male. And it is women who suffer as a result, including forced marriages for teenage girls when they should be getting educated and male polygamy supported by the mullahs. My mum would turn in her grave if she knew Sharia was here. This is England, how can this be happening? People in Pakistan are fighting for it not to happen there. The fundamentalists are looking down at you because you do not want to be like them. You get grass thrown in your face. You cannot be a good person unless you are reading the Koran, unless your children are and you are living as an Asian woman should. But you know what? I am a human being. God gave me a brain equal to the brain he has given you, and I am not going to submit and pray behind you just because you are a man. Muslim women aren't supposed to make waves. I have been told not to say too much. But I'll be damned if I let another jerk put the fear back in me again. The bottom line for my agenda is to eradicate the radicals. We need to say 'wake up, you have to understand you are not being taught the right thing'.

(Interview by Mary Ann Sieghart, *The Times(2)*
9 February 2007, selected)

Gina Khan is widely seen as a champion of moderation, pluralism and tolerance. She is hailed as a peacemaker. Yet her aim is uncompromising – to 'eradicate the radicals' by eliminating their discursive claim to speak for Islam.

With reference to works like Mark Jurgensmeyer's, *Terror in the Mind of God: The Global Rise of Religious Violence* (2001), Hugo Slim similarly advocates the study of 'violent beliefs' in order to 'know your enemies' and defeat them:

The flurry of new books on charismatic Christianity in Africa, on Islamist theology and the increasingly routine monitoring of cults shows that it is both possible and important for secular political and military analysts to engage with and understand religious ideology and the political and military programmes that flow from them. Faced with the texts and creeds of certain groups, secular analysts and policy-makers may still react by saying 'Do people really believe this stuff?' But confronted with repeated suicide attacks in the Middle East and child abductions in northern Uganda, the answer is obvious to many ordinary people on the front line: 'Yes, they do'. The burden of credulity is now on the side of the secular analysts. It makes sense to believe that religious movements do believe this stuff and to examine why they do, where such belief might lead and how best it may be challenged.

(Slim 2005: 23)

The Director of the Cambridge University Security and International Society Mindset Project, set up in the wake of the 9/11 attacks in New York and Washington, explains the purpose of the project:

One of the main aims of the newly established research programme for Security and International Society at Cambridge University is to try to understand the mindset of those who threaten our security ... Bin Laden and his fellow-travellers are so dangerous, because, like Stalin and Hitler, they combine obsessional conspiracy theories about their opponents (including myths of Jewish world conspiracy) with great tactical and operational skill in mounting attacks against them.

(Interview, *The Times* 5 December 2002)

Here is the reason given by the editor for re-publishing an English translation of Hitler's *Mein Kampf* in 1991:

Mein Kampf is lengthy, dull, bombastic, repetitious and extremely badly written. As a historical picture of Hitler's life up to the time he wrote it, it is also quite unreliable. Most of its statements of fact and the entire tenor of the argument in the autobiographical passages are demonstrably untrue. Why then revive *Mein Kampf?* Firstly, it is an introduction to the mind and methods of Adolf Hitler. It is a mind at once concise and repetitive, a mishmash of *idées reçus* and insights, a second-rate mind of immense power, the mind of a man whose early death would have made Europe a safer place to live in for all its citizens. The second reason for its study is that we may know and recognise the arguments of the enemies of democracy in our midst. 'Oh that my enemy had written a book', said Job. Hitler did. It was there for people to read. Despite the omissions from the first British edition, bits of it were circulated to the British cabinet and made available through the British pamphlet press. *Mein Kampf* is not in any sense the work of a civilised man who thought peace a desirable or normal state of international relations. It does not only raise the historical question of why its British readers did not recognise this and know that in Hitler they faced an implacable enemy. It faces us in the post-Cold War era with a similar question. Are there enemies of peace in power in the world today? Are we trying to recognise them?

(Watt 1991: xi–lxi omissions not marked).

What would we as peacemakers have done in 1925 when *Mein Kampf* first appeared, knowing that it would help to propel its author to power a few years later? Picking up a theme from Chapter 3, would we have aimed to 'deepen mutual understanding' or 'expand sympathy and imagination' or tried to promote acceptance of 'the validity of competing narratives', or followed Voltaire in disagreeing with what Hitler said but 'defending to the death his right to say it', or acted on Jefferson's advice to rely on truth to dispel error because 'truth is great and will prevail if left to herself'? I do not think that we would have done any of these things. I think that as peacemakers we would have done everything in our power, not just to refute Hitler in the open court of public opinion, but to ensure that his discourse never reached its intended audience at all.

Peacemakers have enemies too.

Note

1 With his usual perspicacity, Clausewitz himself was well aware of this – in the sentence immediately following his famous observation that war is 'a continuation of political intercourse, with the addition of other means', he adds that the 'main lines along which military events progress, and to which they are restricted, are political lines that continue throughout the war into the subsequent peace' (von Clausewitz, 1976/1832: 75).

Part III

Radical disagreement and the future

Theoretical and practical implications

In Part III, the enquiry moves away from the question of radical disagreement and conflict resolution to the theoretical and practical implications of taking radical disagreements seriously in general. This means revisiting the terrains of discourse analysis and conflict analysis that were bracketed at the end of Part I. How much of the phenomenology, epistemology and praxis of radical disagreement survives the process of unbracketing? And how adequate are discursive and conflict analytic theories to what the phenomenological investigation shows?

Part III looks to the future. It asks what the theoretical and practical implications of taking radical disagreement seriously, as illustrated in Part II, are. Chapter 9 unbrackets discourse analysis. Chapter 10 unbrackets conflict analysis. The epilogue reviews the book reflexively in the light of this.

9 Radical disagreement and human difference

Critical, constructivist and post-structural theorists in the West vie with each other in claiming that their approach maximizes space for the celebration of human difference. Yet the undervalued phenomenology of radical disagreement shows the sense in which human difference is more different than that. The phenomenology of radical disagreement in no way contradicts the insights of discourse analysis. But nor do the understandings characteristic of western discourse analysis exhaust what the study of linguistic intractability in intense political conflict shows.

At the beginning of Part I, the phenomenon of radical disagreement was located at the intersection of the three great spheres of human difference, human discourse and human conflict. Human discourse and human conflict have featured prominently in this book. It is time to revisit the question of human difference.

Chapter 6 noted how a number of discourse analytic philosophers claim that their readings optimize the liberation of diversity and maximize space for the celebration of human difference. Jürgen Habermas strongly rebuts accusations that his theory implies a hegemony of social coordination that stifles dissent and smothers what it purports to emancipate: 'Nothing makes me more nervous' than the imputation that the theory of communicative action 'proposes, or at least suggests, a rationalist utopian society' (Habermas 1982: 235). He wants to claim that, on the contrary, only the idealizations presupposed in 'the intersubjectivity of linguistically achieved understanding' can open up the space for divergent voices to be heard:

> Linguistically attained consensus does not eradicate from the accord the differences in speaker perspectives but rather presupposes them as ineliminable ...
> More discourse means more contradiction and difference. The more abstract the agreements become, the more diverse the disagreements with which we can non-violently live.
>
> (Habermas 1992: 140)

Michel Foucault has already been quoted in similar vein in Chapter 6:

> The freeing of difference requires thought without contradiction, without dialectics, without negation; thought that accepts divergence; affirmative thought

whose instrument is disjunction; thought of the multiple – of the nomadic and dispersed multiplicity that is not limited or confined by the constraints of similarity .... What is the answer to the question? The problem. How is the problem resolved? By displacing the question .... We must think problematically rather than question and answer dialectically.

(Foucault in Bouchard and Sherry (trans.) 1977: 185–6,
quoted Flynn 1994: 42)

In Chapter 6, an adequacy test was applied to see whether putative philosophies of radical disagreement proved to be satisfactory when compared to examples of radical disagreement. I suggested that neither Habermas nor Foucault can in the end be called philosophers of radical disagreement. I now call this the *first adequacy test*:

1   Does the theory offer a satisfactory account of radical disagreements in which it is not itself directly involved?

In this chapter, I will briefly apply two further adequacy tests:

2   Does the theory succeed in taking account of its own involvement in radical theoretical disagreement, or even attempt to do this?
3   Does the theory succeed in taking account of its own involvement in radical political disagreement, or even attempt to do this?

There is no space to do more than touch on the *second adequacy test* here, but I have yet to find a philosophy that passes it. The main empirical data is provided by an investigation into the relationship between what the philosophies in question say *about* radical disagreement, and what happens when there is radical disagreement *between* them. This is the *odium scholasticum*, only slightly less ferocious than the *odium theologicum*. Stephen White, for example, notes how many readers of *The Philosophical Discourse of Modernity* 'are perplexed at the intensity and relentlessness of Habermas' attack on his opponents' (1995: 5). The Habermas-Foucault radical disagreement is well known, while Michael Kelly ends his study of the radical disagreement between Habermas and Gadamer by concluding:

> The debate between Hans-Georg Gadamer and Jürgen Habermas had a rather ironic feature in that its path and conclusion seemed to contradict their notions of philosophical discourse. The path did not conform to Habermas' notion of communicative action oriented to understanding, because Habermas' interest in the dialogue was admittedly to establish his differences with Gadamer and, as a result, his action in the debate was more instrumental than communicative; and the conclusion did not conform to Gadamer's notion of a dialogue that culminates in a fusion of horizons, for the two participants were farther apart at the end of the dialogue than they had been at the start.

(Kelly 1995: 139)

I suggest that this is not just a 'rather ironic feature' of a specific example of theoretical radical disagreement, but a feature of radical disagreement between philosophies in general. The fact that in agonistic dialogue participants find that they are 'farther apart at the end of the dialogue than they had been at the start' sums up the whole of what Chapter 5 shows. Its relevance for the project of managing radical disagreement in intractable conflicts lies in what happens – what possibilities may be opened up – if the participants come fully to realize this.

However subtle and self-aware the philosophies in question may be – including anti-essentialist and anti-foundationalist philosophies – in the vortex of radical disagreement, three characteristic locutions in particular may recall the moments of radical disagreeing illustrated in Chapter 5. They are hallmarks of the *didacticism* of radical disagreement:

1   the predominance of the present indicative tense (this is so);
2   the recurrence of the trope 'not ... rather ...' (that is not so);
3   the preponderance of the form 'It used to be thought that ... now I can reveal ...' (I look across the field of contestation to the far horizon).

If the philosophy in question is too coy to engage explicitly with the opposition in this way (we may think of the playful withholdings of Derrida in his fierce radical disagreement with Searle), it is illuminating to turn to the *third adequacy test*. Does the philosophy succeed in taking account of its own involvement in radical political disagreement, or even attempt to do so? This is, perhaps, the decisive adequacy test, since it is, in the end, the no doubt crude and simplistic 'either–or' choices of intense political confrontation that crush linguistic equivocation and generate the brutal and uncompromising nature of its chief verbal manifestation – radical disagreement.

Consider the example of Habermas' backing for the 1999 intervention in Kosovo in support of the SPD/Green government, of which he was widely seen as unofficial 'philosopher-king'. This was not couched in the 'purely hypothetical language' of discursive ethical argumentation, but in the direct language of justification, refutation and admonition. Foucault's response to the threat of Soviet intervention in Poland in 1982 was similarly forthright, with no reflexive reference to 'regimes of truth' in his unqualified recommendation for action:

> For ethical reasons, we have to raise the problem of Poland in the form of a non-acceptance of what is happening there, and a non-acceptance of the passivity of our own governments.
>
> (Foucault in 'Politics and Ethics: an Interview': 377, quoted Norris 1994: 190)

Derrida rejected the US-led reordering of global priorities post-1989 in uncharacteristically straightforward prose. His radical disagreement was with Francis Fukuyama as he scornfully rejected the 'end of history' thesis and demanded a 'New International' to reignite the struggle against injustice:

For it must be cried out, at a time when some have the audacity to neo-evan-
gelize in the name of the ideal of a liberal democracy that has finally realized
itself as the ideal of human history: never have violence, inequality, exclusion,
famine, and thus economic oppression affected as many human beings in the
history of the earth and of humanity.

(Derrida 1994: 85)

As a further example, it is instructive to compare the philosophy of Emmanuel
Levinas – the philosopher of 'the other' *par excellence* – with his own political
involvement in intractable conflict and radical disagreement. Levinas insists on the
priority of absolute respect for the other, not as a reciprocal relation with 'Thou'
as envisaged by Martin Buber, but as a 'pre-ontological absolute'. For Levinas,
my very existence is an act of violation in the presence of the vulnerability of the
'face' of the other. My responsibility is concomitantly boundless, and precedes
any considerations of justice that only spring into being with the advent of a third
(Levinas 1998).

So what happens when this philosophy confronts a concrete example of radical
disagreement – for example, disagreement between Israelis and Palestinians about
the creation of the state of Israel – in which it is itself politically involved?

Levinas openly supported the project of the Israeli state ('this return to the land
of our forefathers marks one of the greatest events of internal history and, indeed,
of all History'), but only to the extent that it genuinely embodied the values pre-
served down the centuries in the heritage of Jewish scripture – Israel is 'a State
that should embody a prophetic morality and the idea of its peace'. At the time of
the Sabra and Chatila massacres in Lebanon in 1982, Levinas was asked how his
philosophy related to the controversy surrounding those events:

Q: Emmanuel Levinas, you are the philosopher of the 'other'. Isn't history, isn't
     politics the very site of the encounter with the 'other', and for the Israeli, isn't
     the 'other' above all the Palestinian?
A: My definition of the other is completely different. The other is the neighbour,
     who is not necessarily kin, but who can be …
Q: I'd like to ask you whether Israel is innocent or responsible for what happened
     at Sabra and Chatila.
A: Let me begin with our immediate reactions on learning of this catastrophe.
     Despite the lack of guilt here – and probably there, too – what gripped us right
     away was the honour of responsibility. It is, I think, a responsibility which the
     Bible of course teaches us, but it is one which constitutes every man's respons-
     ibility towards all others, a responsibility which has nothing to do with any
     acts one may really have committed. Prior to any act, I am concerned with the
     Other, and I can never be absolved from this responsibility …

(Interview 28 September 1982, Hand (ed.) 1989: 294, 290)

The 'pre-ontological honour of absolute responsibility towards the Other' does not extend to include the consequences of an action – support for the creation of the state of Israel – that was 'the great catastrophe' for an existing concrete other. Within the context of radical disagreement, the philosopher of the other is the philosopher of the other who does not answer back.

There is no space here to go deeper into post-positivist discussions of difference, whether critical (Hoffman 1987; Linklater 1998) or post-structural (Walker 1993; Bleiker 2001), nor into attempts to navigate the tension between them, for example, via concepts of hybridity (Bhabha 1994) or the solidarity of the agents affected, whether as individuals, movements or communities (Jabri 2007). The no doubt immodest claim here is that taking the phenomenon of radical disagreement seriously may in some measure help to temper what is at times a somewhat didactic tendency in the former (critical theory), and a relativist tendency in the latter (post-structuralism), while politically grounding what can be a predilection for abstraction in both.

My conclusion in relation to human difference – including difference of culture, gender and class – is that, however subtle, complex and self-cancelling the philosophy in question may be – whether Bakhtin's *heteroglossia* or Bourdieu's *heterodoxa* or Derrida's *différance* – this does not touch what the simple phenomenon of radical disagreement shows. However disjunctively, dilemmatically or problematically we may speak of human difference, however much our philosophy may disparage the clumsy eruptions of conflicting binaries, or expose their prior equivocated self-erasure in the very notion of iteration itself, the differences manifested in the crude, simple and no doubt naive, exchanges of radical disagreement – insolubly welded as they are to the crisis of contested action – are more different than that.

In the rest of the chapter, I briefly indicate a few of the things that follow from Part II of this book with regard to:

- attempts by democratic theory and meta-ethical pluralism to accommodate radical disagreement and difference;
- media principles of neutrality in the reporting of intractable conflict and radical disagreement;
- a return to the critical theoretic, gender and culture critiques in their invocation of radical difference to undercut the very idea of the viability and ethical legitimacy of a phenomenology of radical disagreement.

Radical disagreement, difference and democracy

The long-standing interest in the handling of difference and diversity in democratic theory confronts particular difficulties when it addresses continuing radical disagreements of the sort outlined in Chapter 8 which need to be accommodated in settlements between undefeated conflict parties. In these circumstances, an uncompromising assertion of classical liberalism that regards the challenge from those who reject status quo norms as 'not a very grave one' needs to do more work:

Why must a political value be made justifiable to those who are scarcely interested in rational debate about justification anyway? A liberal political system
need not feel obliged to reason with fanatics: it must simply take the necessary
precautions to guard against them.

(Larmore 1987: 60)

More promising is the thinking of those who do advocate including a larger area
of political disagreement within the realm of public discourse via an extension
of liberal 'principles of accommodation' (for example, Amy Gutmann and Denis
Thompson 1996). This includes those who positively extol the virtues of diversity
and disagreement in enriching democratic life, for example, in relation to minority
rights (Kymlicka 1995) and those who accept the irreducible agonistic pluralism of democratic politics, albeit domesticated within a 'shared adhesion to the
ethico-political principles of liberal democracy' that turns enemies into adversaries
(Mouffe 2000: 102).

Monique Deveaux argues in *Cultural Pluralism and Deliberative Justice* that
few of these authors in the end do justice to the actuality of radical disagreement.
Gutmann and Thompson, for example, 'rely problematically on an unspecified
impartial standpoint from which to judge the practices and conduct of moral discourse' (Deveaux 2000: 105). Most forms of discursive democracy (Dryzeck 1990)
'fail to take seriously the implication of citizens' deep disagreements on questions
of moral value in pluralistic societies' (Deveaux 140). Even agonistic forms of
democracy can be said to assume that 'some kind of common bond must exist between the parties in conflict' for hostility to be productive, as Paul Muldoon (2008:
124) puts it, quoting Mouffe (2005: 20).

As a result, very much in line with the argument in this book, Deveaux insists
that the emphasis has to shift from hypothetical models of consent to 'the requirements of actual dialogue':

> This step is perhaps the most critical amendment of discourse ethics in my
> view, for it seems likely that procedures based on a commitment to secur-
> ing actual agreement will take seriously the need to solicit and include the
> voices and perspectives of cultural minorities ... In particular, I suggest that
> by seeking to secure citizens' actual agreement on procedures for debate and
> decision making, and even on procedures to manage *disagreements*, we might
> better ensure the inclusion and consent of diverse groups in plural, democratic
> states'.

(Deveaux 2000: 145, 166 original italics)

The phenomenology of radical disagreement advocates doing exactly that in the
context of intractable conflict. And, if there is a settlement, this is carried forward
into the ensuing raw political arrangement, where detailed constitutional working
out is not fully determined in advance – the 'paradoxical reality' embodied in the
agreement still has to be resolved – and is likely indefinitely to remain a 'work in
progress'. As seen above, conflict parties are in this sense still enemies.

In view of this, Deveaux's final position is disappointing:

> Although I do not advocate jettisoning reasoned argumentation or the attempt to reach agreements, I suggest that as an ideal for deliberation in pluralistic societies, strong consensus is simply impracticable. Theorists of deliberative democracy should instead devote more of their attention to the problem of how we might secure reasonable agreement or compromise on *procedures* for deliberation, which is still a difficult task.
>
> (Ibid.: 140)

The trouble here is that in the nexus of settlement between undefeated conflict parties, radical disagreement extends precisely to the foundational principles and procedures which define the constitutional framework in the first place. This is not finally determined in advance, but is worked out in the continuing struggle between enemies. The constitution itself becomes a site for antagonistic contestation, and within this, the procedural rules are part of what is at issue. Even Mouffe, who with great insight places ineradicable antagonism at the heart of her politics, expects the resulting agonistic pluralism to create a space for opponents to respect each other as adversaries, not enemies *because* there is shared 'civility' based on a residuum of common ethico-political democratic principles.

That cannot be presumed in the accommodation of continuing radical disagreement in many post-war settlements. It is worth spelling this out. In intractable *ideological* conflicts – what SIPRI calls 'government' conflicts – the very form of democratic politics may still be in question. Is Sharia law, for example, compatible with democracy? This raises the question of what democracy is (as already quoted in Chapter 6):

> In the American form of democracy any issue is allowed to be put to a vote of the people, and the majority decision prevails upon all. Can we Muslims put an issue that has already been decided for us by Allah up for a vote and accept the will of the majority if they vote against the will of Allah? Of course we cannot, so therefore we can never accept democracy as defined, practised and promoted by America. Islam offers a political system that is based on consultation and consensus that allows each individual's voice to be heard, but can never make a decision against the will of Allah. The nature of this political process is such that it could easily be described as an Islamic democracy.

And in intractable *ethno-nationalist* or secessionist conflicts – what SIPRI calls 'territory' conflicts – the very definition of the polity within which democratic processes are to be conducted in the first place is what is at issue. If Northern Ireland is the electorate, the Unionists win; if the whole of Ireland is the electorate, the Republicans win. This applies, with infinite variety, to innumerable other conflicts such as appeals to the democratic rights of Falkland Islanders in relation to the challenge to the prior legitimacy of this electorate in the Malvinas conflict, or justifications for army action based on the democratic rights of the majority Turkish electorate in relation to the democratic rights of the minority Kurdish electorate claimed as prior by the secessionist PKK. Possessors appeal to status quo democracy, disparaged as an accident of history and anti-democratic abuse of power by the challengers. Here – in a manner familiar from Chapter 5 – foundational distinctions between democratic legitimacy and *force majeure* are themselves caught up at the heart of the radical disagreement through the involvement of the distinction between the distinction invoked and what it does/does not distinguish. This constitutes the core of the linguistic intractability. As such, it confronts theories and understandings of radical democracy with some of their most testing practical challenges.

So radical disagreement in ideological (government) conflicts and secessionist (territory) conflicts of the kind explored in Part II continue to pose deep problems for procedural approaches to handling human difference like Deveaux's, and for agonistic forms of radical democracy like Mouffe's. The suggestion here is not that these models are in themselves deficient, but that there is great scope for testing and exploring them further in relation to the project of containing ongoing radical disagreements within political frameworks that make the non-violent accommodation of human difference possible.

Radical disagreement, difference and meta-ethical pluralism

In applied ethics, the topics of difference and disagreement feature most prominently in relation to the question of moral conflict – especially 'conflicts of value' and the meta-ethical debates associated with them.[1] In the meta-ethical realm, the fact of moral conflict and disagreement has traditionally been used by cultural and ethical relativists as a stick with which to beat ethical absolutists (Mackie 1976). But the fact of ethical disagreement is just as often invoked by ethical pluralists to discredit the claims of ethical subjectivists and ethical relativists in their turn (Walzer 1983; Kekes 1993).

Hinman (2003), for example, argues that difference and disagreement are 'sources of moral strength':

> The fact that different moral theories point to different courses of action is not necessarily bad; indeed, the disagreement can help us ultimately to arrive at the best course of action.
>
> (Hinman 2003: 57)

For Hinman, in a conflictual world, action is guided best by a pluralist stance that values cultural and moral disagreement while avoiding the pitfalls of relativism in line with four principles:

1 the principle of understanding that encourages us to try to comprehend the moral practices of another person or culture before passing judgement;
2 the principle of toleration that persuades us to allow space for ethical and cultural variation in the pursuit of moral vision;

3 the principle of standing up against evil that leads us to debar repugnant acts
   that flout pluralistic values;
4 the principle of fallibility that induces us to retain humility in the face of human
   diversity.

How does this relate to the phenomenology, epistemology and praxis of radical
disagreement? I think that it does not relate very closely at all.

The phenomenology of radical disagreement does not pronounce in general on
meta-ethical controversies such as those between relativists and rationalists (Hollis
and Lukes eds 1982), or between communitarians and absolutists (Rasmussen ed.
1990), since none of these positions is immune and all may be invoked by conflict
parties in the course of their agonistic dialogue. And this extends to what happens
(what is said) *in* those meta-ethical debates themselves – not when they form
part of a mere intellectual game of setting-to-partners, but when they emerge in
deadly serious political conflicts where real-life decisions are thereby passionately
contested.

In these radical disagreements, relativist and communitarian philosophies are
just as forthright as rationalist and absolutist philosophies. Yet, disappointingly,
a pluralist like Hinman shies away from commenting further on this because it
threatens to break through the stipulative rules for public decision-making that
define the pluralism that he advocates:

> Sometimes, if the disagreements are too great and the possibility of genuine
> dialogue and compromise too small, the system of checks and balances can
> immobilize us, preventing us from choosing any course of action at all.
>
> (Hinman 2003: 57)

But radical disagreement does not arise primarily from a mere decision-making
impasse, nor can the antagonists just throw up their hands and walk away because
an overarching system of checks and balances does not resolve their differences.
It is this that *defines* their disagreement as radical. And they cannot 'agree to
disagree' when they are locked together in the passionate and bitter embrace of
mutually thwarted action:

| 'This is the true way.'

'That is your opinion and I respect it. My opinion is that there are many ways,
one of which is yours.'

'Far from respecting my opinion, you take no account of it at all. You refer to
one way among many, but I am speaking of the one true way. If you understood what I was saying, you would see for yourself and believe.'

'Your way is true for you and mine is true for me. Each has a partial view.'

'But it is your idea of what we each have a partial view of that I deny. You do not seem to realize that perspectivism is itself a perspective – and, as it turns out, a false one.'

'I am not advocating perspectivism. I am simply recognising that we disagree with one another – something that you are either unable or unwilling to do.'

'On the contrary, I am the one who takes our disagreement seriously. I at least acknowledge that what you say is a direct contradiction of everything that I believe. That is why I repudiate it so vehemently and am trying so hard to show you where you have gone wrong. You, on the other hand, do not even realize that what you 'take account of' as 'my opinion' is simply not my opinion at all.'

'But does it not cross your mind that there may be other ways than yours?'

'I am sure that there are innumerable other ways – but only one is the true way. Does it not cross your mind that there could be a way other than the fashionable one of which you have been persuaded – namely, that the world is full of equivalent philosophies, among which are yours and mine?'

'You are so bigoted that you do not even conceive of the possibility of your own bigotry.'

'Do you call a person who has come to recognize the truth a bigot? A bigot is a person who is too blind to see either reality or that he does not see reality. You are the bigot.'

'Well, let us at least agree that what you believe to be the true way, I see as one among many. Neither of us, it seems, really understands what the other is saying.'

'We understand each other perfectly. I know exactly what you are saying and doing. I know why I must stop you acting accordingly before it is too late.'

'You are beyond the reach of reason. I will have to prevent you from going on harming others.'|

And this is not a philosophy.

Radical disagreement, difference and the media

At the beginning of his interview with Rowan Williams, Archbishop of Canterbury, in the *Humphrys In Search Of God* series on the BBC, the British broadcaster, John Humphrys, said that in this case he was off the hook, because he did not have to be impartial. Normally 'although interviewers don't have to observe many rules, we are required to be impartial, not to express our own convictions' (*Radio 4* 31 October 2006). This is the BBC convention for objective news reporting as understood by one of its most prominent interviewers.

So what is the difference between an interview in which the BBC rules do apply, and an interview, like this one, where they do not? We might expect the former to be more constrained and the latter to be more controversial. But what if the non-impartial interview *does not*, but the interview bound by the BBC's impartiality rule *does* concern a radical disagreement?

When the BBC's objectivity and impartiality rules are lifted, but there is no radical disagreement, as in the case of the interview with the Archbishop of Canterbury, the result can be – at any rate in my view – somewhat tame and bland. Although, as an agnostic, the interviewer was challenging the interviewee to convert him – which he failed to do – the exchanges were polite and deferential. There were no serious political implications. The same was true of the equally decorous interviews with prominent Jewish and Muslim interviewees in the same series (Humphrys 2007).

In contrast, at almost the same time, Humphrys interviewed a young radical British Muslim (Abu Izzadeen) on the *Today* news programme (22 September 2007). Here the full BBC objectivity and impartiality convention applied. But because this was a radical disagreement with highly contentious political implications, the emotion, drama and confrontation easily broke through the constraints. The BBC convention was shown to be itself already involved.

Here is a short extract from the interview followed by all the emails that were read out immediately after it (JH is John Humphrys, AI is Abu Izzadeen). The BBC controlled the studio, decided what questions should be asked ('on programmes like this the presenter asks the questions and the guest answers the questions'), determined when the interview should start and end, chose which portions of it should be broadcast, and selected the emails from listeners to be read out at the conclusion.

JH: If you're not happy with this country a lot of people would say ....

AI: Who says I'm not happy with this country. I love this country. Allah created the whole universe.

JH: You're telling me it's led by a tyrant. You don't approve of the rules and the way in which this country functions.

AI: That's correct.

JH: Then why can you not go somewhere where Islam is the law?

AI: Oh I see. It's to be mass deportation for those who are in this community ....

JH: Did I suggest that?

AI: I'm asking you a question.

JH: There is a convention on programmes like this during which the presenter asks the questions and the guest answers the questions. If this country is so offensive to you and to some of your friends, you don't have to stay here. You can move somewhere where there is Islamic law. You can go to Saudi Arabia.

AI: Let's look at the reality. As a Muslim I believe Allah is the one who created the whole universe. He created the UK. It doesn't belong to you. It doesn't belong to the Queen. It doesn't belong to the Anglo-Saxons.

JH: I suggest it doesn't belong to you either.

AI: It belongs to Allah, the creator. And he put us on the planet earth to live wherever we want and implement the Sharia rules. If I live in the UK I will call for Islam. Democracy means sovereignty for man. And as a Muslim we believe sovereignty for the Sharia. Therefore I would never take part in a democratic election.

JH: Forgive me, that is your view. You want Sharia law in this country. Right, then I'll tell you what you do. Let me get a word in. I'll tell you what you do. You stand as a member of parliament, you encourage your friends and your colleagues to stand as members of parliament, and you try to change the law in this country democratically. That's the way we do things in this country. Unlike, for instance, Saudi Arabia, where they do have the sort of law of which you approve. Now, if you want to change the way this country functions, why can you not do it in a democratic way? What's wrong with that? And, if not, what are you doing here?

ALAN NEWLAND: I am outraged at the time you have given to this madman. I am outraged at the insult to the Muslim community you have perpetrated by allowing this man even to appear to represent even a tiny minority of extreme Muslim youths.

JANE PARSONS: I suppose you are right to give airtime to this man, but I have to say I had to keep switching the radio off because I was so angry. He twisted everything to make out that a crusade was being waged against Islam by Britain and America. I do not agree with the invasion of Iraq and went on the march before it happened but I deplore the way some Muslims have hijacked the issue to make out that it is a war against Islam.

BEVERIDGE SUTHERLAND: If he represents Islam, I say deport the lot of them. Then again all organised religion has hate and fear of others at its core.

HUMPHREY TREVELYAN: It was encouraging to hear the *Today* programme invite a young radical Muslim to express his views about John Reid's lecture to the Muslim community. Many non-Muslims in this country would have found Reid's patronising and overbearing remarks distasteful and hypocritical.

DOMINIC MITCHELL: I congratulate you on the interview. By allowing his true colours to shine through you revealed the torrid depths of his extremism. I'm sure it was a repugnant experience, but thank you anyway.

MARGOT CUNNINGHAM: It was truly alarming to hear such a fanatic express his hate for our government and our democratic system. It leaves one wondering how many more Muslims think like that and how the government can even begin to tackle it.

VIV RAINER: Muslims like him will fight according to Muslim theology to make the UK subject to Sharia law. The question now is just how much of a minority are they? As I said, it's frightening.

Radical disagreement and the gender and culture critiques revisited

Finally, I return to the radical gender and culture critiques of the phenomenology of radical disagreement. For the issue of gender and culture in relation to conflict resolution in general, see Ramsbotham, Woodhouse and Miall (2005): 265–74 and 302–15 respectively.

At the beginning of this book, I noted how the radical gender critique, particularly in the form of difference feminism, cuts the ground from under the very idea of a phenomenology of radical disagreement by identifying it, lock, stock and barrel, with the symbolic (thetic) order that the pre-symbolic (semiotic) transgression of the thetic subverts. Let this stand. The simple point made now, having followed through the implications of nevertheless taking the phenomenology of radical disagreement seriously in Part II, is that radical disagreements *between* feminism and patriarchy, clearly evident in many of the most vicious conflicts across the world, appear to share precisely the characteristics noted with reference to intractable conflict and radical disagreement in general. It extends to a highly complex, but for all that also a very vigorous, radical disagreement, *between* the gender and the culture critiques. This revolves around the fact that many, if not most, non-western cultures are even more patriarchal than western cultures. So radical feminism, despite its best efforts, is widely interpreted as a western export in the radical disagreements that surround intense political conflicts in those parts of the world.

I will end this chapter with another look at the radical culture critique. In the search for a characteristic sample, it seems reasonable to look to Cultural Studies, the interdisciplinary university field that takes human culture as its main topic (the other alternative would be anthropology). So the question is: how does Cultural Studies describe itself, and what does it say about the phenomenon of radical disagreement in intractable conflicts that are such a striking feature of human cultural behaviour in general? Does the account given by Cultural Studies undercut the enterprise of the phenomenological investigation of radical disagreement, and show up what was explored in Part II as *parti pris* to a discredited and bankrupt epistemology?

To answer this question, I take one of the best-known student textbooks in the field – Chris Barker's *Cultural Studies: Theory and Practice* – and collect all those passages that tell students what the interdisciplinary field of Cultural Studies itself is. What follows quotes these passages verbatim, but does not indicate all the breaks:

> Cultural studies is an interdisciplinary or post-disciplinary field of enquiry that explores the production and inculcation of maps of meaning. Representationalist epistemology has largely been displaced within cultural studies by the influence of poststructuralism, postmodernism and other anti-representationalist paradigms. Common sense, and realist epistemology, understands truth to be that which corresponds to or pictures the real in an objective way. Constructionism, of which cultural studies is a manifestation, argues that truth is a social

creation. Cultural studies has argued that language is not a neutral medium for the formation of meanings and knowledge about an independent object world 'existing' outside of language. Rather, it is constitutive of those very meanings and knowledge. Thus, we make the switch from a question about truth and representation to one concerning language use. Cultural studies seeks to play a de-mystifying role, that is, to point to the constructed character of cultural texts and to the myths and ideologies which are embedded in them. It has done this in the hope of producing subject positions, and real subjects, who are enabled to oppose subordination. These concepts all stress the instability of meaning, its deferral through the interplay of texts, writing and traces. Consequently, categories do not have essential universal meanings but are social constructions of language. This is the core of the anti-essentialism prevalent in cultural studies. That is, words have no universal meanings and do not refer to objects that possess essential qualities. One way we can understand this approach ... is by practising the art of deconstructing key binaries of western thinking. Thus, throughout the book, I put forward a particular binary [such as true/false] for students to deconstruct. Either/or binaries are dissolved by denying that the problem is best described in dualistic terms at all.

(Barker 2003: 7, 31, 33, 34, 54, 85)

It may seem remarkable that the phenomenon of intractable cross-cultural conflict and radical disagreement does not feature in Barker's book at all. But it is not hard to see why. As noted in Chapter 1, the explicit prior assumptions that dismiss representationalist, common sense, realist, essentialist epistemologies, and substitute post-structural, postmodern, constructionist and deconstructionist epistemologies are pre-emptive and wholesale. What is swept away includes just those features – naïve, simplistic and uncritical though they no doubt are – that Part II of this book showed to be characteristic in radical disagreement – including reference to binaries such as truth, falsehood, justice, injustice, and to claims about how things are and should be in the external world.

We may remind ourselves of the example of the revolutionary Palestinian discourse of national determination, freedom and liberation. This lies at the heart of the linguistic intractability of the Israeli-Palestinian conflict. The Palestinian discursive struggle is to make the Palestinian discourse the 'primary language within which the Palestinian issue is discussed', not because it is a narrative, but because it is true:

What is centrally at issue is not a mere Palestinian narrative, but a series of incontrovertible facts – facts of expulsion, exclusion, dominance and occupation bitterly lived out by Palestinians day by day over the past 60 years and still being endured at the present time. This is not a narrative. It is a lived reality. Finding the best strategy for ending this lived reality is the main purpose of this Report. Transforming the discourse within which it is discussed is a major part of that effort.

(Palestine Strategy Group 2009: 15)

The phenomenology of radical disagreement shows why it is misleading even to refer to this as a 'Palestinian discourse' in the first place.

But the self-description of Cultural Studies as defined in Barker's book rules all of this out from the beginning. Cultural Studies already knows how words can and cannot be used and how they are to be understood. It immediately translates questions of truth, representation (reality) and justice into locutions about language use. It deconstructs 'either/or binaries' by denying from the outset that the problem – in this case the problem of Israeli occupation of Palestinian land – is 'best described in dualistic terms at all'. So the radical disagreement is not allowed to get off the ground in the first place.

Instead Cultural Studies, as presented here, self-descriptively reifies itself and substitutes its own epistemology by fiat. In doing so its language evinces the three rhetorical hallmarks of didacticism: the pervasiveness of the present indicative tense, the recurrence of the trope 'not ... rather', and the predominance of the discursive form 'it used to be thought ... but now we can reveal'. In this way, it re-imports the binaries that have ostensibly been expelled. So now it is the whole of Cultural Studies that finds itself engaged in a titanic conflict and radical disagreement with all those cultures – I suggest a majority including many western examples – that explicitly reject secular post-structuralism of this kind as anathema.

But that is another story.

Note

1 See, for example, Nagel, T. (1979) 'The fragmentation of value' in *Mortal Questions*, 128–41; Williams, B. (1981) 'Conflicts of values' in *Moral Luck*, 71–82; Hampshire, S. (1983); Stocker, M. (1990).

10 Radical disagreement and human survival

A survey of possible upcoming conflict formations suggests that the phenomenon of radical disagreement will continue to generate linguistic intractability.

Taking radical disagreement seriously – learning how it can be acknowledged, explored, understood and managed – is not the least of the requirements for human survival in an irredeemably agonistic world.

Looking to the future, what conflict formations are appearing over the horizon? What role is radical disagreement likely to play in the discursive sphere? What can, and should be done, to anticipate and manage linguistic intractability? In this chapter, the field of conflict analysis surveyed in Chapter 2 is unbracketed.

Life on earth began about 3,500 million years ago. Homo sapiens emerged less than 200,000 years ago. Short of an unforeseeable intervening cosmic catastrophe, the earth could remain habitable for up to another 5,000 million years, until the sun, having consumed its inner hydrogen, begins to expand into a red giant and incinerates the earth in the process. How long can the human species survive? Let us begin modestly with the next 100 years. What needs to happen to prolong human existence that long? Setting aside the medical battle with future generations of viruses, what 'man-made' threats loom?

Prediction of the future in complex environments is hazardous. Few can guess what will happen even ten years ahead when there are sudden discontinuities. Which experts foresaw the Wall street crash in 1919, or the outbreak of the second world war in 1929, or the Iranian revolution in 1969, or the collapse of the Soviet Union in 1979? On some projections, the Chinese GDP per capita will reach half that of the United States soon after the middle of this century. Given population discrepancy, this means that total Chinese GDP will be twice that of America. What are the implications? It will be the first eclipse of the West for 500 years. Will it usher in a genuine 'clash of civilisations', not so much Samuel Huntington's politico-military free-for-all, but a 'transvaluation of all values' as the assumption that western norms are now global norms is tested to destruction? This scale of future change is beyond present computation. Nevertheless, I will end this book by proposing three linked predictions of a general kind. First, human history will continue to be conflictual – there will be no 'end of history'. Second, the chief linguistic aspect of human conflict will continue to be radical disagreement. Third, in order to manage linguistic intractability and avert future disaster, the phenomenon of radical disagreement will need to be acknowledged, explored and understood better than it is at the moment.

Radical disagreement and future conflict

All four of the main types of large-scale conflict looked at in Chapter 2 are likely to recur in the foreseeable future, and all four are likely to go on being associated with radical disagreement. To be succinct, I will focus on the role of the state in each case, because, whatever other levels of analysis may be prominent, it is at state level at the moment that the crisis is, in the end, usually played out. States are still the chief actors on the international stage, and the chief satisfiers of human needs in the domestic arena. This is not to underestimate the increasing power and significance of transnational forces or the implosions that have engulfed or threaten to engulf vulnerable states. If the state system evolves into something else with the passing of western hegemony, this is another eventuality that is beyond present projection. Inter-state conflicts are conflicts between states. Ethno-national conflicts are conflicts to determine the identity of the state. Ideological governance conflicts are conflicts to decide the nature of the state. Economic conflicts are conflicts to control the resources of the state.

Interstate conflict

Realists wrongly discount the significance of radical disagreement in interstate conflict. In Chapter 2, mention was made of Thucydides' Melian Dialogue in his *History of the Peloponnesian War*. This is usually seen as the *locus classicus* of the realist view. The Athenian generals dismissed the moral arguments of the Melians and asked them to decide in accordance with the reality of the discrepancy in power. But the Melian dialogue, invented though it was by Thucydides, can just as well be seen as itself a radical disagreement. Given the discrepancy in power in favour of the Athenians, it was in the *interest* of the Athenians to argue (and no doubt at the same time believe) the realist case. This was a stick with which to beat their main opponents, the Spartans, through accusations of hypocrisy:

> Of all the people we know the Spartans are most conspicuous for believing that what they like doing is honourable and what suits their interests is just.
> (Thucydides 1954: 363)

We do not have a record of how the Spartans would have replied. But in that radical disagreement, integral to the linguistic intractability accompanying and structuring the Peloponnesian war, the realist position itself would have been part of what was disputed. Such, too, I suggest, is likely to be the case in any future geo-political confrontations between China and India, or between China and the United States. Even if Thucydides' prediction is borne out, and 'the growth of Chinese power and the fear this causes in America' makes conflict inevitable, in the discursive sphere just as in the case of earlier confrontation with the Soviet Union – and the current 'war on terror' – the 'battle for hearts and minds' will be at the centre of the physical struggle. In the political conflicts of his day, Machiavelli was a passionate Florentine/Roman republican. Radical disagreement is still the chief verbal manifestation of intractable interstate conflict.

Ethnonationalist conflict

Given the continuing mismatch between state borders (some 200 states) and the geographical distribution of peoples (in some estimates up to 5000 groups), there is no prospect of the two coinciding. Even breaking up the current state system would not help because, however small the fragments, there are still smaller minorities cut off within them. So ethno-nationalist conflict can be expected to persist. In this case, I do not think that the further suggestion that this will be marked by radical disagreement in the linguistic sphere is likely to be denied. Radical disagreement centres on disputed questions of identity and rights. As to the scale of ethno-nationalist and other kinds of conflict that would accompany the collapse of states the size of Pakistan or Nigeria or Indonesia – let alone India or China – only experience of the aftermath of the break-up of the Soviet Union or former Yugoslavia may give an indication.

Ideological government conflict

It is much harder to predict future ideological contests to determine the nature of government – fascist versus democratic, communist versus capitalist, religious versus secular. What will follow? Few predicted the increase in religious conflict over the past 30 years. Perhaps it is when existing systems of government prove incapable of meeting needs and delivering desired goods that the ground is fertile for the rise of alternatives. The fascist and communist tide was on the rise in the 1930s during the great depression which destroyed middle-class incomes and the bases for centrist politics. In the Arab world, it was into the vacuum left by the failure of nationalist and socialist experiments in the 1950s and 1960s that Islamist political ideology has rushed. At transnational level hierarchical-imperial structures such as those underpinned by United States economic and foreign policy interests elicit various forms of globalized reaction. I think that we simply have no idea what future ideological configurations may arise. But, whatever they are, here again it hardly seems contentious to say that the phenomenon of radical disagreement will be prominent.

Economic conflict

Some conflict analysts claim that statistical indicators of need deprivation do not correlate closely with the incidence of armed conflict in comparison with indicators for economic incentives. As a result they argue that economic 'greed' causes major armed conflict more than 'grievance':

The combination of large exports of primary commodities, a high proportion of young men, and economic decline drastically increases risk. Greed seems more important than grievance.

(Collier 2000: 110)

This leads to a setting aside of verbalized 'grievance' explanations and a concomitant discounting of the significance of radical disagreement:

I should emphasise that I do not mean to be cynical. I am not arguing that rebels necessarily deceive either others or themselves in explaining their motivation in terms of grievance. Rather, I am simply arguing that since both greed-motivated rebel organizations will embed their behaviour in a narrative of grievance, the observation of that narrative provides no informational content to the researcher as to the true motivation for rebellion.

(Collier 1999: 1)

But this controversy has run its course to the point where Paul Collier himself acknowledges that whatever the 'true motivation' may be, those wanting to prevent war or support post-war peacebuilding need, after all, to address expressed grievances seriously; he tries to save his argument by distinguishing between 'objective' and 'subjective' grievances:

This requires at a minimum that the grievances be addressed, even if though on average they are not objectively any more serious than those in peaceful societies. If, indeed, group grievance has been manufactured by rebel indoctrination, it can potentially be deflated by political gestures. While grievances may need to be addressed objectively, the main purpose of addressing them is probably for their value in changing perceptions.

(Collier 2001: 159)

Even in economic conflicts, verbalized grievance, and hence the phenomenon of radical disagreement, remains significant after all.

Future drivers of conflict

Behind all this lie major global drivers of future conflict. Here the connection with the phenomenon of radical disagreement is, as it were, at one remove – except in respect of the international struggles to define them and to determine what to do about them. The global drivers of future conflict fuel the conflict complexes and conflict configurations from which the axes of radical disagreement themselves emerge, and contribute to the reinforcement of systemic linguistic intractability.

It is easy to be overwhelmed by the scale of the gloomy prognostications. They seem to start so far back and to build to such a size that the late-emergent phenomena of protest, conflict party formation and radical disagreement seem no more than the froth on the surface, itself already shaped from the outset by the economic, political and cultural forces that have produced it. On the other hand, if the articulation of human choices has any purchase at all in the shaping of the future, then once again a site for radical disagreement has been defined in the ensuing political struggles.

Doom-laden lists of future global drivers of conflict include the following.

Economic inequality

The vast deprivations, exclusions, co-optations and controls that make up the slowly evolving lineaments of late capitalist global political economy are seen to remain impervious to protest and reform. Always the victims are the 'bottom billion' no matter what convulsions may shake the upper echelons, as in the recent 'credit crunch'. This huge unfairness seems to be reinforced rather than undermined by the evolution of international institutions, from the state system itself to UN agencies and the International Financial Institutions that purport to embody universal emancipatory norms, and to work to implement 'millennial goals' in the interest of the dispossessed.

According to the World Institute for Development Economics Research (WIDER):

> while the richest 10% of the adults of the world own 85% of global household wealth, the bottom half collectively owns barely 1%. Even more strikingly, the average person in the top 10% owns nearly 3,000 times the wealth of the average person in the bottom 10%.
>
> (WIDER 2006, quoted Rogers 2007: 90)

Three areas – North America, Europe and the rich Asia-Pacific (Japan, South Korea, Taiwan, Singapore, Australia, New Zealand) – own 88 per cent of global household wealth. Rapid recent economic growth in countries like China and India is 'lifting millions out of poverty', although wealth discrepancy is still extreme, and rising expectations and relative deprivation are recognized by students of revolution as perhaps more dangerous than habitual and apparently ineluctable poverty.

Much greater relative population growth in poorer parts of the world concentrates increasing numbers of unemployed young people – particularly young men – in politically fragile, often autocratic and repressive, states without hope of betterment. Kept on the margins of global capitalism, and largely excluded from rapid development in the richer areas, a huge pool of recruits for revolutionary movements, and often violent, black market operations, is continually being replenished and deepened. On some estimates more than 40 million new jobs would need to be created in the Arab Middle East alone to neutralize this. These populations are increasingly concentrated in cities. In 1975, one third of the world's population lived in cities. By 2025, it is likely to be two-thirds. In some poor countries, half the population is under 18. Even in oil-rich Saudi Arabia two-thirds are under 30, of whom a third are unemployed.

The environment

The linked effects of material scarcity, climate change, and natural resource depletion are widely projected to have major political impacts. Thomas Homer-Dixon predicted some time ago a looming concatenation of severe environmental constraints and human conflicts (1991; 1994), with 'simple scarcity' conflicts over water, forests, fishing and agricultural land, 'group-identity conflicts' triggered by large-scale population movements (climate change will disproportionately affect tropical and sub-tropical landmasses where most of the world's population lives), and 'deprivation' conflicts caused by relative depletion of natural resources. There are any number of predictions in this area, from war in the Arctic over the hunt for oil and gas, to 'water wars' to control disputed aquifers that lie under and across international borders (the Tigris affects Iran, Iraq, Syria, Turkey; the Nile affects Burundi, DRC, Egypt, Eritrea, Ethiopia, Kenya, Rwanda, Sudan, Tanzania, Uganda.

Drivers of future conflict are seen to be systemically interconnected. A combination of environmental pressure and the global socio-economic divide, for example, is predicted in some estimates to be likely to accelerate migratory pressures possibly by a factor of ten over the next decades. Existing political structures may be unable to control them.

Gender oppression

From a different angle of analysis, the continuing plight of a high proportion of one half of the human family, oppressed by structures and traditions of patriarchy, is highlighted as a deep source of future conflict, and a site for emancipatory struggles that will challenge most of the dominant power structures, attitudes and behaviours that are in one way or another based on it.

The passing of Western hegemony

Here is the predicted looming 'transvaluation of all values', as the Western liberal values that have been dominant for so long – democracy, human rights, free markets, secularism, developed civil societies, individualism, the state system itself – are challenged by the rising economic and political power, and sheer demographic weight, of non-western societies, polities and cultures. At the beginning of the twentieth century, Europe contained 25 per cent of the world's population. By the middle of this century, this is predicted to fall to 7.5 per cent. In 1950, the combined Arab population was 60 million compared with 120 million in Britain, France and Spain, the three main imperial powers in the region. By 2000, the population of Iraq alone, which had been 2 million in 1918 compared to 45 million in the UK, had reached 30 million. The average age in Iraq was 18 in 2000; in Europe it was 38 (Ehrman 2009). Will the main declared values on which the existing international system is based evolve into truly global values, or will they turn out to have been merely 'western'? If so, what will replace them?

Weapons development

Into this complex systemic set of actual and potential conflict formations flow ever-evolving military technologies and proliferating supply routes. These weapons range from numerically by far the largest killers – knives and small arms – up to the potentially catastrophic weapons of mass destruction. Looking a hundred years ahead, the odds on biological, chemical or nuclear weapons technology at some point falling into the hands of governments or groups willing to use them are impossible to calculate, but frighteningly easy to imagine. Linked to this, are the extraordinary prospects for enhanced governmental control via new generations of surveillance technologies, 'non-lethal' crowd control weapons, and methods of persuasion.

Putting all this together, the question is: can existing economic and political structures contain and manage these enormous stresses, particularly at a time when the revolution in communications is making the huge discrepancies between the resources available to the haves and the have-nots increasingly obvious? Given political convulsion in the state system, or a possible future economic collapse, as at one time threatened in 2008, it is not hard for pessimists to envisage the possibility of a break-up of the institutions in the international system as we have known them, and the onset of a chaotic and warring global anarchy (the 'Mad Max' scenario).

Conclusion

But none of this is inevitable. The advent of the new Obama administration in the United States has heartened those who look to a further evolution of liberal cosmopolitanism to guide humanity through the present turbulence. Criticism from the right that this lacks hard-headed realism, and from the left that it fails to address structural global inequalities are still to be argued out, as are a complex of as yet sporadically developed critiques from non-western, non-liberal parts of the world. Will world economic and political institutions be reformed to meet basic human needs more adequately – particularly those of the 'bottom billion'? Will humanity learn to live within a sustainable environment for the benefit of future generations? Will the aspirations of women in all their variety be recognized and acted upon to the same extent as those of men? Will the eirenic elements in the Hindu/Buddhist, Confucian, Judeo-Christian and Islamic civilizations – as well as secular and other traditions – prevail and provide mutual meaning and hope for those who live by those values? Will the constant development of ever-more lethal weaponry be controlled? Or will the opposites of all these happen?

What is the main battleground where future wars of words associated with the most intractable global conflict formations, and with the main concerted efforts to overcome them, are likely to be fought out? The ongoing revolution in global communication strongly suggests that it will be via the mobile phone and the internet, perhaps even putting global access into the hands of the most disadvantaged for the first time in history once literacy levels, the cheapness of the technology, and the interest of providers in increasing the global market make this possible.

Still in its infancy, but developing at astonishing speed, who can tell what forms the World Wide Web may ramify into over the next century? It seems likely that it will be the locus for political struggles of all kinds in which the balance between defence (shutting it down and controlling it) and emancipation (circumventing restrictions) will ebb and flow. This is a vast global laboratory for understanding and managing the associated radical disagreements. Across the internet, the struggle for values will be played out – for example, the battle of languages such as Mandarin challenging English for pre-eminence.

Part I of this book identified a gap in the analysis of complex conflict systems. The phenomenon of radical disagreement, the chief verbal manifestation of intractable political conflict, does not appear in monological third-party analysis or complex systemic maps. As a result, a careful tracing of patterns of competing discourses embedded in the dynamic conflict system is missing from the analysis. Mental models are described subjectively, and the discursive battle is consequently dismissed as merely epiphenomenal or functional for the deeper sociological, cultural, psychological or political drivers of conflict. Recommendations for discursive transformation based on this analysis take the form of the promotion of dialogue for mutual understanding. Although this achieves remarkable results when conditions are propitious – outstanding grass-roots dialogue work creates the whole foundation for future transformation – it is not surprising that in times of maximum intractability at political level it proves impotent.

The suggestion in Part II of this book is to look in the opposite direction in these circumstances by taking the phenomenon of radical disagreement itself as the main focus of attention. Radical disagreement introduces a different order of complexity. It is a systemic and emergent manifestation in which the whole is dramatically different from the sum of its parts. In light of this, insights gained from the phenomenology and epistemology of radical disagreement can better inform the practice of managing agonistic dialogue. A greater focus on the strategic engagement of discourses can sustain communication even during times of maximum intractability, helping to build capacity for challengers, assisting possessors to decide if, when and how it is best to settle, and aiding those who seek to manage conflict non-violently. In terms of emancipation, inclusion and respect, it can give voice to those involved in political struggles who often are not heard, and can encourage them to speak in their own words, not words put into their mouths by third parties, however expert or well-intentioned. The fact that in the phenomenology of agonistic dialogue conflict parties find that they are not nearer but much further apart than was thought, and the fact that in the epistemology of agonistic dialogue third parties find that there is no adequate theory or philosophy of radical disagreement may themselves eventually turn out to be transformative discoveries. This book has aimed to open up the topic. It makes no claim to have developed it very far. Its empirical base is still very small. But I think that the potential is great.

Part III looks to the future. It suggests that the phenomenon of radical disagreement gives insight into the nature of human difference that monological accounts – however subtle – cannot match. It predicts that the phenomenon of radical disagreement will not go away, and it proposes that awareness and knowledge of agonistic dialogue may help to some extent to neutralize the most devastating consequences of linguistic intractability. At the moment, the phenomenon of radical disagreement is dismissed as naive, simplistic and superficial. But, if so, it is a naivety that confounds third-party explanation however sophisticated, a simplicity that defies expert analysis however complex, and a superficiality that nevertheless reaches right down to the bottom. Faced with the prospect that human history will continue to be conflictual, and that the chief linguistic aspect of human conflict will continue to be radical disagreement, taking the phenomenon of radical disagreement seriously – learning how it can be acknowledged, explored, understood and managed – is not the least of the requirements for human survival in an irredeemably agonistic world.

Epilogue
Having the last word

At the end of Chapter 5, the exploration of agonistic dialogue suggested that what shows this to be *my* opinion in a radical disagreement is that it is a *true* opinion. A *true* opinion is *my* opinion. In the epilogue, it is usual for the author to address the reader directly. This is the author's last word. All at once, the author becomes reflexive. In didactic books, the author anticipates the reader's objections in advance. The author is writing under the moment of description. In the pre-imagined radical disagreement between author and reader, the moment of description plays the function outlined in Chapter 5. The author refers to the work and to the reader's criticism of the work and thereby absorbs the consciousness of self-distance and irony. The author expresses modesty in the face of the listener's expected response, or is braced for criticism, or takes the opportunity to clear up objections with polite condescension. But the function of the last word is to include all of this in the beam of light that the book shines into the future. The book is a window through which, having accounted for and thereby neutralized opposition, the author can once again finally enjoy the peaceful experience of looking to the far horizon – and pointing at how things are.

These are Hans-Georg Gadamer's last words in *Truth and Method*:

> But I will stop here. The ongoing dialogue permits no final conclusion. It would be a poor hermeneuticist who thought he could have, or had to have, the last word.
>
> (1960/1986: 579)

Gadamer refers to *Truth and Method* and to the reader's response to *Truth and Method*. He says that within the terms of his book, neither *Truth and Method* nor the reader's criticism of *Truth and Method* is, or can be, the last word. That is Gadamer's last word. He foresees and has accounted for the future and the posthumous existence of *Truth and Method* into the future.

This is how Theodor Adorno addresses his anticipated critics in *Negative Dialectics*:

> The author is prepared for the attacks to which *Negative Dialectics* will expose him. He feels no rancor and does not begrudge the joy of those in either camp

[Marxist or anti-Marxist] who will proclaim that they knew it all the time and now he was confessing.

(1966/2004: xxi)

In expectation of radical disagreement, Adorno refers to *Negative Dialectics* and to expected readers' attacks on *Negative Dialectics*. In so doing, he refers to the fact that the attacks will come from the two camps into which he has penned his critics. His last word anticipates the future and the nature of his readers' reactions.

And here is Jürgen Habermas' final communication in his postscript to *Between Facts and Norms*:

> There is a sense in which an author first learns what he has said in a text from the reactions of his readers. In the process, he also becomes aware of what he meant to say, and he gains an opportunity to express more clearly what he wanted to say. I find myself in this position hardly one year after the appearance of my book ... Certainly the interpreter enjoys the advantage of understanding a text better than the author himself, but on the occasion of a new printing, the author may be permitted to take the role of an interpreter and attempt to recapitulate the core idea that informs the whole book as he sees it. This also allows him to clear up some of the objections that have been raised in the meantime.
>
> (1992/1996: 447)

In response to radical disagreement, Habermas refers to *Between Facts and Norms* and to readers' criticisms of *Between Facts and Norms*. He points to the fact that the interpreter understands a text better than the author, that the author can become interpreter in response, and that in this case the last word in the new postscript to *Between Facts and Norms* clarifies what the original text says and clears up some of the objections raised against it. He is able, in his new last word, to reaffirm and strengthen his previous last word. Both together can now project themselves confidently into an already anticipated future.

So it must be with this book. In my last word, I address the reader. I refer to my book and to the reader's future criticism of my book. I write under the moment of description. In doing so, I anticipate the reader's objections, by saying, for example, that I cannot anticipate them. That is, after all, what this book predicts. Like all polemical authors who anticipate radical disagreement, I try to neutralize my reflexive awareness of my own mortality in this way, and thereby make a bid for immortality. This book is a *window* and through it my last word can point at what lies beyond. See Figure E.1.

Readers react in different ways. Acceptance brings happiness to the author. Abstention or faint praise brings disappointment. Indifference brings a sense of loneliness. But what about outright rejection?

So far I have referred to myself and to 'the reader'. But now I hand the microphone over to – you. And all at once the kaleidoscope of reflexive terms (this book, I, you, temporal references) is affected. This is not what I anticipated at all. You

Figure E.1 The window

refute what is written here. You see that this book contains all the tell-tale marks of didacticism – the prevalence of the present indicative tense, the recurrent phrase 'not ... rather', the general form 'it used to be thought that ... now I can reveal'. You point to errors of fact, misreadings of texts, superficiality of judgement, and contradictions in argument. And now this book is a *picture* – namely a *false picture* – that is shown up as such by how things are. That is what you point at in refuting this book. See Figure E.2.

But this is still my last word. I have not, in reality, handed the microphone over yet. Perhaps this is the situation:

'First I as author write this book, then you as reader criticize it.'

But now it is plain why this description fails. When you seize the microphone and I seize it back, our radical disagreement becomes a struggle to control the microphone. This affects all the reflexive terms. Familiar landmarks defined by them slide. What do 'this book', 'I', 'you' and the temporal references refer to? In the radical disagreement, they are contested. This book is not separate from the radical disagreement about it. The distinction between author and reader is already hopelessly equivocated.

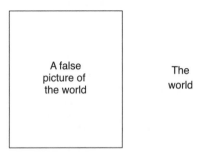

Figure E.2 The picture

At first I want to say that in our radical disagreement, this book is, and is not, *both* a window *and* a (false) picture. But now this third-party description fails too. There is no room for it. So is this book a *mirror*? See Figure E.3.

If this book is a mirror, then what this book says is that in our radical disagreement, neither you nor I appear in the mirror at all.

Figure E.3 The mirror

Glossary

Given the unusual nature of the subject, it has not been possible to avoid either coining new terms or interpreting existing terms in new ways. All usages are explained where they appear, but it also seems helpful to collect some of these terms together here.

Linguistic intractability   Intractable conflict is conflict that resists settlement and transformation. Linguistic intractability is the verbal aspect of intractable conflict.

Radical disagreement   Radical disagreement is the chief linguistic manifestation of intense political conflict. It is the key to linguistic intractability

The bar line notation and the limits of radical disagreement   Bar lines mark out examples of radical disagreement in written notation. If there is not enough in common, the bar lines are empty. This is mutual misunderstanding. The parties are talking about different things. If there is too much in common, the bar lines disappear. This is mutual convergence. Either way, there is not yet or no longer a radical disagreement. These are *limits* to radical disagreement.

The phenomenon of radical disagreement   The phenomenon of radical agreement is what is said in the exchanges between conflict parties. It is what appears between bar lines in written notation.

The phenomenology of radical disagreement   The phenomenology of radical disagreement is the study of (the phenomenon of) radical disagreement. It is the study of what conflict parties say in intractable conflicts. Any third-party verbal contributions are fed back for comment into these exchanges. In the end, it is the conflict parties who undertake the exploration.

The sociology, psychology, politics, etc. of radical disagreement   In contrast, the sociology, psychology and politics of radical disagreement are the study of the social, psychological and political origins and functions of radical disagreement. These are descriptions, analyses, interpretations and explanations of other people's texts, utterances, speech acts and discourses by third-party experts.

The epistemology of radical disagreement   The epistemology of radical disagreement is the study of what third parties (analysts or interveners) say about radical disagreement. In the epistemology of radical disagreement, what these parties say is tested by applying it to examples of the radical disagreements that they purport to describe, interpret, explain or transform.

Relations of interest, relations of power and relations of belief   Relations of interest are the contradictory aspirations of conflict parties in intractable conflicts. Relations of power are the relative capacities of conflict parties to fulfil their aspirations. Relations of belief are the radical disagreements that both express and fuel these struggles. Relations of belief in intractable conflicts are not juxtapositions of announced conviction (beliefs and belief systems) considered separately and attributed to conflict parties accordingly, but the clash of claim and counter-claim (recommendation, justification, refutation) in the crucible of dynamic conflict.

The polylogical and the monological   The polylogical refers to the fact that radical disagreement is made up of contributions by many speakers in dynamic interconnection. Radical disagreement is systemic and emergent – the whole is greater than the sum of its parts. The monological refers to the fact that third-party accounts (including this book) are single voiced. Demonstrations of the discrepancy between these two terms reveal key insights into linguistic intractability in the epistemology of radical disagreement. The polylogical nature of radical disagreement is distinct from more general forms of dialogism (heteroglossia) or intertextuality.

Agonistic dialogue   Agonistic dialogue is the dialogue of struggle; it is the dialogue between enemies in intense and intractable conflicts. It is that part of radical disagreement in which conflict parties directly engage each other's utterances.

Dialogue for mutual understanding   Dialogue for mutual understanding is the form of dialogue favoured in conflict resolution (settlement and transformation). Its aim is to overcome radical disagreement.

Dialogue for strategic engagement   Dialogue for strategic engagement is the form of dialogue promoted in the management of intractable political conflicts when settlement and transformation are premature. Its aim is to explore the strategic implications of radical disagreement.

The strategic engagement of discourses   The strategic engagement of discourses (SED) is the result of success in the promotion of dialogue for strategic engagement. The strategic engagement of discourses operates at three levels: intra-party radical disagreement; inter-party radical disagreement; and radical disagreement among and within third parties, as well as between third parties and conflict parties

The hexagon of radical disagreement   The hexagon of radical disagreement is the simplest model for two-party composite radical disagreement. It defines six axes of radical disagreement within and between conflict parties and illuminates the SED aim of combining inclusive intra-party strategic dialogue tracks with inter-party and third-party strategic engagement.

Extremism of ends and extremism of means   Extremism of ends is intransigence in relation to strategic goals. Extremism of means is intransigence in choosing violent means to achieve strategic goals. The distinction between these two concepts is a key to managing continuing radical disagreement nonviolently even when dialogue for mutual understanding so far fails.

References

Abu-Nimer, M. (1999) *Dialogue, Conflict Resolution and Change: Arab-Jewish Encounters in Israel*, Albany, NY: SUNY Press.

Abu-Nimer, M. (2003) *Nonviolence and Peacebuilding in Islam*, Florida: University Press of Florida.

Adorno, T. (1966/2004) *Negative Dialectics*, trans E. Ashton, New York: Continuum.

Al' Alwani, T. (1997) *The Ethics of Disagreement in Islam,* trans A. Hamid, Herndon, VA: The International Institute of Islamic Thought.

Alon, I. (2007/9) *A Linguistic Analysis of the 2002/2007 Arab Peace Initiative Documents.* Available online at: http://www.peace-security-council.org/ articles.asp?id=763

Althusser, L. (1970/1971) 'Ideology and ideological state apparatuses (notes towards an investigation)' in *Lenin and Philosophy and Other Essays*, trans. B. Brewster, London: New Left Books.

Anderson, B. (1991) *Imagined Communities: Reflections on the Origin and Spread of Nationalism.* (2nd edition) London: Verso.

Adrey, R. (1966) *The Territorial Imperative*, London: Collins.

Arnswald (2002) 'On the certainty of uncertainty: language games and forms of life in Gadamer and Wittgenstein', in Malpas, *et al.* (eds) *Gadamer's Century*, Cambridge, MA: MIT Press, 25–42.

Atkinson, J. and Heritage, J. (eds) (1984) *Structures of Social Action: Studies in Conversation Analysis*, Cambridge: Cambridge University Press.

Aughey, A. (2002) 'The art and effect of political lying in Northern Ireland', *Irish Political Studies*, 17(2): 1–16.

Augsburger, D. (1992) *Conflict Mediation Across Cultures*, Louisville, KY: Westminster/ John Knox Press.

Avruch, K., Black, P. and Scimecca, J. (1991) *Conflict Resolution: Cross Cultural Perspectives*, Westport, CT: Greenwood Press.

Axelrod, R. (1984) *The Evolution of Cooperation,* New York: Basic Books.

Azar, E. (1990) *The Management of Protracted Social Conflict: Theory and Cases*, Aldershot: Dartmouth.

Barash, D. (2000) *Approaches to Peace*, Oxford: OUP.

Barker, C. (2003) *Cultural Studies: Theory and Practice* (second edition), London: Sage.

Bar-On, M. (2006) 'Conflicting narratives or narratives of a conflict?' in R. Rotberg *Israeli and Palestinian Narratives of Conflict*, Bloomington, IN: Indiana University Press, 142–73.

Barthes, R. (1957/1993) *Mythologies*, London: Vintage.

Bashir, B. (2009) 'Reference Report on the Regaining the Initiative Project', unpublished.

Berdal, M. and Malone, D. (eds) (2000) *Greed and Grievance: Economic Agendas in Civil Wars*, Boulder, CO: Lynne Rienner.

Berger, P. and Luckmann, T. (1966) *The Social Construction of Reality: A Treatise in the Sociology of Knowledge*, New York: Doubleday and Co.

Benhabib, S. (1992) *Situating the Self: Gender, Community, and Postmodernism in Contemporary Ethics*, Cambridge: Polity.

Bhabha, H. (1994) *The Location of Culture*, London: Routledge.

Bieber, F. and Daskalovski, Z. (eds) (2003) *Understanding the War in Kosovo*, London: Frank Cass.

Billig, M. (1991) *Ideologies and Beliefs*, London: Sage.

Blair, J. and Johnson R. (eds) (1980) *Informal Logic: The First International Symposium*, London: Edgepress.

Blake, R. and Mouton, J. (1970) 'The fifth achievement', *Journal of Applied Behavioral Science*, 6(4): 413–26.

Blake, R. and Mouton, J. (1984) *Solving Costly Organizational Conflicts*, San Francisco: Jossey-Bass.

Bleiker, R. (2001) 'The aesthetic turn in international political theory', *Millennium* 30(3): 509–33.

Bohm, D. (1996) *On Dialogue*, London: Routledge.

Booth, K. and Dunne, T. (eds) (2002) *Worlds in Collision: Terror and the Future of Global Order*, Houndmills, UK: Palgrave Macmillan.

Bouchard, D. (ed.) and Sherry, S. (1977) *Language, Counter-Memory and Practice: Selected Essays and Interviews*, Ithaca, NY: Cornell University Press.

Boulding, K. (1962) *Conflict and Defense: A General Theory*, New York: Harper and Brothers.

Boulding, K. (1990) *Three Faces of Power*, London: Sage.

Bowell, T. and Kemp, G. (2002) *Critical Thinking: A Concise Guide*, 2nd edn, London: Routledge.

Bradford, B (2004) 'Managing disagreement constructively', online source Handout 9.

Broome, B. (1993) 'Managing differences in conflict resolution: the role of relational empathy' in D. Sandole and H. van der Merwe (eds) *Conflict Resolution Theory and Practice: Integration and Application*, Manchester: Manchester University Press, 97–111.

Brown, C. (1992) *International Relations Theory: New Normative Approaches*, Hemel Hempstead, UK: Harvester Wheatsheaf.

Brown, C. (2002) 'Narratives of religion, civilization and modernity' in K. Booth and T. Dunne (eds) *Worlds in Collision: Terror and the Future of Global Order*, 293–302.

Brown, C. (2007) 'Tragedy, 'tragic choices' and contemporary international political theory', *International Relations*, 21(1): 5–13.

Burgess, H. and Burgess, G. (1996) 'Constructive confrontation: a transformative approach to intractable conflicts', *Mediation Quarterly* 13(4), Summer: 305–22.

Burgess, G. and Burgess, H. (1997) *Constructive Confrontation: A Strategy for Dealing With Intractable Environmental Conflicts*, Working Paper 97–1, www.colorado.edu/conflict.

Burns, D. (2006) 'Evaluation in Complex Governance Arenas: The Potential of Large-Scale System Action Research' in B. Williams and I. Imam, *Using Systems Concepts in Evaluation*, Fairhaven, MA: American Evaluation Association, 181–95.

Burr, V. (1995) *An Introduction to Social Constructionism*, London: Routledge.

Burton, J. (1968) *Systems, States, Diplomacy and Rules*, London: Macmillan.

Burton, J. (1997) *Violence Explained*, Manchester: Manchester University Press.

Carnegie Commission on Preventing Deadly Conflict (1997) *Preventing Deadly Conflict*, Washington D.C.: Carnegie Corporation of New York.

Center for Monitoring the Impact of Peace (2000/2001) *Report: Jews, Israel and Peace in Palestinian School Textbooks* (November 2001); *Arabs and Palestinians in Israeli Textbooks* (September 2000), New York: CMIP.

Chagnon, N. (1983: 3rd edn) *Yanomamo: The Fierce People*, New York: Holt, Reinhart and Winston.

Chanteur, J. (1992) *From War to Peace*, Boulder Co.: Westview Press.

Charteris-Black, J. (2005) *Politicians and Rhetoric: The Persuasive Power of Metaphor*, New York: Palgrave.

Cheshire, L. (1985) *The Light of Many Suns*, London: Methuen.

Chilton, P. (2004) *Analysing Political Discourse: Theory and Practice*, London: Routledge.

Cohen R. (1991) *Negotiating Across Cultures: Communication Obstacles in International Diplomacy*, Washington D.C.: United States Institute of Peace.

Cole, P. and Morgan, J, (eds) (1975) *Syntax and Semantics: Vol. 3. Speech Acts*, New York: Academic Press.

Coleman, P., Vallacher, R., Nowak, A. and Bui-Wrzosinska, L. (2008) *Intractable Conflict as an Attractor: Presenting a Dynamical-Systems Approach to Conflict Escalation and Intractability*, draft chapter for *Systemic Thinking and Conflict Transformation*, Berlin: Berghof Foundation (forthcoming).

Collier, P. (1999) 'Doing Well Out of War', Paper Given at London Conference on Economic Agendas in Civil Wars, April 26–7.

Collier, P. (2000) 'Doing well out of war: an economic perspective', in M. Berdal and D. Malone (eds) *Greed and Grievance*, Boulder, CO: Lynne Rienner, 91–111.

Collier, P. (2001) 'Economic causes of civil conflict and their implications for policy' in C. Crocker, F. Hampson and P. Aall (eds) *Turbulent Peace: The Challenges of Managing International Conflict*, Washington, DC: United States Institute of Peace.

Collier, P. and Hoeffler, A. (2001): *Greed and Grievance in Civil War*, World Bank Development Research Group.

Cox, R. (1981) 'Social forces, states and world orders: beyond international relations theory', *Millennium Journal of International Studies*, 10(2): 126–55.

Davey, R. with J. Cole (1993) *A Channel of Peace: The Story of the Corrymeela Community*, Grandville, MA: Zondervan.

Davidson, D. (1984) 'On the very idea of a conceptual scheme', in *Inquiries into Truth and Interpretation*, Oxford: Clarendon Press, 183–98.

Dawkins, R. (1989) *The Selfish Gene*, Oxford: Oxford University Press.

Dédaic, M. and Nelson, D. (eds) (2003) *At War with Words*, New York: Mouton de Gruyter.

Deleuze, G. and Guattari, F. (1976/1981) 'Rhizome', trans P. Foss and P. Patton, *I & C*, 8, 49–71.

Derrida, J. (1994) *Spectres of Marx: The State of the Debt, the Work of Mourning, and the New International*, trans P. Kamuf, London: Routledge.

Dershowitz, A. (2005) *The Case for Peace: How the Arab-Israeli Conflict Can Be Resolved*, Hoboken, NJ: John Wiley & Sons Inc.

Deveaux, M. (2000) *Cultural Pluralism and Dilemmas of Justice*, Ithaca, NY: Cornell UP.

De Waal, F. (1989) *Peacemaking Among Primates*, Cambridge, MA: Harvard UP.

Deutsch, M. (1949) 'A theory of cooperation and competition', *Human Relations* 2, 129–52.

Deutsch, M. (1973) *The Resolution of Conflict: Constructive and Destructive Processes*, New York: Yale University Press.

Deutsch, M. (2000) 'Cooperation and competition' in M. Deutsch and P. Coleman (eds) *The Handbook of Conflict Resolution: Theory and Practice*, San Francisco: Jossey-Bass, 21–40.

de Zulueta, F. (2006) *From Pain to Violence: The Traumatic Roots of Destructiveness*, second edition, Chichester: John Wiley.

Dollard, J., Doob, L., Miller, N., Mowrer, O. and Sears, R. (1939) *Frustration and Aggression*, New Haven: Yale UP.

Doyle, M. and Sambanis, N. (2006) *Making War and Building Peace: United Nations Peace Operations*, Princeton, NJ: Princeton University Press.

Drew, P. (1992) 'Contested evidence in courtroom cross-examination: the case of a trial for rape' in Drew and Heritage *Talk at Work: Interaction in Institutional Settings*, 470–520.

Drew, P. and Heritage, J. (eds) (1992) *Talk at Work: Interaction in Institutional Settings*, Cambridge: Cambridge University Press.

Dryzek, J. (1990) *Discursive Democracy: Politics, Policy and Political Science*, New York: Cambridge University Press.

Dudouet, V. (2006) *Nonviolent Resistance and Conflict Transformation in Power Asymmetries*, Berlin: Berghof Research Center for Constructive Conflict Management.

Duffield, M. (2001) *Global Governance and the New Wars: The Merging of Development and Security*, London: Zed Books.

Dukes, F. (1996) *Resolving Public Conflict: Transforming Community and Governance*, Manchester: Manchester University Press.

Edwards, D. and Potter, J. (1992) *Discursive Psychology*, London: Sage.

Ehrman, R. (2009) *The Power of Numbers*, Buckingham: University of Buckingham Press.

Evans, R. (1997) *In Defence of History*, London: Granta.

Fairclough, N. (1989) *Language and Power*, Harlow, UK: Longman.

Fanon, F. (1961) *The Wretched of the Earth*, London: Penguin.

Festinger, L. (1957) *A Theory of Cognitive Dissonance*, Stanford: Stanford UP.

Filardo, L. (2008) 'A comparative study of the discursive legitimisation of the Agreement by the four main Northern Irish parties through time', *Ethnopolitics*, 7(1): 21–42.

Filardo, L. (forthcoming 2010) 'Legitimising through language: political discourse worlds in Northern Ireland after the 1998 Agreement' in K. Hayward and C. O'Donnell (eds) *Political Discourse and Conflict Resolution*.

Finnis, J., Boyle, J. and Grisez, G. (1987) *Nuclear Deterrence, Morality and Realism*, Oxford: Oxford University Press.

Fisher, A. (1988) *The Logic of Real Arguments*, Cambridge: Cambridge University Press.

Fisher, Roger, Ury, W. and Patton, B. (1981/1991) 2nd ed. *Getting to Yes: Negotiating Agreement Without Giving In*, New York: Penguin.

Fisher, Roger, Kopelman, E. and Schneider, A. (1994) *Beyond Machiavelli: Tools for Coping with Conflict*, Cambridge Mass.: Harvard University Press.

Fisher, Roger and Shapiro, D. (2005/7) *Building Agreement Using Emotions As You Negotiate*, London: Random House.

Fisher, Ronald (1997) *Interactive Conflict Resolution*, Syracuse, New York: Syracuse University Press.

Fitzduff, M. (1989) *A Typology of Community Relations Work and Contextual Necessities*, Belfast: Community Relations Council.

Floyer Acland, A. (1995) *Resolving Disputes Without Going to Court*, London: Century.

Flynn, T. (1994) 'Foucault's mapping of history' in G. Gutting (ed.) *The Cambridge Companion to Foucault*, Cambridge: CUP, 28–46.

Follett, M. (1940) in H. Metcalf and L. Urwick (eds) *Dynamic Administration: The Collected Papers of Mary Parker Follett*, New York, Harper.

Foucault, M. (1977) *Language, Counter-Memory and Practice: Selected Essays and Interviews*, trans D. Bouchard and S. Sherry, Ithaca NY: Cornell University Press.

Foucault, M. (1980) *Power/Knowledge: Selected Interviews and Other Writings 1972–1999*, trans C. Gordon, New York: Pantheon.

Fowler, R., Hodge, B., Kress, G., Trew, T. (1979) *Language and Control*, London: Routledge & Kegan Paul.

Frost, M. (1996) *Ethics in International Relations: A Constitutive Theory*, Cambridge: CUP.

Fry, D. and Bjorkqvist, K. (eds) (1997) *Cultural Variation in Conflict Resolution: Alternatives to Violence*, Mahwah, NJ: Lawrence Erlbaum Associates.

Gadamer, H-G. (1975) *Truth and Method*, London, Sheed and Ward.

Gadamer, H-G. (1960/1986) *Truth and Method*, second revised edition, New York: Continuum.

Galtung, J. (1996) *Peace By Peaceful Means: Peace and Conflict, Development and Civilization*, London: Sage.

Galtung, J. (2000) *Conflict Transformation by Peaceful Means (the Transcend Method)*, Participants' and Trainers' Manual, New York: United Nations.

Galtung, J. (2004) *Transcend and Transform*, London: Pluto Press.

Gantzel, K. and Schwinghammer, T. (2000) *Warfare Since the Second World War*, London: Transaction Publishers.

Garfinkel, H. (1967) *Studies in Ethnomethodology*, Englewood Cliffs, NJ: Prentice-Hall.

Gergen, K. (1973) 'Social psychology as history', *Journal of Personality and Social Psychology*, 26, 309–20.

Gergen, K. and Gergen, M. (1984) *Historical Social Psychology,* Hillsdale NJ: Lawrence Erlbaum Associates.

Gilligan, C. (1982) *In A Different Voice*, Cambridge MA: Harvard UP.

Gilligan, C. (2002) *The Birth of Pleasure*, New York: Knopf.

Glasl, F. (2008) 'Enriching conflict diagnosis and strategies for social change: a closer look at conflict dynamics' in Körppen *et al.* (eds), 43–51.

Gleick, P. (1995) 'Water and conflict: fresh water resources and international security' in S. Lynn-Jones and S. Miller (eds) *Global Dangers*, 84–117.

Goodall, J. (1986) *The Chimpanzees of Gombe: Patterns of Behaviour*, Cambridge, Mass.: Harvard UP.

Grice, H. (1975) 'Logic and conversation' in P. Cole and J. Morgan (eds) *Syntax and Semantics: Vol. 3. Speech Acts*, New York: Academic Press, 41–58.

Groebel, J., Hinde, J. and Hinde, R. (eds) (1989) *Aggression and War: Their Biological and Social Bases*, Cambridge: Cambridge University Press.

Gulliver, P. (1979) *Disputes and Negotiations: A Cross-Cultural Perspective*, New York: Academic Press.

Gurr, T. (2000) *Peoples Versus States: Minorities at Risk in the New Century*, Washington DC: US Institute for Peace.

Gutmann, A. and Thompson, D. (1996) *Democracy and Disagreement*, Cambridge Mass.: Harvard UP.

Gutting, G. (ed.) (1994) *The Cambridge Companion to Foucault*, Cambridge: Cambrige University Press

Habermas, J. (1979) *Communication and the Evolution of Society*, Boston: Beacon Press.

Habermas, J. (1981a/1991) *The Theory of Communicative Action Volume I: Reason and the Rationalization of Society*, trans T. McCarthy, Cambridge: Polity Press.

Habermas, J. (1981b/1987) *The Theory of Communicative Action Volume II: The Critique of Functionalist Reason*, trans T. McCarthy, Cambridge: Polity Press.

Habermas, J. (1982) 'A reply to my critics' in Thompson, J. and Held, D. eds *Habermas: Critical Debates*, London: Macmillan.

Habermas, J. (1992/1996) *Between Facts and Norms*, Cambridge: Polity Press.

Habermas, J. (1992) *Postmetaphysical Thinking*, Cambridge, Mass.: MIT Press.

Halabi, R. and Sonneschein, N. (2004) 'The Jewish-Palestinian encounter in time of crisis', *Journal of Social Issues*, 60(2): 373–89.

Hall, E. (1976) *Beyond Culture*, New York: Doubleday.

Hampshire, S. (1983) *Morality and Conflict*, Cambridge, MA: Harvard UP.

Hampson, F. (1996) *Nurturing Peace: Why Peace Settlements Succeed or Fail*, Washington, DC: US Institute of Peace.

Hand, S. (ed.) (1989) *The Levinas Reader*, Oxford: Blackwell.

Harrison, N. (ed.) (2006) *Complexity in World Politics: Concepts and Methods of a New Paradigm*, New York: State University of New York.

Hayward, K. and O'Donnell, C. (eds) (forthcoming 2010) *Political Discourse and Conflict Resolution*, London: Routledge.

Hendrick, D. (2009) *Complexity Theory and Conflict Transformation: An Exploration of Potential and Implications*, University of Bradford Working Paper 17, Bradford UK: Centre for Conflict Resolution.

Heritage, J. (1984) *Garfinkel and Ethnomethodology*, Cambridge: Polity Press.

Hinman, L. (2003) *Ethics: A Pluralistic Approach to Moral Theory*, Belmont, CA: Thomson (Wadsworth).

Hoffman, M. (1987) 'Critical theory and the interparadigm debate', *Millennium* 16, 231–49.

Hollis, M. and Lukes, S. (eds) (1982) *Rationality and Relativism*, Oxford: Basil Blackwood.

Homer-Dixon, T. (1991) 'On the threshold: environmental changes as causes of acute conflict', *International Security* 16(2): 7–16.

Homer-Dixon, T. (1994) 'Environmental scarcities and violent conflict: evidence from cases', *International Security*, 19(1): 5–40.

Honig, B. (1993) *Political Theory and the Displacement of Politics*, Ithaca, NY: Cornell UP.

Howard, M. (1984) *The Causes of Wars*, Cambridge, MA: Harvard University Press.

Howarth, D. (1998) 'Discourse theory and political analysis' in E. Scarborough and E. Tannenbaum (eds) *Research Strategies in the Social Sciences: A Guide to New Approaches*, Oxford: Oxford University Press, 268–93.

Howarth, D., Norval, A. and Stavrakakis Y. (eds) (2000) *Discourse Theory and Political Analysis: Identities, Hegemonies and Social Change*, Manchester: Manchester University Press.

Humphrys, J. (2007) *In God We Doubt: Confessions of a Failed Atheist*, London: Hodder & Stoughton.

Hutchby, I. (1992) 'The pursuit of controversy: routine scepticism in talk on talk radio', *Sociology*, 26, 673–94.

Hutchby, I. and Wooffitt, R. (1998) *Conversation Analysis*, Cambridge: Polity Press.

Irigaray, L. (1977/1985) *This Sex Which Is Not One*, Cornell University Press.

Jabri, V. (1996) *Discourses on Violence: Conflict Analysis Reconsidered*, Manchester: Manchester University Press.

Jabri, V. (2007) *War and the Transformation of Global Politics*, London: Palgrave.

Janis, I. (1972) *Victims of Groupthink*, Boston: Houghton Mifflin.

Jervis, R. (1976) *Perception and Misperception in International Politics*, Princeton, NJ: Princeton UP.

Johnson, D., Johnson, R. and Tjosvold, D. (2000) 'Constructive Controversy', in M. Deutsch and P. Coleman (eds) *The Handbook of Conflict Resolution: Theory and Practice*, 65–85.

Jones, D. (1999) *Cosmopolitan Mediation? Conflict Resolution and the Oslo Accords*, Manchester: Manchester University Press.

Jones, P. and Carey, C. (2003) *Disagreement and Difference*, special issue of the *Critical Review of International Social and Political Philosophy*, 6(3): 154–64.

Jurgensmeyer, M. (2001) *Terror in the Mind of God: The Global Rise of Religious Violence*, Berkeley, CA: University of California Press.

Kahane, A. (2007) *Solving Tough Problems: A Creative Way of Talking, Listening and Creating New Realities,* Berrett-Koehler.

Kekes, J. (1993) *The Morality of Pluralism*, Princeton: Princeton UP.

Kelly, M. (1995) 'The Gadamer/Habermas Debate Revisited: The Question of Ethics' in D. Rasmussen (ed.) *Universalism Vs Communitarianism: Contemporary Debates in Ethics*, Cambridge, MA: The MIT Press, 139–59.

King, M. L. (1963) *Lincoln Memorial Address*. Reprinted in Safire, W. (ed.) (1992) *Lend Me Your Ears: Great Speeches in History*, New York: WW Norton.

King, S. (2000) 'A Global Ethic in the light of comparative religious ethics' in Twiss and Grelle (eds) *A Global Ethic: The Declaration of the Parliament of the World's Religions*, 118–40.

Klug, T. (2008) 'The Last Chance Saloon' *Palestine–Israel Journal of Politics, Economics and Culture*, 15(2): 161–65.

Körppen, D., Schmelze, B. and Wils, O. (eds) (2008) *A Systemic Approach to Conflict Transformation: Exploring Strengths and Limitations*, Berlin: Berghof Research Center for Constructive Conflict Management: Berghof Handbook Dialogue Series.

Kress, G. and Hodge, B. (1979) *Language as Ideology*, Routledge & Kegan Paul.

Kriesberg, L. (1982) *Social Conflicts*, Englewood Cliffs, NJ: Prentice-Hall.

Kriesberg, L., Northrup, T. and Thorson, S. (eds) (1989) *Intractable Conflicts and Their Transformation*, Syracuse, NY: Syracuse University Press.

Kristeva, J. (1986) *The Kristeva Reader*, ed. T. Moi, Oxford: Basil Blackwell.

Küng, H. (1978/1980) *Does God Exist? An Answer for Today*, trans. E. Quinn, London: Collins.

Küng, H. (ed.) (1996) *Yes To A Global Ethic*, New York: Continuum.

Küng, H. and Kuschel, K-J. (eds) (1993) *A Global Ethic: The Declaration of the Parliament of the World's Religions*, New York: Continuum.

Kuttab, J. (1988) 'The pitfalls of dialogue', *Journal of Palestine Studies*, 17(2): 84–108.

Kymlicka, W. (1995) *Multicultural Citizenship: A Liberal Theory of Minority Rights*, Oxford: OUP.

Kymlicka, W. and Bashir, B. (eds) (2008) *The Politics of Reconciliation in Multicultural Societies*, Oxford: Oxford University Press.

Labov, W. and Fanshel, D. (1977) *Therapeutic Discourse: Psychotherapy as Conversation*, New York: Academic Press.

Laclau, E. and Mouffe, C. (1985) *Hegemony and Socialist Strategy*, London: Verso.

Lakoff, G. and Johnson, M. (1980) *Metaphors We Live By*, Chicago, IL: University of Chicago Press.

Larmore, C. (1987) *Patterns of Moral Complexity*, Cambridge: CUP.

Laurence, W. (1946) *Dawn Over Zero*, New York: Knopf.

Lederach, J.P. (2003) *The Little Book of Conflict Transformation*, Intercourse Pa.: Good Books.

Lederach, J.P. (2005) *The Moral Imagination: The Art and Soul of Building Peace*, Oxford: Oxford University Press.

Levinas, E. (1998) *Entre Nous: On Thinking-Of-The-Other*, trans. M. Smith and B. Harshav, London: Athlone Press.

Levinson, S. (1983) *Pragmatics*, Cambridge: Cambridge University Press.

Lewin K. (1935) *A Dynamic Theory of Personality*, New York: McGraw-Hill.

Lewin K. (1947) 'Frontiers in group dynamnics', *Human Relations* 1, 5–41.

Linklater, A. (1998) *The Transformation of Political Community*, Cambridge: CUP.

Locke, J. (1690/1975) *An Essay Concerning Human Understanding*, Oxford: Oxford University Press.

Lorenz, K. (1966) *On Aggression*, New York: Harcourt, Brace and World.

Lynn-Jones, S. and Miller, S. (eds) (1995) *Global Dangers*, Cambridge, MA: MIT Press.

Macdonell, D. (1986) *Theories of Discourse*, Oxford: Blackwell.

Mackie, J. 1976: *Ethics: Inventing Right and Wrong*. London: Penguin.

McDowell, J. (2002) 'Gadamer and Davidson on understanding and relativism' in Malpas *et al.* (eds) *Gadamer's Century*, 173–94.

Malpas, J., Arnswald, U. and Kertsche, J. (eds) (2002) *Gadamer's Century: Essays in Honour of Hans-Georg Gadamer*, Cambridge, MA: MIT Press.

Mead, M. (1940) 'Warfare is only an invention – not a biological necessity', *Asia*, 40, 402–5.

Mertus, J. (1999) *Kosovo: How Myths and Truths Started A War,* Berkeley, CA: University of California Press.

Mitchell, C. (1981) *The Structure of International Conflict*, London: Macmillan.

Mitchell, C. and Banks, M. (1996) *Handbook of Conflict Resolution: The Analytical Problem-Solving Approach*, London: Pinter/Cassell.

Montefiore, S. (2007/8) *Young Stalin*, London: Weidenfeld and Nicolson.

Montville, J. ed. (1990) *Conflict and Peacemaking in Multiethnic Societies*, Lexington, MA: Lexington Books.

Morgenthau, H. (1948 4th edn 1967) *Politics Among Nations: The Struggle for Power and Peace*, New York: Knopf.

Mouffe, Chantal (1999) 'Deliberative democracy or agonistic pluralism', in: *Social Research*, (66)3: 745–58.

Mouffe, C. (2000) *The Democratic Paradox*, London: Verso.

Mouffe, C. (2005) *On The Political*, London: Routledge.

Mourad, K. (2004) *Our Sacred Land: Voices from the Palestine-Israeli Conflict*, Oxford: Oneworld.

Muldoon, P. (2008) '"The very basis of civility": on agonism, conquest and reconciliation', in Kymlicka and Bashir, 114–35.

Musab, A (2003) Article from *Kcom Journal*, online source (no longer available).

Nagel, T. (1979) *Mortal Questions*, Cambridge: CUP.

Neuberg, A. and Waltman, M. (2006) *Why We Believe What We Believe: Uncovering Our Biological Need for Meaning, Spirituality and Truth*, New York: Free Press, Simon and Schuster.

Nicolic, L. (2003) 'Ethnic prejudices and discriminations: the case of Kosovo', in F. Bieber and Z. Daskalovski (eds) *Understanding the War in Kosovo*, London: Frank Cass.

Nietzsche, F. (1974) *The Gay Science*, trans. W. Kaufmann, New York: Vintage.

Nordstrom, C. (1994) *Warzones, Cultures of Violence, Militarisation and Peace*, Canberra: Australian National University.

Norris, C. (1994) '"What is enlightenment?": Kant according to Foucault', in G. Gutting (ed.) *The Cambridge Companion to Foucault*, Cambridge: Cambridge University Press, 159–96.

Northrup, T. (1989) 'The dynamic of identity in personal and social conflict' in L. Kriesberg, T. Northrup and S. Thorson (eds) *Intractable Conflicts and Their Transformation* Syracuse, NY: Syracuse University Press, 35–82.

Nye, J. (2002) *The Paradox of American Power: Why the World's Only Superpower Can't Go It Alone*, Oxford: OUP.

Palestine Strategy Group (2008) *Regaining the Initiative: Palestinian Strategic Options for Ending Israeli Occupation*, London: Oxford Research Group. Text in Arabic and English: www.palestinestrategygroup.ps

Parekh, B. (2002) 'Terrorism or intercultural dialogue', in K. Booth and T. Dunne (eds) *Worlds in Collision: Terror and the Future of Global Order*, Houndmills, UK: Palgrave Macmillan, 270–83.

Parker, I. (1992) *Discourse Dynamics: Critical Analysis for Social and Individual Psychology*, London: Routledge.

Pécheux (1975/82) *Language, Semantics and Ideology: Stating the Obvious*, trans. H. Nagpal, London: Macmillan.

Pinker, S. (2002) *The Blank Slate*, London: Penguin Books.

Pioneers of Change Associates (2006) Bojer, M. and McKay E. *Mapping Dialogue*, with German Technical Cooperation, www.pioneersofsocialchange.net.

Pomerantz, A. (1984) 'Agreeing and disagreeing with assessments: some features of preferred/dispreferred turn-shapes', in J. Atkinson and J. Heritage (eds) *Structures of Social Action: Studies in Conversation Analysis*, Cambridge: Cambridge University Press. 79–112.

Potter, J. and Wetherell, M. (1987) *Discourse and Social Psychology: Beyond Attitudes and Behaviour*, London: Sage.

Potter, J. (1996) *Representing Reality: Discourse, Rhetoric and Social Construction*, London: Sage.

Pressman, J. (2003) 'Visions in collision: what happened at Camp David and Taba?', *International Security*, 28(2): 5–43.

Priest, G. (2002) *Beyond The Limits Of Thought*, Oxford: Clarendon Press.

Pugh, M., Cooper, N. and Turner, M. (eds) (2009) *Whose Peace? Critical Perspectives on the Political Economy of Peacebuilding*, Houndmills, UK: Palgrave/Macmillan.

Quine, W. and Ullian, J. (1970) *The Web of Belief*, Random House.

Ramsbotham, O. (1987) *Choices: Nuclear and Non-Nuclear Defence Options*, London: Brassey's.

Ramsbotham O., Woodhouse T., and Miall H. (2005) *Contemporary Conflict Resolution*, Cambridge: Polity Press.

Rapoport, A. (1989) *The Origins of Violence*, New York: Paragon House.

Rasmussen, D. (ed.) (1990) *Universalism Vs. Communitarianism: Contemporary Debates in Ethics*, Cambridge, MA: The MIT Press.

Richmond, O. (2005) *The Transformation of Peace*, London: Palgrave.

Richmond, O. (2008) *Peace in International Relations*, Abingdon: Routledge.

Ricigliano, R. (2008) 'Planning for systemic impact', draft chapter for Berghof *Systemic Thinking and Conflict Transformation* (forthcoming).

Risse, T. (2004) 'Global governance and communicative action', *Government and Opposition* 39(2): 288–313.

Rogers, C. (1980) *A Way of Being*, Boston: Houghton Mifflin.

Rogers, P. (2000) *Losing Control: Global Security in the Twenty-First Century*, London: Pluto.

Rogers, P. (2007) *Towards Sustainable Security: Alternatives to the War on Terror*, Oxford Research Group International Security Report, London: Oxford Research Group.

Ropers, N. (2008) 'Systemic conflict transformation: reflections on the conflict and peace process in Sri Lanka', in D. Körppen, B. Schmelzle and O. Wils (eds) *A Systemic Approach to Conflict Transformation: Exploring Strengths and Limitations*, Berghof Research Center for Constructive Conflict Management, 11–41.

Rorty, R. (1988) *Contingency, Irony and Solidarity*, Cambridge: Cambridge University Press.

Rose, H. and Rose, S. (eds) 2001: *Alas Poor Darwin: Arguments Against Evolutionary Psychology*, London: Vintage.

Rosenau, J. and Earnest, D. (2006) 'Signifying nothing? What complex systems theory can and cannot tell us about global politics', in: N. Harrison (ed.) *Complexity in World Politics: Concepts and Methods of a New Paradigm*, New York: State University of New York.

Ross, D. (2004) *The Missing Peace: The Inside Story of the Fight for Middle East Peace*, New York: Farrar, Straus and Giroux.

Ross, M. (1993) *The Culture of Conflict: Interpretations and Interests in Comparative Perspective*, New Haven: Yale University Press.

Rotberg, R. (ed.) (2006) *Israeli and Palestinian Narratives of Conflict: History's Double Helix*, Bloomington IN: Indiana University Press.

Roth-Cline, M (2004) 'Half measures', online source (no longer available).

Rothman (1992) *From Confrontation to Cooperation: Resolving Ethnic and Regional Conflict*, Newbury Park, Calif.: Sage.

Rothman, J. (1997) *Resolving Identity-Based Conflicts in Nations, Organizations, and Communities*, San Francisco: Jossey-Bass.

Rouhana, N. (2006) 'Zionism's encounter with the Palestinians: the dynamics of force, fear and extremism', in R. Rotberg (ed.) *Israeli and Palestinian Narratives of Conflict*, Bloomington Il: University of Illinois Press, 115–41.

Rouhana, N. and Körper, S. (1996) 'Dealing with dilemmas posed by power asymmetry in intergroup conflict', *Negotiation Journal*, 12(4).

Ryder, C. and Kearney, V. (2001) *Drumcree: The Orange Order's Last Stand*, London: Methuen.

Sacks, (1984) 'Notes on methodology' in J. Atkinson and J. Heritage (eds) *Structures of Social Action: Studies in Conversation Analysis*, Cambridge: Cambridge University Press. 21–7.

Said, E. (1986) 'Burdens of interpretation and the question of Palestine', paper presented to the conference of the International Society of Political Psychology, Amsterdam.

Said, E. (1995) *Peace and its Discontents*, London: Vintage.

Sandole, D. (1999) *Capturing the Complexity of Conflict: Dealing With Violent Ethnic Conflicts in the Post-Cold War Era*, London: Routledge.

Sandole D. and van der Merwe, H. (eds) (1993) *Conflict Resolution Theory and Practice: Integration and Application*, Manchester: Manchester University Press.

Saunders, H. (1999) *A Public Peace Process: Sustained Dialogue to Transform Racial and Ethnic Conflict*, New York: Palgrave.

Schäffner, C. and Wenden A. (eds) (1995) *Language and Peace*, London: Routledge.

Schofield, V. (1996) *Kashmir in the Crossfire*, London: I.B. Tauris.

Scriven, M. (1976) *Reasoning*, New York: McGraw-Hill.

Searle, J. (1969) *Speech Acts: An Essay in the Philosophy of Language*, Cambridge: Cambridge University Press.

Singer, D. (1996) 'Armed conflict in the former colonial regions; from classification to explanation', in L. van de Goor, K. Rupesinge and P. Sciarone (eds) *Between Development and Destruction; An Enquiry into the Causes of Conflict in Post-Colonial States*, New York: St Martin's Press, 35–49.

Singer, D. and Small, M. (1972) *The Wages of War, 1816–1965: A Statistical Handbook*, New York: Wiley.

SIPRI Yearbook: 2008, Oxford: Oxford University Press for the Stockholm International Peace Research Institute.

Slim, H. (2005) 'Violent beliefs', *RUSI Journal*, April 2005: 20–3.

Sperber, D. and Wilson, D. (1986) *Relevance: Communication and Cognition*, Oxford: Blackwell.

Staub, E. (1989) *The Roots of Evil: The Origins of Genocide and Other Group Violence*, Cambridge: CUP.

Stewart, J. and Thomas, M. (2005) 'Dialogic listening: sculpting mutual meanings' in J. Stewart (ed.) *Bridges Not Walls: A Book About Interpersonal Communication*, 9th edn, New York: McGraw-Hill, 192–210.

Stocker, M. (1990) *Plural and Conflicting Values*, Oxford: Clarendon Press.

Strategic Foresight Group (2009) *Cost of Conflict in the Middle East*, Mumbai: SFG.

Stroh, D. (2002) *A Systemic View of the Israeli-Palestinian Conflict*, in *The Systems Thinker*, 13(5): 2–7.

Taylor, C. (2002) 'Understanding the other: A Gadamerian view on conceptual schemes' in Malpas *et al.* (eds) *Gadamer's Century*, Boston: MIT Press, 279–98.

Thompson, J. 1984 *Studies in the Theory of Ideology*, Cambridge: Polity Press.

Thompson, J. 1990: *Ideology and Modern Culture*, Cambridge: Polity Press.

Thucydides (1954) *History of the Peloponnesian War*, trans Warner, R., London: Penguin.

Toulmin, S. (1958) *The Uses of Argument*, Cambridge: Cambridge University Press.

Turnbull, C. (1978) 'The politics of non-aggression', in A. Montagu (ed.) *Learning Non-Aggression: The Experience of Non-Literate Societies*, Oxford: Galaxy Books, 161–221.

Twiss, S. (1993) 'Curricular perspectives in comparative religious ethics: a critical examination of four paradigms', *The Annual of the Society of Christian Ethics*, 249–69.

Twiss, S. and Grelle, B. (eds) (2000) *Explorations in Global Ethics: Comparative Religious Ethics and Interreligious Dialogue*, Boulder, CO: Westview Press.

US/Middle East Project (2008) *A Last Chance for a Two-State Israel–Palestine Agreement*, New York: http://www.usmep.us.

Van Dijk, T. (1993) 'Principles of critical discourse analysis', *Discourse and Society*, 4(2): 249–83.

Volkan, V. (1988) *The Need to Have Enemies and Allies: From Clinical Practice to International Relationships*, Northvale, NJ: Jason Aronson.

Volkan, V. (1990) 'Psychoanalytic aspects of ethnic conflicts', in J. Montville (ed.) *Conflict and Peacemaking in Multiethnic Societies*, Lexington Mass.: Lexington Books, 81–92.

Volkan, V. and Harris, M. (1992) 'Negotiating a peaceful separation: a psychopolitical analysis of current relationships between Russia and the Baltic Republics', *Mind and Human Interaction*, 4(1): 20–39.

Volkan, V. and Harris, M.(1992) 'Vaccinating the political process: a second psychopolitical analysis of relationships between Russia and the Baltic states', *Mind and Human Interaction*, 4(4): 169–90.

Volosinov, V.N. (1930/1973) *Marxism and the Philosophy of Language*, trans L. Matejka and I.R. Titunik, New York: Seminar Press.

von Clausewitz, C. (1976/1832) *On War*, trans and ed. M. Howard, M. Paret and P. Paret, Princeton, NJ: Princeton University Press.

von Neumann, J. and Morgenstern, O. (1944) *Theory of Games and Economic Behavior*, New York: Wiley.

Walker, R. (1993) *Inside/Outside: International Relations as Political Theory*, Cambridge: CUP.

Wallensteen, P. (2002) *Understanding Conflict Resolution*, London: Sage.

Waltz, K. (1979) *Theory of International Politics*, New York: McGraw-Hill.

Walzer, M. (1977; 2nd edn 1992) *Just and Unjust Wars: A Moral Argument With Historical Illustration*, New York: Basic Books.

Walzer, M. (1983) *Spheres of Justice: A Defense of Pluralism and Equality,* New York: Basic Books.

Warnke, G. (1987) *Gadamer: Hermeneutics, Tradition and Reason*, Stanford: Stanford University Press.

Wasserstrom, B. (2001) *Divided Jerusalem: The Struggle for the Holy City*, London: Profile Books.

Watt, D. (1991/1964) *Mein Kampf*, trans. Manheim, R., London: Pimlico.

Wehr, P. (1979) *Conflict Regulation*, Boulder, CO: Westview Press.

Wheen, F. (2004) *How Mumbo-Jumbo Conquered the World*, London: Harper/Collins.

White, S. (1995) *The Cambridge Companion to Habermas*, Cambridge: CUP.

Whyte, J. (1990) *Interpreting Northern Ireland*, Oxford: Clarendon Press.

Williams, B. (1981) *Moral Luck*, Cambridge: Cambridge University Press.

Williams, B. (2002) *Truth and Truthfulness*, Princeton: Princeton University Press.

Williams, R. (2004) *Analysing Atheism: Unbelief and the World of Faith*, London: Lambeth Palace Press Office.

Wils, O., Hopp, U., Ropers, N., Vimalarajah, L. and Zunzer, W. (2006) *The Systemic Approach to Conflict Transformation: Concepts and Fields of Application*, Berghof Foundation for Peace Support.

Wittgenstein, L. 1961 *Tractatus Logico-Philosophicus*, D. Pears and B. McGuinness (eds), London: Routledge.

Woodrow, P. (2006) *Advancing Practice in Conflict Analysis and Strategy Development; Interim Progress Report*, Reflecting on Peace Practice Project, Cambridge, MA: CDA Collaborative Learning Projects.

Wright, S. (1998) *Language and Conflict: A Neglected Relationship*, Bristol: Multilingual Matters Ltd.

Zalzberg, O. (2009) 'Report on the Time is Ripe Project', unpublished.

Index

Note: page numbers in **bold** refer to figures and tables.